LEOPARD IN MY LAP

LEOPARD IN MY LAP

LEOPARD
IN MY LAP

★

MICHAELA
DENIS

Photographs by Armand Denis

THE COMPANION BOOK CLUB
LONDON

*Made and printed in Great Britain
for The Companion Book Club (Odhams Press Ltd.)
by Odhams (Watford) Limited*
S.656.ZT

THIS edition, issued in 1956, is for members of The Companion Book Club, 8 Long Acre, London, W.C.2, from which address particulars of membership may be obtained. The book is published by arrangement with the original publishers, W. H. Allen & Co., Ltd

"A blessed companion is a book"—JERROLD

CONTENTS

CONTENTS

ILLUSTRATIONS

ILLUSTRATIONS IN COLOUR

ILLUSTRATIONS IN BLACK AND WHITE

8

LEOPARD IN MY LAP

CHAPTER ONE

CUPID IN THE CLOUDS

AT THE heart of all adventure lies self-fulfilment.

I didn't know this when I was fashion-designing and moving among a smart set in New York. The lure of the big city held me and swept me more or less limp from one week to the next. I loved my work, but my life was really a tangle of ragged ends. Something vital was missing.

There were times when my whole being protested against the empty social round through the city's concrete canyons and under its bright lights. Then I would stay at home and lock my door against the world.

Love and marriage, they say, always lie at the bottom of a woman's thoughts. I can honestly say that I had no such ideas—at least, not consciously. But my sophisticated friends did the conventional thing and dangled eligible young men before me. I couldn't have been less interested.

Outside my work I had two passions—travel books and animals. I had grown up with them and they had helped to form my character and outlook. The most wonderful hours of my youth had been spent dreaming over maps in travel books and pretending that our domestic pets were wild creatures in forests.

But there was nothing I could do about making these dreams real. We have to take life as we find it and to make our own opportunities within the scope allotted. But new prospects are apt to open up unexpectedly. Then suddenly the whole world is transformed.

It happened to me at a party in New York. I had accepted the invitation as a matter of course. It was just another party where I should see friends and indulge in small-talk, drink a couple of Martinis, and return home without a ripple on the surface of my thoughts and feelings.

As soon as I entered the room, however, I became conscious of something different. A very tall man rose from his chair and took my hand as our hostess murmured our names. His was Armand Denis.

My heart leapt. This was Armand Denis, the famous explorer, whose travels in the wild areas of the world had brought him fame and the gratitude of all animal lovers, for he was not a hunter but a student and photographer of the untamed creatures of forest and jungle.

I was rather overcome and had little to say for myself. Armand Denis has a magnetic personality which draws people to him naturally. I made no attempt to resist. In less than a minute after meeting him I knew that I was in love; but I had not the slightest idea as to what he thought of me.

So it came about that not long afterwards I found myself in South America, sitting next to Armand Denis in a large sedan car, driving over the Andes. Before and below us stretched a scene of unparalleled magnificence. Ahead lay our destination—Potosi, the highest town in the world. The way to it was strewn with death-traps. This was the worst season of the year for car travel among the precipitous mountains. For days it had rained; now snow was falling. Over the terrifying complex of hairpin bends and crumbling paths stretched the immense grey, snow-laden sky, and below, between the great peaks, depths of unfathomable steel-blue.

Armand was silent and calm. I glanced at him and marvelled at his imperturbability. We had just passed through a nerve-shattering experience. The road over which we drove had been dynamited for repair and no warning notices had been put up. Suddenly before us yawned a horrifying drop into the blue chasm. I stiffened into a column of ice. Armand, with only crumbling inches to spare, urged the car forward without a tremor.

Now all the ice in me had thawed to an emotional pulp. I was suffering from a violent reaction. But Armand sat there, maddeningly aloof, threading his way round sickening bends with a matter-of-fact mastery. Not a flicker of feeling had passed over his handsome face. Nothing, it seemed to me, could fray those steel nerves or weaken that iron will. I was desperately in love with him.

Every day, I knew, car loads of Indians were flung to their death along this route. Thousands of feet below lay wreckage and bones plucked clean of flesh by the condors. Of condors I will tell more later. Armand must have guessed what was passing through my mind, for he turned his face to me and said:

"Potosi is straight ahead. The Indians around here call it 'the mountain of silver'. When the Spaniards first conquered them, they were forced to work the silver seams. Do you know how much the Indians were paid for their labour? You'd be surprised. They were allowed to take part in the Christmas processions of the Spaniards. That's all. . . . Of course, those were the days before trade unions."

The last touch is typical of Armand. He has a nice quiet sense of humour to lighten his scholarship and knowledge and to add to his deep sympathy for all living things. As we drove on, the old question came to my mind —where was I really going with him? Potosi is just a place on the map. I meant—where were we going in another, a less physical, sense? I didn't even know what he felt about me.

The snow was now falling so heavily that Armand had to call a halt for the night. The roads were blocked and it would have been certain death to go on. The cold was paralysing. At an altitude of 13,000 feet cooking was out of the question. It would have been an exhausting business to boil water or to cook an egg; we ate sardines and drank soda water.

Armand decided that we should sleep in the cars. He said good-night to me and went to join one of his men in a truck behind. As I pulled on my heaviest sweater and started to adjust the blankets, I noticed that the snow had stopped. An enormous moon rose, flooding the eerie landscape with silver light which was swallowed up by the black void where the road ended. All around, the ghostly sentinels of the mountains towered into the luminous sky. I settled down to sleep with these majestic images in my mind.

An insistent tapping on the car window woke me. I shook off the invisible chains of sleep reluctantly. The tapping continued. Opening my eyes, I glanced at my wrist-watch and saw that it was four o'clock. Tap, tap, tap, and then a voice said:

"Open up, open up, please!"

It was Armand, muffled to the neck against the early morning cold. His face expressed nothing at all. I wound the window down.

"Would you consider a proposal of marriage?" he said.

Still half-asleep, I couldn't grasp the meaning of his words. I stared at him bemused, wound up the window and fell asleep again. Half an hour later he returned and repeated the performance. He got no more sense out of me than before. Sleep held me under the surface of full consciousness. Again, at five o'clock, he returned. The window was wound down, the question put, followed by silence on my part and the winding up of the window once more.

This preposterous comedy of errors, played among those snowy Andean peaks, under the large silver eye of the moon, had run its course, and after the third act the curtain finally fell. When I really awoke at seven-thirty, with the noises of the busy expedition in my ears, I was

14

sure that I had been dreaming. I had, in fact, dreamed of Armand for so long that I was convinced the whole thing was fantasy.

The breakfast off more sardines and soda water was real enough. So was Armand's presence when he settled down beside me in the car and let in the clutch to begin the last lap to Potosi. I was still living the comedy and sat silent. Armand, also, seemed struck dumb until he said:

"We'll be in Potosi at ten-thirty."

That was all. Just a routine comment. Of course I had been dreaming.

The hotel where we rested was the prototype of every Spanish hotel in Bolivia. Needless to say, it had a patio. Characters that might have strayed from some corny Latin-American musical moved around, but the courtesy of the people was not theatrical, it was drawn from centuries-old tradition.

After lunch I went to my room to freshen up. I was wearing the usual expedition outfit of slacks, shirt and sweater, and knew of no reason to change them. But when I returned to the patio something unusual was happening. Bodo, Armand's cameraman, was having his shoes shined. Considering the dust and dirt, and the hard work that lay ahead of us, this seemed a little eccentric. I hung around for a time and then returned to my room.

Presently there was a knock on the door. I opened it and there stood Armand.

"Are you ready?" he asked.

"Ready for what?" I said.

"You must have forgotten. We have a date. We are getting married to-day. Remember?"

"No," I said out of sheer surprise, meaning yes.

"Yes," said Armand for me.

Within three minutes I was dressed in a vintage English suit, one of the wonderfully tailored things that defy time and the brain-storms of French *haute couture*. These were the early days of Dior's "New Look", but

15

nothing mattered now. The dream had vanished and I was face to face with the reality. This was the beginning of my first self-fulfilment out of adventure with Armand.

Together, accompanied by Bodo and another member of the expedition, we made our way to the Town Hall.

"We're cutting it fine," said Armand. "They close at six. We have twenty minutes. Hurry!"

The registrar was a sepulchral figure, cast by nature in the mould of a funeral attendant. His face and body were mere anatomies. He would have served admirably for demonstration purposes in a medical lecture-room. But the two pellets of coke that were his eyes glowed when he learned that Armand and I desired to be married that evening.

Then the light went out of his eyes and his skeleton jaws snapped.

"Under Bolivian law you must have Bolivian witnesses," he said with grim satisfaction.

Bodo acted as translator and took up our cause for an immediate marriage warmly. I listened fascinated. Rich gobbets of words, punctuated and, it seemed, ejected by gutturals, spattered the room, until at last the registrar said in an implacable tone:

"Mañana, eh? Ritorno mañana?"

We knew what that meant: come back to-morrow. I looked at Armand miserably. Deep in me was the fear of a bad omen. But Bodo wasn't taking no for an answer. He dashed out of the registrar's room, waving to us and shouting, "It's all right. I'll be back soon."

The registrar surveyed us gloomily. He shot out a few luscious sentences at us and, when we made no attempt to answer him, shrugged his whole body violently as if to scare us with the rattle of his bones. When we stuck our ground, he put his head between his hands and stared at us with his dead coke eyes, as if meditating on two prize objects of human folly.

Bodo was back in ten minutes, pushing two surprised

16

Bolivian citizens before him. One, a well-dressed and rather snooty man, we learned later, was the manager of the Bolivian-American Club; the other was apparently the town drunk.

The registrar, realizing that he was now on the spot, sighed and reached for a book, but he remained seated. The ceremony proceeded; it was almost as dream-like as Armand's proposal. Armand kept on whispering something to me all through the proceedings, but I couldn't catch the drift of his words.

Just before the end of the ceremony, a young man came into the room with a pair of trousers over his arm. Armand's whispered words suddenly fell into a rational form:

"The registrar . . . *he's got no pants on!*"

Now the registrar *knew we knew*. His reaction was surprising. His sallow face flushed crimson and the colour seemed to chase years from his face. He might have had a blood transfusion. We moved towards him and thanked him, and he blessed us in return. I couldn't resist a peek under the table. In contrast to his sober and conventional top were two skeleton legs adorned with silk socks and suspenders.

The drunken witness was overcome with emotion. As Armand and I kissed, he broke away from Bodo's supporting arm and reeled towards us. Snatches of words and song fell from his lips as he advanced with outstretched arms towards my husband.

"For heaven's sake!" exclaimed Armand.

But before he could take evasive action the drunk held him in an alcoholic embrace and then turned towards me. Out of good manners, I tried not to shrink. A reek of spirits smote me in the face, but I avoided the final ordeal by side-stepping and catching his hand—just in time to prevent him from falling flat on his face.

Inflamed by Pisco, the raw alcoholic concoction Bolivians drink, he wished me the great joy of giving birth to a hundred sons. We followed the local custom by giving presents to the witnesses; on the drunk we bestowed a bottle of his favourite brew which we carried as emergency fuel for our lamps.

Of course, a revolution was in progress in Bolivia. This involves all kinds of activities by armed soldiers and may be dangerous. Most of the soldiers we saw were stockily built, generally a foot shorter than me, dressed in khaki and armed with weapons which might have been exhibited in a museum to illustrate the evolution of warfare.

I was fantastically happy. We spent a dream day in Potosi after our marriage and then resumed our journey into the clouds, climbing, always climbing, until the earth appeared to slip away from us altogether. Our mood was one of aerial bliss.

But the world always insists on coming back. It is never very far away, even in our most transcendent moments. And it returned to us in the form of a barrier across the road, manned by soldiers who looked very much on their toes. The chain was lowered for us to pass, and the guard, who was talking to a man, answered our inquiry whether we could proceed by a gesture which we construed as waving us on. So we continued without let or hindrance.

Half an hour later the driver of our truck behind spoke to us on the intercom (we had the same system of inter-communication as police cars) and warned us that we should probably be arrested at the next military post. The guard had apparently not given us permission to proceed, as we had imagined, and had alerted all military posts by telephone.

"This may be ugly," said Armand.

"But we're all right. We've nothing to do with their affairs," I said innocently.

"I know, but that doesn't mean a thing. . . . Let's hope for the best."

18

The next barrier loomed up. As soon as the soldiers saw us they manned their machine guns and kept us in their sights.

"They look jittery," said Armand. "I hope they keep their nerve."

They were shaking with excitement and fear. As soon as we reached the barrier one of them thrust a gun through the open window. Its muzzle waggled against my shoulder; the man couldn't hold it still. I instinctively behaved as I would when dealing with a nervous wild animal that could be dangerous. I caught hold of the barrel and very slowly and gently pushed it away. The soldier made no attempt to resist my action.

There was a lot of shouting and running around until we were ordered to get out of the car and stand in front of the machine guns. Then we were marched, still under their sights, into a small whitewashed adobe hut which acted as the jail. Armand jabbered with our captors, and learned that we were regarded as dangerous revolutionaries and would have to spend the night in prison.

It would have been intolerable but for the innate human decency of the prisoners. Whole families, including their pets, were packed into a room not more than fifteen feet square. There was some attempt to segregate the sexes. One of the guards drew aside a blanket, revealed a dozen or more Indian women behind it, and politely pointed to me to join them. Children and dogs emerged. Everybody was scratching. So I gave the guard to understand that I would prefer to spend the night with my husband. This seeming proof of wifely devotion drew forth nods and smiles of approval from the visitors.

Music and sentiment are always near the surface of Latin-American human nature. Someone produced a guitar and we all joined in a song. Armand got a bottle of Pisco from the car and the drink went round. Jailers and prisoners were united in good fellowship. We forgot the possibility that we might be shot in the morning!

I drew near to Armand under the spell of this spontaneous happiness.

"How good it is to be together," I whispered—"even here."

"Yes," he said, and pointing to a group of merrymaking prisoners and jailers, he added: "What a lesson for the world! Here they were a few hours ago ready to cut each other's throats because of political differences—and look at them now! A little music, a drink of Pisco, and some sentiment, and they are brothers and sisters."

"But to-morrow?"

"Um. That's different. I don't know."

Sentiment played a fine part in our disposal. A general arrived in the morning and we were taken before him for questioning. When he learned that we had been married only the day before, he was shocked and apologized deeply, begging our forgiveness and referring in the most gracious terms to the misfortunes of war. He would do all in his power to ensure our safe passage, he told us; and he presented us with a very large document, impressively sealed and bearing his signature in full. The autograph measured fully five inches across and probably contained his genealogical tree stretching back to the time of Ferdinand and Isabella.

We thanked the general and departed full of confidence; but alas, when we reached the Argentinian frontier and produced the document to the local Bolivian officials, we got a shock. They took one look at the signature, whipped out automatics and ordered us out of the car. We were placed under arrest again. These were the revolutionaries and they were after our general's blood. His name was poison to them.

Hours of grilling followed before they decided that we were just foreigners and probably mad anyhow. They sent us packing—with imprecations against our general—towards the Argentinian customs.

Loaded as we always are on our journeys, customs

inspections are generally wearisome and annoying. Every detail of equipment has to be inspected and the serial numbers of cameras, sound recorders, etc., checked.

I rely largely on smiles; but this time the formula didn't work. The Argentinian officials had been made uneasy about us by the fuss on the Bolivian side. Just as they were about to give us the okay, an alarm clock in one of my suitcases went off. I had packed it in a hurry between a dried head and an ancient hand-axe, wrapped in my undies, but I'd forgotten to switch off the alarm. Everybody scrambled for cover. Under the suspicious eyes of the officials, I somehow felt guilty.

I watched them exchange glances and knew the message they were flashing—*time-bomb*!

These Argentinian customs men are of an exquisite courtesy which seldom degenerates into rudeness. Fear can bring strain to their features but never to their manners. Armand rushed in with the explanation:

"It's an alarm clock," he said, proceeding to open and unpack the case. The sight of the clock allayed the alarm of the officials and we crossed into Argentina followed by their smiles.

There is no perfect country in the world. The good ones are those in which the advantages outweigh the disadvantages. That is all.

To some, South America is a paradise. And so it is in many respects. But not if you are in the habit of leaving motor cars unattended for any length of time— especially in the hours of darkness in remote places.

If you do so you are apt to lose hub-caps, windscreen wiper blades, and any other removable parts. A detachable spare tyre, for instance, is a temptation that a South American professor of ethics could hardly resist—at least, that's how things looked to our foreign eyes.

So, as there were no lock-up garages to be found in any but the larger cities to accommodate our trucks, we made it a rule to sleep in them, and at least a couple of miles out of any town.

But one evening, Armand and I, dog tired after a long day's driving, decided we could not face another night stretched out on the floor of the truck. We took a room at a hotel which boasted of beds and electric lights; the drivers took off with the trucks, to drive the usual two miles out of town, promising to pick us up in the morning; we settled down for a long night's sleep. There were indeed beds: there were lumpy mattresses and pillows. There was no electric light, but there was some electric wiring and an empty socket, in which a candle had been stuck. Within minutes we were stretched out on the lumps and I had blown the candle out.

Within minutes again I was wide awake, scratching. I heard Armand sit up, tearing at his skin.

I said, "Mosquitoes!"

He said, "There are not that many mosquitoes in the world. Where is a match?"

A desperate search produced one match in the pocket of my slacks. Groping, Armand lighted the candle. He lifted his pillow. Under it was a black army of round insects, squirming. I had never seen anything like them. "Are they ladybirds?" I asked.

Armand was grim. He said, "Lady bed bugs, perhaps— but bed bugs they are." I looked down and saw to my horror that fresh echelons were advancing across the floor.

"Look!" I cried. "The place is alive with them!"

Each bug was as big as a ladybird. They seemed to move with the blind purpose and unbroken rhythm of creatures destined to inherit the earth.

Armand scrambled into his clothes after shaking them vigorously.

"Sit on that chair," he directed, "and keep your feet off the ground whatever you do. I will find the trucks and come and get you. Don't move until I come back."

He dashed out of the room and I crouched on the hard

wooden chair, my knees drawn up to my chin. Fascinated, I watched the evolutions of the invading army of bugs.
.   Outside I heard the fierce barking and snarling of dogs. Armand! Had he been set upon by those savage famished dogs we had seen before we went to bed? They looked starved and desperate. The noise gradually faded in the distance. After what seemed hours I heard a car stop outside and a few minutes later Armand came into the bedroom.

"Come along," he said. "We'll get out of this."

We collected our belongings and tiptoed down the stairs to the truck. There we settled down for the night.

"What happened?" I asked Armand before going to sleep.

"The dogs chased me all the way. It was bad because everything was pitch-dark. I thought I would never find those trucks. I shouted to the drivers but they never woke up. Bodo was asleep, too. I pushed him out of the way and got the car going, and here we are."

"Where's Bodo?"

"Still asleep. He's out to the world. We might be bandits taking him for a ride."

The sun rose in blinding splendour and we were soon on our way to Salta through some of the most magnificent mountain country in the world. The sunlight was a golden probe which seemed to expose all the sores and warts of our human condition. I felt and no doubt looked pretty rough; my handsome husband's dishevelment made him even more attractive to me, though he might have shaved with more care.

After nearly an hour's silence, he suddenly said:

"In a couple of days we shall be in Buenos Aires. That seems to be the end of the road of our South American journey. What should we do next?"

I knew that sooner or later the question would come. I had awaited it for months, and an answer had long been forming within me. Now was the time for me to speak out.

I say that the answer had been forming within me for months. That is really an understatement. I should have said years—from the time, in fact, when I was a small girl playing with domestic animals in a London garden; for I am London-born and it was my subsequent work as a fashion-designer that took me to the United States.

My father, an archaeologist, died when I was a baby, and I was brought up by my English grandmother, a matriarch of the old school, who ruled with a rod of iron. Decisive of speech and inflexible of will, she said "no" more easily than she said "yes"; but I learned to respect her stern principles.

I was often in trouble. My love of animals was so intense that I used to lure our neighbours' pets into our garden and there hold a sort of zoological court. The proceedings were not always happy. Cats, I discovered, were not compatible with birds, so I had to have "cat days" and "bird days". Sometimes I had "insect days"—much to the discomfort of my mother who disliked insects as well as spiders and snakes; and snakes were what I wanted more than anything—except lions!

I devoured animal books; one of them definitely gave me an African fixation. Night after night I would lie awake with the Dark Continent stretched out like a marvellous living rug, whose foliage and creatures were alive. My young imagination soared. Lions dominated these African scenes and were the lords of my dreams.

Forbidden to acquire unusual pets, such as snakes and lions, I created in self-defence a little girl named Connie, whose fabulously rich parents presented her with a private zoo packed with gorgeous reptiles and black-maned lions. This fantasy became so real that I begged my grandmother to set about procuring a lion for me "like Connie's", but she insisted that "the government wouldn't allow it".

Out of this passionate attachment to animals came the desire and finally the determination to travel. I studied art and design because I thought fashion-designing would give me a chance to satisfy my wanderlust; and, in fact, I made such rapid progress that I was soon able to get a job in New York. The money I saved there was spent on a solo trip to South America. This South American trip was to lead to the greatest adventure of my life: I returned to New York married to Armand.

I looked at him now, intent upon his driving, his fine firm profile at once decisive and sensitive. A man in a million, I thought, on whom the gods seemed to have showered all the gifts, physical, mental and moral. He also had loved animals from his earliest years.

"My father," he told me once, "used to take me to the Antwerp Zoo and encourage me to stroke the lions' manes through the bars of their cages. He used to impress on me that even the wildest animals could be tamed by love and patience. I've never forgotten his words."

Armand, still intent on his driving, seemed not to expect an answer to his question—"What shall we do next?" But presently I should make a suggestion and we could discuss it, weighing the pros and cons. I was very happy at this moment, very deeply in love, and I gave myself up for a while to recalling the circumstances and events which had helped to make my husband the remarkable man he was in body and mind.

"You know," he went on during that early conversation, "the Antwerp Zoo is one of the best and oldest in the world. Right up to the time of the war, I was often there, studying this or that animal, noting its habits and special characteristics. . . . We grow up in the image of what we were before we were fourteen years of age. I was an animal lover early on and shall always be one."

But the First World War tore Armand away from his zoological interests. Although much under military service age, he at once joined the Belgian Army, had many adventures, escaped from internment in Holland and finally made his way to England. There he went to Oxford and read chemistry for his B.A. The outcome was a Research Fellowship to continue his studies in California.

In the United States he became an expert in radio and electronics and joined the research staff of the Eastman Kodak Company, in Rochester, N.Y. Among his many inventions of this time are automatic film printers and one of the basic methods of automatic volume control of radio receivers.

Underneath the surface of this successful scientific life was a restless desire for travel and the study of nature, more especially animals. The camera was the instrument through which he could express himself; and much of the money he earned by his inventions were spent on cameras, film and pioneer sound-recording equipment. Bali was the setting for his first picture; under the title *Kriss* in Europe, *Goona Goona* in America, it achieved success and convinced Armand that he had found his true *métier*. Many films followed from Malaya, Ceylon, Sumatra, Burma, Nepal and the Belgian Congo.

My musings were broken by Armand's voice.

"This is Salta," he said, waving a hand towards some delightful buildings. "I wouldn't mind settling here. They have taste and an artistic conscience. It's an offence here to build a house that doesn't conform to the Spanish colonial style—an excellent idea. The preservation of tradition, you know. And of character, too."

I wondered in what part of the world our own house would eventually be built, or whether we would ever stay long enough in one country to build at all.

"You were saying," I reminded Armand as we drove through charming Salta, "that we are coming to the end of the road."

"Yes," he said, "in South America—for the time being. We've all the material we want for *Wheels Across the*

Andes and *Mystery of the Incas,* and I think they'll make two fine films. Now we've got to break new ground . . . There's plenty of time to decide."

There was; for we were making for Rio, after Buenos Aires. From there we were to take a slow Belgian freighter to Antwerp—for a rest. We needed a rest badly. But I needed something even more badly, and at once—an assurance that our next trip would be to Africa. So I said one word without bothering to explain or comment:

"Africa."

Armand gave no sign of having heard; but for no reason at all he accelerated the car—that is, no reason apart from the mention of Africa. He had a habit of accelerating when he was excited.

CHAPTER TWO

AFRICA AT LAST

WE HAD been in New York a month, following our rest in Antwerp, when Armand looked up from the desk on which he had been writing some notes and said:

"Michaela, did you say Africa?"

My heart jumped.

"Yes, that's what I said."

"Then Africa it shall be. We'll make our next picture there."

"Lions?" I asked.

"Lions, and in fact the whole boiling. I've a rough plan worked out here." He pointed to his notes.

We were in our tiny Greenwich Village apartment. It was hung with trophies of Armand's expeditions and I could hardly find space for some of the Ecuadorean and Peruvian designs I had brought back from the trip described in the foregoing chapter.

We lived almost as roughly here as on a location in the backward areas. A bed and an old armchair comprised the bulk of the furniture; the desk was a pure extravagance. We had no money for home comforts. Every penny we possessed went into equipment.

Life in that apartment was truly hell. The refrigerator threw off noxious fumes which gave us splitting headaches. There was no cold water, only hot, for the cold water pipe had given up the ghost. One day while I was reading a book a spear fell off the wall and stuck, quivering, into the floor. It was that sort of place.

As soon as Africa had been decided upon, we began to buy safari clothes and go through the necessary physical chores—visits to doctors for inoculations, to the dentist for a check-up.

A cable came from Hollywood, from Sam Zimbalist to Armand, asking him to fly to Hollywood at once.

He went off alone and in a few days I received the news that he had been asked to accept the job of technical adviser on *King Solomon's Mines*. This was wonderful but—wives were not allowed to accompany film units. Armand remembered me and was on the point of refusing the assignment when he met Deborah Kerr, who was to star in the film.

"I got a shock," he told me later. "When I saw Deborah on the set at some distance, I thought you had flown out to Hollywood to pay me a surprise visit. She was so like you."

My likeness to Deborah touched off a bright idea in Armand's fertile mind. At the next story conference on the picture he threw out the suggestion that he knew a girl who was her double. Sam Zimbalist bit; the first result was a cryptic telegram to me in New York:

SEND MEASUREMENTS LOVE ARMAND.

What was happening? Knowing nothing, I thought for a moment that Armand was having a joke with me; but he is not the sort of man who cables jokes. So I wired back:

THIRTYSIX BUST TWENTYFOUR WAIST THIRTYSIX AND A HALF HIPS FIVE FOOT SIX AND A HALF HEIGHT ONE TWENTY POUNDS WEIGHT LOVE MICHAELA.

The expression on the telegraph clerk's face was worth watching.

After a few hours came the clincher:

MEASUREMENTS PERFECT YOU ARE TO DOUBLE FOR DEBORAH KERR CONTRACT FOLLOWING LOVE ARMAND.

So it was Africa—after all these hopes and fears. For

29

King Solomon's Mines was to be filmed in Kenya, one of the lands of my dreams. Kenya, home of the lion.

Our preparations for an African journey had already been completed; we were ready to move at once. We flew to Brussels. The deadline date for arrival in Nairobi was easy to make—or so we thought. But to get reservations on a plane going there was not easy: it was, in fact, next to impossible. We just had to sit tight and wait for cancellations.

I was strung up to breaking point.

I had lived and breathed Africa all my life, and on our way there. Now we were stuck, unable to get a plane.

Armand took it all with maddening calm, but as day after day passed, without plane seats, his brows began to wrinkle with annoyance.

The cloud—the hoodoo, I had begun to call it—lifted when we got a plane as far as Nice. From there we hopped to Rome, Malta and Greece. In Athens we were bundled into a plane bound for Cairo.

From above the Mediterranean I got my first sight of Africa. I was so filled with emotion that I had to press my handkerchief into my eyes. Armand said, pointing to the window:

"Well, there's your land of dreams. . . . And mine, too."

"I know," was all I could say.

My first experience in Egypt was rather embarrassing. Visiting the ladies' room in Cairo's Mena Hotel, I was struck by the absence of attendants. I began to wash my hands when I *felt* something behind me. Turning, I saw two huge Egyptians, in baggy trousers and fezzes, and with MENA HOTEL inscribed on their blouses, advancing towards me with smiling but grim intent.

One of them made a grab for my leg. I felt like screaming and struck out with my wet hands. But my legs were grabbed in spite of my resistance, and to my horror they began to soap and wash them. When they reached my knees, I panicked and shouted "Stop!" tore myself away and ran.

Armand was waiting in the vestibule. I panted out the details of my unnerving experience.

"Curious," he said. "It must be a local custom. . . . Never heard of it. Nothing like that happened in the men's room. I wonder why?"

He laughed all the way to the airport over the incident.

At the airport there was a passport queue. I joined it while Armand took charge of the baggage. Hidden somewhere beneath the fat of the Egyptian passport officer there must have been an ardent Antony pining for his Cleopatra. His manner was, to say the least, flirtatious. He turned on me moist ox-like eyes and examined my passport, lingering over the photograph.

"This is destiny," he said in a hoarse voice. "We were born on the same day. . . . When do you return?"

"I'm afraid I shan't be returning," I said in business-like tones.

"I find that impossible to believe," he replied, tapping the passport with a fat forefinger. "There's something fateful in our birthdays."

"Well, I'm going to Kenya to make films with my husband."

He wasn't at all put out. He bowed deeply and looked soulfully into my eyes.

"All Egypt is yours!" he exclaimed gallantly.

I thought this had gone on long enough and looked around for Armand.

"Ah, here is my husband," I said.

But Antony instantly left his post, swept us both to the head of the queue, and with a flourish handed us into the plane.

"All Egypt is yours!" he repeated fervently, as the door of the plane began to close.

Armand looked at me quizzically.

"I wonder if that includes the Pyramid of Cheops," he said solemnly, as we took our seats. "If so, we've got that permanent home you're always talking about."

I told Armand what had led up to the remark. All he said was:

"That birthday stunt is neat. Wonder how many times a day he pulls it off?"

From the window of the plane I saw my childhood travel books come to life. Here were the originals of the coloured plates that used to stir my imagination: stretches of flat yellow desert and ahead, in the far distance, mysterious limestone hills, and beyond, a mere stain on the sky, a dark mist that might be the edge of a forest leading into the very heart of my dreams. Many hours passed.

Armand told me: "We are nearly in Nairobi."

Looking down, I saw a series of black circles on the golden earth. I asked Armand what they were.

"Maniattas," he replied. "The Masai build a circle of thorn bushes to enclose their huts which, by the way, are made of cow-dung. At night the cattle are brought into the enclosure. The idea is to protect them from lions.

"The Masai are nomads. When the grass in an area has been eaten, they move on. But they are less nomadic than they used to be. They are learning a little about soil conservation from the British, who have tried to teach them about the dangers of over-grazing . . . but, you know, the Masai really prefer to go the way of their ancestors centuries ago."

Nairobi was an anti-climax after my thrilling view of Africa from the sky; but even its matter-of-fact buildings and air of European efficiency could not damp my romantic ardour. This was Africa, I told myself, as we walked to the car which took us to the New Stanley Hotel, and I had already a sense of belonging. I had lived

A Papua maiden being tattooed by her mother; this is always done when girls reach puberty. The necklaces are of dogs' teeth

When we filmed this jungle close-up the elephant charged us. We got away — but saw it stamp on our lunch-basket

Ochre - painted Aborigines mimic animals in their dances. I was never embarrassed by the nudity of these "children of nature"

We film flying foxes on the Great Barrier Reef; the creatures had been driven from the mainland by drought

through all this before so intensely that it was like coming home.

But the figures that walked about the Nairobi streets! These were indeed like figures in a dream—bearded Sikhs, superbly aloof; Indians from the Punjab and Gujerat, eternally graceful like the figures in the frieze; tall slender Masai Morani, dressed in cowhide and decorated with red paint; bowed Kikuyu women carrying enormous bundles.

The hotel enchanted me. As I moved about our room, unpacking what we should need at once, I felt that I was entering a new dimension of life—expansive, joyous, free. But Armand came in later with dubious news.

"What do you think?" he said. "They've already got two doubles here for Deborah Kerr. . . . It's a rather awkward situation."

I stared at him and dropped the stuff I was unpacking on the bed.

"And," he went on, "the whole unit is under orders to leave the hotel to-morrow."

"Oh, no! Why?"

"The management are highly displeased about something. So they say they want the rooms."

I at once sought out the hotel manager. He was polite but firm. He needed the accommodation. I pointed out our predicament. Could a whole Hollywood unit be ejected, simply because of some little international misunderstanding?

"Come," I said. "We English pride ourselves on our sense of fair play. . . . I'm English and can take it. But it's bound to look bad to the others."

The fair play appeal did the trick and the unit were allowed to stay on. But presently yet another double for Deborah arrived—making, with me, the fourth. The situation could become embarrassing. A decision had to be made. They did not look a bit like Deborah. Moreover, I was under contract. Curtis, the production chief, finally decided that jobs would be found for the other girls.

The unit rapidly grew into a colony. With the arrival of Andrew Marton, director of action scenes, head cameraman Bob Surtees, director Compton Bennett, and later of Stewart Granger, Deborah Kerr, Richard Carlson, and the rest of the company, more than fifty people had to be accommodated.

Yet another double had to be found, but not for Deborah—a double for old Nairobi. A little town called Machakos was chosen. I was gradually becoming soaked in Africa and this move helped to take me deeper into the astonishing and beautiful reality.

The native dances held me spellbound. The script of the film called for a great ceremonial dance. For three days hundreds of magnificent men and women of the Masai, Kikuyu and Wakamba tribes abandoned themselves to dances that seemed to transcend the body and became entrancing evolutions of the spirit. "Out of this world" is a catch phrase that can aptly be applied to these amazing performances.

One day I was sitting among some Masai women, trying to learn their language; they motioned to me to join them in the great *Ngoma,* as we say in Swahili, meaning the Great Dance. The dancers formed two lines, the men with their backs to the women. I imitated the women's steps as best I could, but when the men turned to face their partners my opposite number stopped dead in his tracks. His eyes were full of superstitious fear. He must have thought a Masai girl had been transformed by magic into a white woman. For a few seconds the dance hung suspended, but a ripple of laughter from the ranks of the dancers broke the suspense and, with joyous shouts and much teasing, we began to step out again.

Thud, thud, thud the drums beat into the brain, banishing all rational thought. A column of dust rises from the hundreds of pounding feet. A state of ecstasy is reached where the dance becomes the sole object of existence. I had heard much of the mystical experiences that come from magical practices, and now I understood. Africa was yielding up to me one of the ancient secrets of its people, and in the frenzy of the dance I became one with them.

I took over a drum and while beating it I underwent a new emotional experience. A strange compelling power seems to issue from the primitive instrument; one feels that one is controlling the souls of the dancers. My drum beating drew a tall Wakamba warrior towards me. He danced and bounded round me as if held to me by a chain whose links were formed of drum beats. While he was dancing round and round a white girl approached me, accompanied by a young man. It was Deborah Kerr and her husband, Tony Bartlett. The introduction was managed between drum beats, for I didn't want to break the rhythm.

The Africans were delighted that a white woman should dance with them. When the dance was over they lined up in hundreds to shake my hand. From that moment these people became my friends, and I knew that I should never feel strange and apart from Africans as long as I lived.

I had engaged a young boy of nine to carry my make-up case. The money I gave him put him in a higher earning category than his father. He seemed devoted to me. About a year later, when we were leaving Nairobi for a safari from East to West Africa, he came to see me. His manner told me that something was on his mind. I thought he might need money and offered him some. He refused it.

He stood before me, hanging his head, his dark eyes clouded with trouble.

"Tell me," I said.

He murmured some words, the purport of which was that I should adopt him.

"But your mother and father," I said, "wouldn't they be very sad to lose their son?"

As he did not reply, I raised his chin in my hand and said:

"I will be your aunt—the sister of your mother."

All the misery vanished from his face. He bade me good-bye happily and went away, singing.

To return to the filming. My job as Deborah's double meant long hours, Sunday-less weeks, relentless travelling by chartered planes, cars or buses. Worst of all, it meant almost continuous separation from my husband. I perforce had to be with the second unit; Armand was usually away on long reconnaissance trips by plane to the Congo, to Ruanda, to the lion country in the Masai Reserve. He was still away as the first anniversary of our wedding drew near. I wanted desperately to be with him when it came round. The MGM people were good enough to give me permission to visit him; this was really an important concession on their part and I was very grateful to them.

I had to fly there. The only plane I could get was an Auster, a tiny two-seater affair; but as soon as I saw the pilot my doubts vanished. He was a competent-looking young man named Macdonald, with a short, trimmed beard, neatly dressed in a well-cut bush jacket and shorts. He carried a folded newspaper under his arm. "A city man strayed into the bush," I thought; and I could see him in a dark suit, a bowler hat, and holding a tightly rolled umbrella, going to his business near the Bank in the City of London.

He was a fine pilot and very popular. His almost daily trips over desolate African territory were just part of his day's work, but they weren't joy rides. . . . A few months later, his plane caught fire in the air, and he was killed. . . .

We flew over the Longonot and Suswa volcanoes, heading for the plains. The plane bumped, swayed and fluttered in the air-pockets and violent up-currents common in the African skies. Macdonald asked with a poker face and in a matter-of-fact voice if I would like to try my hand at piloting—it was a dual-control machine —but I declined and he gave a deep chuckle. Maybe I looked greener than I felt.

I remember him saying, in the nicest tone: "Perhaps another time, then."

We landed on a handkerchief-sized airstrip in the middle of dense bush. A three-ton truck was waiting for me in the charge of a very large African driver.

"You Memsahib Dennisi?" he asked, politely.

"Yes," I said, pleased with that "memsahib".

"Then we go," he said.

It was my first experience of driving through the bush. To my untutored eyes there was no track at all; the car seemed to plunge into impenetrable bush and through waving grassland. The African driver must have had an uncanny sense of country. His keen eyes picked out tyre marks invisible to me. Every tree and bush seemed to act as a sign-post for him.

Hours passed. The landscape never changed. Bush and grassland, grassland and bush, until I was convinced that we were hopelessly lost. Occasionally we came upon herds of impala and groups of topi. An immense blue sky, broken with theatrical clouds, encompassed our world. Time stood still; a marvellous sense of peace invaded me. Conversation did not break the spell, for I knew as little Swahili as the driver knew English. Lost, I told myself again and again, and unable to do anything about it.

But I was suddenly aroused out of the somnolence of a late African afternoon. The truck took a sharp turn, rounded a clump of trees, and there was the camp—with Armand's tall figure striding towards me.

"What a place!" I said, after our greetings were over. "What a divine place!"

"Yes, this is the real Africa," said Armand. "No hotels, no film locations. Just Africa as it was centuries ago.

37

Unspoilt. Jump into the safari car. We have seven lions on a kill."

For me the peak of fulfilment was reached. We sat in an open safari car and watched lions, whole families of lions, only a few feet away. The look on their faces seemed benign. Watching one magnificent animal I could almost swear that he smiled. I longed to get out and stroke his mane.

In that hour I felt that I was accepted by the vast continent and its wild creatures.

Oh, the music of Africa!

In our tent by the river, my ear began to distinguish between two natural orchestras: by day the melodies of bird songs of such rapturous quality that I sometimes sat entranced for long spells listening to them, and the muted sounds of small animals; by night the soul-shaking symphony of lion roars against the background of the gurgling, high-pitched laughter of hyenas and the croak and chirp of frogs. My ear learned to pick out the woof-woof of the hippo, the snort of the rhino.

One night I was standing outside the tent, listening, when I heard a strange animal call. It sounded like a sudden blast on a trumpet.

"Elephant," said Sid Downey, MGM's white hunter and guide who was standing near me.

"How lucky I am!" I exclaimed. "Admit it, Sid, you and Armand have laid all this specially on for me."

"Not me. It might be Armand's idea of a wedding anniversary present for you. But you certainly have the luck. Africa seems to like you."

Armand's Lion Camp, as I named this place, was a luxurious affair compared with what we were to experience later on. We had African servants to prepare our meals; for breakfast there was orange juice and cornflakes, bacon and eggs. The coffee was wonderful, and we even had a cocktail before lunch.

In the evenings a big fire was lighted. We sat around

it eating our last meal for the day and were in bed by eight o'clock. The river flowed by, and over us was the protecting parasol of a tall, yellow-barked thorn tree. There were a thousand things to do—and to learn. All animals throw off different smells and I became proficient in identifying them. Although my senses were still largely untrained, I knew instantly whether elephants or buffalo were near.

Of course, my stay in this African paradise had to come to an end. I radioed imploringly for extra leave. Back came the answer: I was wanted for urgent filming at Murchison Falls.

I had to tear myself away from the camp, but Armand came with me to make it easier. On the airstrip as the plane came in for me there was born a story of my wifely devotion which later spread over all Africa.

As the plane touched down I noticed that Armand's shirt was unbuttoned to the waist and I began to do it up. To my horror I saw a huge tick gorging in his navel. He looked down and saw it too.

"Stand still," I said, "while I pick this thing out."

At that moment the pilot of the plane—Trench, not Macdonald—taxied up. He saw me perform the operation, which took time and patience, of removing the swollen tick. I had no idea at the time that the death of the tick would start a story which would precede me wherever I went in Africa.

Nairobi again. Most of the unit had already left, to the location at Butiaba. I, with five others who had been left behind for various reasons, was assigned to a chartered plane, and we flew to Entebbe in Uganda. From there we proceeded by car towards the location.

This was very different country from Kenya; it was lush and green and pastoral. The *shambas* (Swahili for gardens) were full of manioc and bananas and leafy trees. At Masindi we received instructions: wait until sent for.

I raged at the futility of things. To think that I had left Armand's Lion Camp to kick up my heels here! It was maddening—but it was film business. The hotel was comfortable and I found solace in a baby velvet monkey which I bought from an African. Its mother had been shot and it looked the loneliest little thing in the world.

It would have died had I not managed to find a feeding bottle and baby food for it. At night the sad little creature slept with me quite comfortably and I carried it around with me all day. I have never forgotten my feelings as I watched its tiny hands, so like those of a human baby, clasping the feeding bottle; they were not much bigger than my thumbnail and perfectly formed.

At last came the call to Butiaba. From there, following instructions, we proceeded by boat up the Victoria Nile to Murchison Falls, surely one of the most dramatic spectacles in the world. Enormous volumes of water gush from two steep clefts of rock with a force that seems to split the cliff asunder. Down roars the torrent into the river to dash itself into foam and spray. And the river swarms with hippos and crocodiles.

We walked to the top of the Falls. Here there is a round pool in which, said the script of *King Solomon's Mines,* Deborah was to bathe after having cut her hair.

I had been sent for all the way from Armand's Lion Camp to do the bathing and hair-washing scene.

True, it was one of the most important scenes in the picture, for in it begins Stewart Granger's awakening interest in Deborah; and I was given very explicit directions.

But at once things went wrong. The bathing suit had been lost. I was told that I would have to do the scene without a bathing suit. But I remembered seeing a flesh-coloured bathing suit being packed with other clothes, and I began to have doubts about its having been lost. When I refused point blank to do the scene without it, of course miraculously it was found.

That scene!

The midday heat was frightful. We dragged ourselves up to the top of the Falls streaming with perspiration. The sun smote us like a golden hammer, flattening body and mind. All the way up the cameraman emitted volleys of abuse against the heat, the location, the scene, and the general condition of man's life on earth. But when it was suggested that he hand over his camera and tripod to an African bearer, he refused to do so on the ground that this would be against trade union regulations.

The sight of the pool frightened me, for I could not swim. It looked very deep.

"How deep is this water?" I asked.

"Oh, four feet or so," I was assured.

But an eight-foot stick failed to reach the bottom, in the place where I was supposed to stand. A shallower place was found. My director got into the water with me and held my hand until we were ready to take the scene. From the side one of the unit men beat the water with a stick to make beautiful circles round me.

I had to lather my hair with a coal-tar shampoo and strong yellow soap. The ordeal lasted for three hours. All the time the sun beat down relentlessly. Towards the end it was sheer agony; finally the director was satisfied and shouted "Cut!" for the last time. I staggered down, my hair like a straw mat, my eyes red and inflamed by the coal-tar.

Suddenly I began to laugh. I had thought of the romantic picture that cinema audiences would see a few months later and contrasted it with the grotesque reality: that is, if the whole scene didn't end on the cutting room floor. It was my last laugh for some time.

When I returned I found that my baby monkey, whom I had left behind while we were filming, had died. As I handed its tiny stiff body over to an African for burial, I felt that something had died in me too, and an oppressive sense of foreboding haunted me for days.

Back in Butiaba, we fell on Curtis like vultures. He had brought the mail with him. There were two letters from Armand.

"I miss you frightfully, dearest," he wrote. "Why not resign and join me here?"

Easier said than done, for transport was already being arranged to take us back to Entebbe, and I hated the idea of letting anyone down, though I was under no illusion that my services were indispensable.

But I climbed into the last car for the journey with regret. That sense of foreboding was still with me. My companions were an assistant director and a cameraman with a mania for speed.

"Faster, faster!" he ordered the native driver.

He didn't want to miss his dinner, he kept saying.

"Get a move on! Step on it!"

Cold and thoroughly miserable, I was dozing. Hours passed. Then instantly I was fully awake and aware of danger. I saw as in a dream the car swerve off the road and charge up a steep slippery bank. In the headlights vast and sinister trees rushed at us like monsters in a nightmare. The next moment I felt that the car had taken off and we were airborne.

Thoughts rushed through my mind with lightning speed, succeeded by powerful visual images. The figure of Armand flew past me.

"What a pity," I remember thinking, "what a pity when there's so much to do. How awful for Armand!"

The small dead monkey swam before me and eluded my grasp. Then I was enveloped in blackness, shot with tiny tongues of flame which formed a circling red mist. I fell, fell fell. . . .

The next thing I remember was a voice saying, "Thank God she's alive!" I was hazily conscious of being dragged feet first—it must have been through a window of the car. As my senses gradually returned I found I was lying on car seats by the side of the road. Something was wrong

42

with my face and instinctively I put my hand across my eyes and nose out of which blood was pouring.

I turned to look at the driver who was lying near me. He had a great cut on his cheekbone and, I learned later, chest injuries.

The other two were vomiting nearby—from shock.

The car was unrecognizable—it had fallen back from the high bank which it had climbed, on to the road, upside down, and crushed. It seemed incredible that we should have come out of it alive.

I rose painfully to test myself and staggered about. I felt no pain in any of my limbs and was satisfied there were no broken bones. But I knew my nose was broken, although the bleeding had nearly stopped.

The speed-crazy cameraman, the one who had kept yelling "Faster! faster!", was the only one of us who was completely unhurt.

Rain was falling. For three hours we waited for help to arrive. Some natives who found us were at first too scared to do anything but roll their terrified eyes from the upturned car to ourselves, dishevelled and blood-stained on the bank.

We begged them to fetch help. After a while they agreed to get their chief's bicycle—it was two miles away —and find assistance. The rain beat down steadily, drenching us. A sort of delirium took hold of me and it seemed hours before a native returned on the bicycle with the news that an African ambulance, which was picking up a man dying of tetanus, would soon come for us.

My face was a bruised and bloody mass of pain. To touch it lightly with my finger-tips was agonizing. I listened to my companions reconstructing the crash. We had hit a tree and my face had been smashed into the back of the seat in front of me.

Finally, the ambulance arrived and we were driven to the native hospital at Kampala where the tetanus victim

—a dreadful sight—was deposited, and then on to the European hospital where my companions were discharged. More than anything I wanted to go to Armand at Entebbe, but the doctor insisted on detaining me.

"Do you realize," he asked, "that your nose is broken?"

"That won't kill me," I replied. "Let me come back in the morning."

"Not only your nose, young lady, but your cheekbone is smashed—and probably the upper jawbone as well. Do you still want to go?"

"Yes," I said. "I must meet my husband."

We compromised. The doctor telephoned to Entebbe and I allowed myself to be put to bed. By a curious premonition Armand had flown to Entebbe by chartered plane that very day and was there when the doctor's phone call came through. By four o'clock in the morning he had reached the hospital, imagining the worst.

He took my hands and kissed me, and I saw his strained face relaxing.

"Darling," he said, "I love you whatever you look like. It's you and not your physical appearance that matters."

These sweet comforting words made me uneasy. I reached for a hand-mirror and glanced into it. A frightful apparition stared back at me. My face was as grotesque as a sculptor's unfinished clay model, lop-sided, out of drawing. One eye was completely closed, the other swollen and discoloured.

I handed the mirror back to Armand. The shock was terrible. As I lay there I felt his hand tightening on mine, and, remembering his words, I slowly regained my calm and felt glad to be alive. All was well so long as Armand loved me.

He stayed all night at the hospital. In the morning I was X-rayed. The doctor was right. Nose, cheekbone and upper jaw were all broken on the right side.

"You'll have to fly to Nairobi to see Michael Wood,"

said the doctor. "He's the finest surgeon in East Africa. But first, you must rest."

Drugs kept the pain in check. I ate enormously and began to feel well. The MGM people were wonderful. Menus were sent daily from Entebbe with sympathetic messages written on the back. There was a stream of visitors from the unit to see me in hospital. I wondered why they showed so much concern when I was feeling so well. Then I realized that for film people an accident to the face is virtually the end of a career.

I mentioned the matter to Armand.

"I don't mind," I said, "so long as you still love me and I can go on expeditions with you."

But the doctors feared a permanent eye injury because the cheekbone had been broken so near to the optic nerve. When my eye finally opened, however, I was overjoyed to learn that their fears were unfounded.

The X-ray photographs which Michael Wood examined in Nairobi left him in no doubt as to the gravity of my injuries.

"We can't operate on you here," he said frankly. "You must be flown to London. There's only one person in the world who can do this job—Sir Archibald MacIndoe, at East Grinstead, in Sussex. I'll cable him to see you as soon as you arrive."

Sir Archibald's fame is, of course, world-wide. Everyone knows of the miracles in plastic surgery he performed on the smashed and burned faces of Battle of Britain pilots. He was a friend of Deborah Kerr and her husband, and they had talked to me about him.

We were to leave at once.

"This is not farewell to Africa, is it, Armand?" I asked as we were packing.

"No, of course not, darling. We'll be back here very soon."

I hated to leave; but this job on my face had to be done. News of my accident had become known outside

Africa and some queer versions of it appeared in the newspapers. In one Hollywood journal, which we saw in Cairo on our way to London, there was a report of my death. It sounded convincing even to me.

"How does it feel being dead?" asked Armand, when we were flying over the Mediterranean into a miraculous sunset.

"Fine," I said, squeezing his hand.

At London Airport we were overwhelmed by transport. An airport ambulance, a Red Cross ambulance, and a chauffeured limousine sent by MGM were waiting for us. We chose the latter and drove straight to the famous East Grinstead hospital.

I stood before the great surgeon with the feeling that he held my future life in his hands.

Sir Archibald, a handsome New Zealander, would be distinguished in any company in the world. In his own hospital he is a scientist who puts the world in his debt. His air of confidence buoyed me up, and from the moment I first saw him I never had the slightest doubt about the outcome of any treatment he proposed.

He advised an immediate operation.

There was a day's rest and preparation. The next morning I was given an injection with a syringe which seemed big enough for a horse, and I was still laughing about it when I lost consciousness. . . .

I opened my eyes.

A voice said: "How do you feel, dearest?"

For a minute or so I could not utter the words that were on the tip of my tongue. I sought his hand but somehow found his face.

Then strength flowed back into me. I half-raised myself from the pillow.

"Take it easy, darling," he said.

Then the words came.

"Armand, I'm terribly hungry."

"We'll soon fix that," he said.

46

Hunger was the measure of my rapid recovery. The operation was a surgical masterpiece. Not the trace of a scar remained. I was healed.

Out of the serene days of my short convalescence loomed Africa again, spreading before me its beauties and terrors.

CHAPTER THREE

FIRST SAFARI

I FACED the world again with my face in bandages. They are not the most comfortable of disguises, but Sir Archibald insisted that I keep them on until Christmas Day.

Joy at my recovery was shadowed by the sadness of having to leave the many good friends I had made at East Grinstead. I looked back at the hospital from the window of the car that was taking me to London Airport with tears in my eyes.

Sir Archibald had said: "Take the utmost care. Avoid any kind of risks. Play safe. Don't remove the splints before Christmas Day."

This was, of course, excellent advice, but I didn't see how I could adhere to it strictly when I resumed the arduous work of filming in Africa. But sitting in the car I was happy to dismiss the future and live just for the present.

I was on my way to London Airport to catch a plane for Antwerp. With my face draped in a georgette scarf, yashmak fashion, I was able to cover up the splint on my nose and so avoid arousing curiosity. In the plane I thought only of my reunion with Armand.

He was staying with his family, and *Maman* had arranged a sumptuous dinner for which the rarest of old Burgundies had been drawn from the cellars. I was about to drink from my half-filled glass, when Armand whispered: "Look before you drink, darling."

I peered into the glass and saw a wedding ring. It was inscribed with the date of our marriage.

48

Right: Riding the rhino

Below: The rare okapi (only six in all the world's zoos) enjoys his bottle of milk

My "lady's maid"—the girl with one expression

Above: Peruvian Indians still play the music and perform the dances, centuries old, of Inca times. These are Chicheros of southern Peru

Right: Colorado Indians; father, mother and daughter. I became a member of their tribe

The funeral of an Indian child in Ecuador contrasts with that of an Aborigine, whose body is trussed in grass and burned

"Oh, Armand, what a lovely surprise!" I cried.

He kissed my hand and my happiness was complete.

The next morning we were on our way to Africa. Rome again, Cairo, Khartum. We flew via Stanleyville to Usumbura to join the MGM unit in Ruanda-Urundi. As soon as we arrived the unit doctor visited me. He was astonished at my rapid recovery.

"This is marvellous," he said. "I was sure it would take six months to get you into action again. What a wonderful piece of surgery!"

On his advice another double for Deborah Kerr had been engaged. He had never anticipated that I should be back so soon and the work had to go on. I thoroughly understood.

We arrived on the day of Christmas Eve. At a party in the director's room the splint suddenly fell off my nose— actually fell off while I was sitting quietly chatting to one of the unit. Without any help from me, the splint had obeyed Sir Archibald MacIndoe's instructions on its own!

We had a wonderful party on Christmas Day. Deborah, Stewart Granger and Dick Carlson cut sandwiches and cooked. Then they blacked their faces, and, dressed as African houseboys, served the dinner. But a number of familiar faces were missing. Vernon, the assistant director who had been in the car crash with me, was still in hospital suffering from shock, and about twenty-five other members of the unit were down with amoebic dysentery.

The problem of Deborah's double was solved by a happy compromise. It was decided that the new girl and myself should share the job. This seemed to me fair and even generous, considering all the circumstances.

The work in Ruanda completed, we flew back to Nairobi. Our next assignment was to climb Mount Kenya. The unit doctor sought me out.

"Take my advice," he said, "and let the other double do this job."

"Oh, but I want to go, doctor!"

"I can't let you take the risk."

"Does than mean you forbid me to go?" I asked.

"Yes, I'm afraid it does. I'm sorry, but there it is," he replied sympathetically but firmly.

I appealed to Michael Wood, the surgeon. He also vetoed the idea. That settled the matter.

I hung around Nairobi disconsolate for a few days. Then came the news that I was to join the unit in a journey to the Wagenia country to shoot a big scene which Armand was to organize.

The route was an exciting one. Our destination was a part of the Congo which we had visited before. It involved a journey by air down that wonderful river which seems to lead, in Joseph Conrad's phrase, into "the heart of darkness".

We landed, and travelled in one of the big canoes towards the chief's village. The talking drums were relaying the news of our impending arrival. A welcoming committee was lined up to greet us. We were surrounded by warriors and a host of chanting Wagenia women, many of whom I had danced with the last time we visited the place.

They seemed delighted to see me. Seizing my arms, they swept me into a dance and we danced our way up to the village in flowing rhythmic movements, imitative of the swing of oars and water currents, which all river people incorporate into their dances.

Armand and I thoroughly enjoyed the work here. It brought me into even closer contact with Africa and I was forming the conviction that this great and mysterious continent would sooner or later become my permanent home.

When the day's work was finished we would often walk beyond the village, sit down for an hour, and discuss our future plans. I shall never forget the magic of those times.

"Kenya's the place to settle down in," Armand concluded. "We'll buy some land there and build our own house."

"What sort of house?" I asked. "I mean what sort of design?"

Then we would begin to argue. Finally we decided that Portuguese architecture would harmonize best with the African landscape. Armand planned and designed the house. It was actually built with stone taken from our own quarry. My contribution to it was the staircase which I designed in the Portuguese style wrought-iron, the motif being a delicate tracery of leaves.

The house, by the way, was finished four years ago. We have yet to live in it in a physical sense. But in imagination I am never far away from it. In the big city where I am now writing it rises before me in all its solitary beauty, this dream house surrounded by the things Armand and I love best—native people and wild animals.

But I am over-running my narrative.

The big Congo scene was finished and *King Solomon's Mines* was nearing completion as far as Armand and I were concerned. It had been a rich, amusing and sometimes frustrating experience. I had seen enough of filmmaking to marvel at the minds of movie moguls.

They are a race apart. Common sense is a commodity they have little use for. They are attracted by the grandiose and the irrational. Sometimes the consequences are ludicrous.

Take the problem of Deborah Kerr's doubles. Deborah was perfectly willing to dispense with doubles in all her scenes, but the film company would not permit her to do so. She is a woman of high intelligence, very nice to work with, and very kind. And she has a large fund of common sense.

After the bathing scene in which I had doubled, Deborah suggested that her hair should be ruffled, since she was supposed to have had a quick shampoo in the open air. Hollywood said no. They took the preposterous view that, whatever the circumstances, she must look glamorous at all times.

The result was that when the film was shown, a strong critical attack was directed against the bathing scene in which Deborah appeared with not a hair of her head out of place!

The making of *King Solomon's Mines* involved me in some amusing incidents with all sorts of queer people in various places.

I remember my encounter with a "line-shooter" whom we met at Livingstone airport one day when Armand and I were flying down to Cape Town. He looked like a professional charmer running to seed. At the moment he was subjecting an attractive air hostess to bombardment.

"You'd be a riot in pictures," he told her. "I'd say a screen test was hardly necessary in your case. . . . You've got it all."

The girl was flattered and looked at him with shining eyes.

"Yes," he went on, "that's how *I* see the matter, and I think I know what I'm talking about. So-and-so and so-and-so and so-and-so" (he mentioned three famous Hollywood executives) "are among my best friends. A word to any one of them and you'd be offered a contract. Take my word for it."

This was no business of mine, but he spoke in a loud exhibitionist's voice and I couldn't help but hear.

"What are you doing here?" asked the girl. "Making a film?"

"Yes, just finished one . . . *King Solomon's Mines* . . . I was directing."

"It must have been interesting."

"Oh, not particularly. Most of these Hollywood pro-

ductions are fakes, you know. Take this picture, for
instance. Not one of the stars set a foot in Africa. . . .
What do you think of that?"

I could stand it no longer. Throwing down the book I
had been reading, I rose from my seat and shouted in a
voice that could be heard all over the airport:

"You are the fake! It so happens that my husband was
technical adviser for the film you've been talking about.
All the stars have spent months in Africa. . . . I was a
member of the unit and I've certainly never seen you
before in my life."

Everybody in the room began to laugh. The air hostess
rose rather stiffly.

"Excuse me," she said to the "line-shooter", "I've no
more time to talk to Hollywood big shots."

Poor man! He was on the same plane with us on the
trip to Johannesburg, all alone and looking very crest-
fallen. A fool; but I felt rather sorry for him.

We had made our plans in New York for our African
safari. The idea was to cross the continent from East to
West—from Mombasa to Matadi—collecting material for
a film during the journey. It was a big undertaking, but
it was to be Armand's fifth overland crossing of the
African continent, and we were not in the least daunted
by the many difficulties that presented themselves when
we actually began to organize. The film material obtained
on this trip eventually became the RKO picture *Below
the Sahara*.

As soon as we landed in East Africa I fell ill with
agonizing stomach cramps and an almost paralysing
fatigue. I knew these were symptoms of bacillary
dysentery. Armand became alarmed when I could no
longer conceal the pain.

"Is it so bad, darling?" he asked anxiously.

"I'm so sorry," I said, "to be such a burden."

I knew that if my suspicions were confirmed, the

53

planned expedition might be held up indefinitely.

I stayed in hospital for three weeks. As soon as I began to move around I fell violently ill again. The specialist whom I consulted pronounced the verdict.

"You're suffering from amoebic dysentery. You should be treated with aureomycin."

But none was available in the Nairobi hospital because of the restriction on dollar imports. Aureomycin was made only in America, and its price was still astronomical. This was a serious situation for us. Armand sat by my bed, holding my hand, when he suddenly exclaimed:

"Why didn't I think of it before! I know where we can get aureomycin. They use the stuff all the time on my chimpanzee farm in Florida. I'll cable for some."

What a relief! I now recalled Armand telling me of the success the University of Miami scientists had with the drug in treating delicate anthropoids at his chimpanzee farm.

"Oh, why didn't we think of it before!" I cried.

The cable went off at once. Back came the reply that a supply of aureomycin was already on its way by air. We were all very happy, but we hadn't taken officialdom into our calculations.

As soon as the drug arrived at the Nairobi airport, the hospital authorities went to get it. Nothing doing. The customs officials asked to see our import licence. We didn't possess one. All right, then. No aureomycin could be released.

We were frantic. I staggered out of bed and got through on the telephone to the chief customs officer. He was hide-bound with red tape. I couldn't move him. In answer to my pleas, he quoted regulations. Finally, I almost shrieked:

"There's a woman here dying of amoebic dysentery."

There was, in fact, a very serious case in the hospital, apart from myself.

"I'm sorry," he said.

54

"Release the drug and we can save her," I pleaded.

There was silence at the other end of the line. There was nothing now to lose, and I put the responsibility squarely on his shoulders.

"Her life is in your hands," I said. "I wouldn't like to be in your place if she dies."

The voice said: "Hold the line."

A few minutes later the voice came through again.

"Very sorry for the hold-up. Send a nurse down straight away."

The matron, who was standing beside me, was over-joyed. She hugged me to her beautifully starched bosom.

The Florida chimpanzee farm had sent enough aureomycin to treat several patients. We made it all available to the hospital, of course. Within a few days all the serious cases were out of danger and showing wonderful improvement.

Soon I was fit and ready to go with the expedition. Native staff is always a problem. We finally decided to take with us our African cook and our African house-boy. I had learned a good deal about such matters since I first came to Africa.

Moslem boys are the best—if you can afford them. Pagans are the next best but also on the expensive side. If you are hard up you have to engage Christian boys. The Moslems are usually good workers and do not drink. The pagans are trustworthy but less so than the Moslems. I regret to say my experience has taught me that Christian Mission boys are often untruthful, apt to steal and to drink.

Many of the Kikuyu have had some sort of Christian training. Only a very few of them, however, have succeeded in replacing their old strict tribal morality with Christian values. This is a tragedy.

They are bewildered at the contrast between precept and practice among their Christian teachers. The missionaries teach them how a Christian should behave, yet they see bullies, bigots, adulterers and drunks among the Christian community. They see white men, claiming to be Christians, steal and lie. Is it any wonder that most native Christians are so in name only? This was certainly true of the ones I had in my household.

Shabani, our Moslem house-boy, turned out to be a treasure. He came up to us as we were leaving a famous little restaurant in Nairobi, greeted us in beautiful English, and produced three references—one from the High Commissioner of Mombasa.

Armand looked at him critically.

"You're a bit fat, aren't you?" he remarked.

Shabani evidently took this for a compliment, for he smiled and replied courteously:

"Thank you, sir. You, too, Bwana, are very fat."

Armand simply couldn't resist this and he engaged Shabani on the spot. Later, when we needed a cook, Shabani produced Mucharia, another Moslem, who did not wear a fez and whose teeth were filed to points in the old Kikuyu fashion.

When the two Moslem boys learned that they were to travel with us and that our destination was the land of the pygmies, they were delighted. I watched their behaviour, fascinated. Every day their sense of importance increased. Big things were happening to them. They had to get passports and injections. A sum of money had to be deposited for them with the authorities in case anything happened to us and they were left stranded.

Shabani became a figure of great importance in his Reserve. He posed as an authority on the Congo. His precious passport, containing his photograph, rapidly increased his circle of admirers. They crowded round him to examine the portrait.

Yet if I showed Shabani a photograph, he would as often as not hold it upside down, and I doubt whether he could pick out its forms or knew what it represented. Many Africans, I have found, are quite unable to recognize a picture and not a few of them are colour-blind.

The Masai, by the way, are different. I have shown them pictures of other parts of Africa and they were very interested in animals not found in Kenya. Other peoples beyond their frontiers also attracted their attention and caused them to jabber excitedly—the Asongo-Meno of the Congo, for instance, who wear their hair in a similar fashion to the Masai.

We were going to make the journey to Stanleyville, in the Congo, in a Dodge truck with a specially built safari body—a cage-like arrangement in which we packed all our provisions and equipment. The two boys usually slept on top of this load. It was amusing to hear them speaking English together whenever other natives could overhear. They put on an impressive act as glamorous foreigners, although Mucharia could only speak about forty words of English.

We had been about a month of the journey when Shabani came to me and said:

"Mucharia is sick, Memsahib."

"What's wrong with him, Shabani?"

"A malaria, Memsahib, very bad."

This didn't mean anything, for Shabani diagnosed every illness as a malaria. But when I saw Mucharia he was feverish and complained of pains in his head and all over his body. It certainly looked like malaria. I offered him paludrine.

"No, Memsahib."

All I could get out of him was that he wanted a special medicine I'd never heard of. He was insistent that he must have this medicine, and no other. Naturally nothing could be done until we reached a place with a hospital. There I asked the doctor for the medicine Mucharia wanted.

The doctor looked at me curiously and said we'd better bring both boys to the hospital for an examination.

"Is that necessary?" I asked, for we wanted to push on.

"Very necessary, I should say," the doctor replied. "Don't you know that what your boy has been asking for is a remedy for venereal disease?"

Horrified, we brought the boys to the hospital. But after they had sheepishly left the surgery, the doctor called us into his consulting room.

"I've done every test I know, and there's absolutely no sign of anything wrong."

We asked Mucharia why he wanted that particular medicine. He explained that one of the boys on his Reserve had been given it when he was ill and it had cured him completely.

"Very very good medicine," said Mucharia fervently.

The boys were very subdued while we drove back to camp, but I knew that Shabani wanted to talk to me.

That evening Shabani hung around. I said: "What is it, Shabani?"

His trusting, humid eyes were full of reproach. He said: "Memsahib, why you and Bwana take us that place?"—meaning the hospital.

I explained as best I could.

He said: "Memsahib, what that man think is wrong with us, Mucharia, and me Shabani?"

I said: "He did not know, Shabani."

Shabani raised his voice a little.

"You know what that man did to us, to Mucharia, and to me Shabani? I tell you, Memsahib. . . ."

"I think you had better not tell me, Shabani."

But nothing would hush him; he had the uninhibited candour of a child. He recounted his awful experience to the ultimate detail, his voice trembling with reproach and outraged dignity. Finally, to my relief, he stopped.

I said: "You must try to forget this, Shabani. You must not think or speak of it again."

"I shall try, Memsahib," he said as he went away shaking his head.

All the boys had an immense respect for Armand. He was to them lord and master and they always seemed rather overwhelmed in his presence. He never said a cross or unkind word to them, but they kept their distance with him. His massive figure undoubtedly impressed them, as it did all Africans. His nickname in Swahili is *Bwana Mkubwa*—Big Master.

But to ask anything of a personal nature or a favour, Shabani and Mucharia always came to me. I was their confidante. They would solicit my opinion on a length of coloured cotton—would it be a suitable present for their wives?

I had always doubted whether Mucharia was really a Moslem. When the Moslem festival of Ramadan came round, I was almost sure that he was either not a Moslem or the worst one I had ever met.

Shabani, on the other hand, rigidly kept the fast, neither washing nor drinking, but Mucharia sat by the river stuffing himself with food.

"Why aren't you fasting, Mucharia?" I asked.

He looked at me with embarrassment.

"Poor Shabani," was all he said. At the same time he was obviously deriving a secret pleasure from Shabani's self-denial.

"Aren't you a Moslem?" I asked.

"No," he replied. "I am Cee-Emm-Essi."

C.M.S. are the initials of the Church Missionary Society. Mucharia had solved the problem of getting the best out of both worlds. He pretended to be a Moslem to get higher wages. He adopted Christianity to acquire some schooling and medical services!

One day when we were in the Congo both boys came to me and asked for a rise in pay. They said they could not manage on their wages. I took up the matter with Armand and we agreed to give them more money. Some time later, however, while chatting to the local Belgian official, we learned that their wages (before the increase)

59

were six times higher than those paid to boys in the Congo.

"This is strange," said Armand. "There must be something behind it. I'd like to know the reason why they wanted that extra money."

I soon found out. While staying at the official *gîte d'étape* in a forest village, I noticed that the household was swarming with strange boys, while Shabani and Mucharia sat around all day, holding court, and looking like Oriental potentates.

"What's going on here?" I asked Armand.

Shabani and Mucharia had gone into business as contractors of labour and were employing local people to do their work for them! They were able to pay the locals out of their extra pay, while keeping their original wages intact.

"This is big business," said Armand with a laugh.

Something had to be done about it. When Shabani's paid local helper came into my tent to make my bed, I sent him away and began to make my own bed.

Shabani ran up to me looking shamed and agitated.

"No, Memsahib," he said.

"Why not, Shabani?" I replied. "I don't mind working. There's nothing shameful or undignified in it, you know. In fact, work is good for one. We live by work—all of us." I finished making the bed, while Shabani wrung his hands in discomfort.

After that the contractors of labour went out of business and resumed their household duties with a zest and cheerfulness that were pleasant to behold.

How that Shabani could eat!

He fell sick with malaria and we had to leave him at Stanleyville with Mucharia to look after him. When we visited him in hospital later he was on the road to recovery but complained that he was not getting enough to eat.

"Lucky I brought this," I said, putting by his bed an enormous bowl of food I had brought.

His eyes lit up and he thanked me warmly again and again.

"Now I shall not starve," he said. "If you hadn't brought this I might have died!"

While we were talking one of the hospital orderlies came in with an even bigger enamel bowl than mine, heaped with curried rice, onions and meat.

"I thought you said, Shabani, that you didn't get enough to eat here."

"Well, Memsahib," he replied with a serious face, "you can see for yourself that there's hardly anything—not enough for a bird."

There was enough in that bowl to feed Armand and me for a week.

We now began to penetrate deeper into the Belgian Congo. With every day the sense of isolation, of remoteness from civilization deepened. In such places subtle changes take place in body and mind. Different people are affected in different ways. Armand and I expand in spirit.

But the boys began to show signs of homesickness; they became listless and moody.

"We'll have to talk them out of this state," remarked Armand.

I told them about the pygmy people we should soon see, and of the strange Watusi, piling story on story which, I said, they could tell their wives and children when they returned home. They were immensely cheered by this, and they begged me to re-tell several stories in the minutest detail. They could see themselves back in the Reserve surrounded by an admiring audience of listeners.

The crossing of rivers by native ferries is one of the most exciting and picturesque features of travelling in Africa. Huge dug-out canoes are lashed together with heavy poles on which a raft is built. With the aid of two planks the car can be driven on to the raft which is then

61

either paddled across by the Africans or towed by cable. It is a tricky business, but relatively few cars end up in the river.

The Africans seem to enjoy this procedure immensely, and while the ferry is being paddled with long, spear-shaped oars they sing rousing, rhythmic songs, the rhythm being kept up by drum beat or the stamping of feet. Once we crossed a very wide river with a group of young women as the other passengers. They wore raffia-cloth bikinis and big copper anklets and bracelets, and their hair was treated with resin and painted red with *ngula*; they made a colourful spectacle. Shabani started to show off. He applauded the girls loudly and began to tell them of his travels with many gestures. He was especially eager to impress the wife of an important Moslem. While in the middle of a story, the raft suddenly lurched and Shabani toppled off into the river. He was quickly pulled out, little the worse for his ducking, but his dignity had suffered.

Shabani evidently possessed a keen sense of the dramatic. He came to me later and recounted his adventure in the water with tears in his eyes. I tried to calm him. "You are safe now, Shabani." "Memsahib," he replied, "I was thinking of you and Bwana going back to my wife and telling her that Shabani was dead. Poor Memsahib, poor Bwana!" he wailed, as the tears ran down his fat face. Trying to divert his mind from the sad fate which had *not* befallen him, I asked him to describe how it felt when he plunged into the river. He rose to the bait and with great animation unfolded the story. "I was walking about the bottom of the river for ten minutes, Memsahib. Fishes were flying around my face and my legs were entangled in the mud. I looked around, saw the bottom of the boat and came up to the surface."

"Are you sure it was ten minutes?" I queried. His round black eyes looked straight into mine, and he nodded with solemn conviction, "Ten minutes, Mem-sahib. Yes, indeed, and maybe more."

At Tshikapa we said good-bye to the boys, and Duncan, Armand's assistant, started with them in the small truck on the long trip back to Kenya. Armand and I went on alone by car to Matadi, down through Portuguese West Africa and finally to Luanda where we embarked for Lisbon.

We had crossed the continent of Africa from east to west. We had visited many exotic peoples and had many strange adventures which I shall relate in another chapter.

CHAPTER FOUR

LIFE WITH THE LIONS

LIONS WERE to be the stars of our film *Below the Sahara*. The screen has never known more elusive actors. Nature and men have combined to make the filming of lions difficult. Our pictures would have to be taken in the dry season and as soon as possible after November's long rains.

But this would also have to be fitted between other seasons, equally critical, in which we planned to film other sequences of almost similar importance. December seemed the best compromise we could achieve, and the shooting schedule was geared to a start in early December.

We had no wide choice of locations. Hunters have denuded of lions vast areas of Africa. In the Cape, in the Atlas mountains, and in many of their former haunts they have been practically wiped out. Almost everywhere else, lions have become so wary as to be practically unapproachable. Armand decided on one of the two reasonably good areas which are normally—during dry season—easily accessible from Nairobi—the Southern Masai Reserve. Here the tsetse fly has kept man out of a region teeming with game, and thus stood guardian over the king of beasts.

We flew to Kenya from South Africa, where for the past month we had been photographing ostriches and white rhino. Our first problem was to engage a safari organizer; for on this safari we should have to take large supplies and a staff of Africans to handle the tents and discharge the rough tasks of camp life. Armand and I had to be free to give all our time to filming.

We quickly found our safari organizer in Bill Forsyte.

64

Congo mother and child

Below: Our little Toowoona—
naughty, mischievous, but
irresistibly charming

The water-carrier uses gourds
of all sizes

Left: Every African's dream is to own a bicycle. This boy has made one for himself

Below: Capturing a porcupine, armed only with a blanket

He was both pleasant and willing, but we had some doubts about the partner whom he introduced to us, an American called Brad, who was said to have worked with an oil company up north. He carried a lot of flesh and was rigged out in a Texan-type fringed jacket and a cowpuncher's hat. Experience had taught us to distrust fancy touches in dress. The competent, we had found, was generally garbed in the serviceable. We hoped, however, that Brad would act as camp manager while Bill scouted for food and lion.

Shabani and Mucharia, our own boys, posed a problem. We had given them leave to visit their families, but when they saw the Africans who had been engaged for the trip, they offered to forgo their leave and come with us. Loyalty or jealousy? Perhaps a mixture of both. Or they may have feared for us when they saw the ape-like *Mpishi*, or cook. We thanked them and sent them off home, though I must confess that I had a strange sense of foreboding when we parted company.

Soon our convoy was on the move. We had five vehicles. A safari truck to carry the boys, a power wagon, the Queen Mary—as we called our large three and a half ton truck — our own little safari conveyance in which Armand and I had crossed Africa, from East to West, a few months before, and a saloon car to carry the fragile equipment—cameras, sound recorders, light meters, and so on.

We headed in the direction of the Great Rift Valley. This huge cleft runs thousands of miles through many countries from the Jordan Valley to below Tanganyika. Before us lay a wide panorama, gloomy and forbidding under an overcast sky. At the bottom of the escarpment we passed a little church, built by Italian prisoners of war, roofed with tiles which were orange in the sunshine; in this shadowed day, however, they were subdued to a dark plum colour.

The grey flannel sky was full of rain, and by the time

we made a left turn to reach the Narok road, it started to fall. Decades of rainy seasons had rutted and scarred the road. Cavities—some of them four feet in depth—made the going difficult. In the distance extinct volcanoes thrust their bulk against the rain clouds. The whole huge valley, which Armand remembered as full of game, appeared now lifeless. The eye searched in vain for signs of living things, but nothing stirred. Bill explained that at one time the place swarmed with Thompson gazelle and zebra, but all wild life had been exterminated to protect some imported domestic cattle. This depressed me, and I was glad when we left the valley behind and entered the Reserve.

Armand must have sensed my feeling of depression, for he said: "Cheer up! We'll soon be coming to one of the loveliest little outposts in Africa—Narok."

Suddenly the sun came out and transformed the landscape, lighting the golden vegetation on either side of the road. Like figures in a dream, two tall and beautifully painted Masai appeared and waved their spears to us as they passed. They were magnificent. One was an elder with a shaven head and a blanket over one shoulder. The other was a Morani, a warrior with the vermilion triangle on his chest, his long hair plastered with red clay and hanging down his back, in the Egyptian fashion.

Our course lay through three deep ravines flanked by sheer walls on which scrub and small acacia seemed to cling for dear life. Then once more the baked sienna plains stretched out before us.

"Narok just ahead," said Armand.

I looked eagerly out of the window. What was I expecting—tall, delicate trees, African thatched huts? Armand had talked about "the loveliest little outpost in Africa". Now, confronted with the reality, I looked at him accusingly and he began to laugh. For Narok is a place of surpassing ugliness—a monument to the power of man to transform a natural earthly paradise into a dead end of corrugated iron and petrol can huts.

We lunched standing at the counter of the *duka* and talked to the Indian who owned it; his command of the English language was extraordinary. But we were soon on the move again and headed towards the Temple-Borhams' place, eleven miles away by the Uaso-Nyero river. Major Evelyn Wood Temple-Borham, M.C., nephew of the famous Field-Marshal Sir Evelyn Wood, was game warden of the Southern Masai.

He came out to meet us, accompanied by his wife Joan and their pets—two half-grown lion cubs, and seven dogs, including a small dachshund which ran between the legs of the cubs. The Temple-Borhams were an impressive couple—Lyn, six foot five, with immense shoulders, dark hair and a military moustache, and Joan, five foot two, with red hair, honey-coloured skin and brilliant blue eyes; he every inch a soldier, she a delicate beauty as exquisite as an eighteenth-century French marquise.

After serving in campaigns in Abyssinia, Burma and India, Lyn took over the game warden job in 1946, when there were only twelve good maned lions left in the Masai Reserve. He at once closed the area to hunters and from that time the lion population began to increase.

These two fascinating people began from scratch. Out of the bush they created a Garden of Eden where they lived in complete concord with wild animal life. In a clearing they built their house and cut themselves off from the world's turmoil of making money and spending it, loving the solitude and the chance of observing nature in all its manifold aspects. Both share the qualities necessary for such a lonely but idyllic life. They had outstanding physical courage and moral strength and an identity of interests. Joan, who came of a line of explorers, soldiers and diplomatists, was as completely dedicated to the preservation of wild life in the Reserve as her husband.

Here, I thought, watching these two simple and

67

magnificent people outside their house in the clearing, and surrounded by their pets, is what more than half the world is looking for and will never find: a new Golden Age. But Lyn and Joan had it because they created it out of their own vision and desires and thus found the reality behind the dream.

They promised all the help they could give us. It must be remembered that all the animals in the Reserve lived in a wild state; they roamed the vast open area as free as were their ancestors before the days of gun and trap. Yet Lyn and Joan moved among them without fear, and they even had a favourite pair of lions which they called Gog and Magog. They said they would introduce us to them.

Early next morning we set out for the Reserve. It was a thrilling experience, moving through an almost trackless country in which man seemed to be an intruder and not a master. But the real surprise came when we suddenly saw three lion cubs, playing like kittens, while a short distance away, in the shade of some trees, lay Gog and Magog, watching. They were superb creatures. One had a golden and the other a black mane; for lions can be blond or brunette.

Of course we wanted pictures of them in action, so we tied some meat at the end of a long rope on the back of our truck and tried to lure them into the open from the shade of the thicket. The cubs came first. They ambled heavily towards the meat and began to play with it, but they were too small to tear it off the rope. All the time Gog and Magog watched the performance with wary interest. Then the mother rose and slowly came towards the meat.

As she neared it we moved the truck away from her. She followed and we played cat and mouse with her. From time to time she would spring, just as a cat will at a piece of paper tied to a string. She seemed to be enjoying the game. She would go down on her haunches, wriggle, and then spring, but she did not manage to get the meat.

Meanwhile, her husband, Gog, had been showing signs of impatience at her failure. Rising lazily from the shade, he surveyed the situation and looked about him, as if to say: "Now I'll show the women and children how it ought to be done."

He put up a terrific performance, springing forward and indulging in some really fearsome acrobatics. At one wonderful moment he rose on his hind legs and batted the meat around as though it were a hot potato. There is no doubt that he was giving this show for his mate and cubs, and his pleasure was unmistakable. He had earned the meat, so we cut the rope and let him have it.

We camped about half a mile away from this scene. The safari boys had just finished erecting the tents when it began to rain. The Temple-Borhams left us after we had promised to take good care of their lions.

The next day dawned on misfortunes. All through the night there had been heavy rain; there were now no signs of lion. For hours we drove in search of them, until we returned to the thicket where we had seen them the day before. There were lionesses and their cubs, but no Gog and Magog. For four days the rain came down and finally they also disappeared.

We had had no luck in feeding them. To get good pictures of lions you have to feed them. The trick is to stake down a carcass in the sun, firmly enough to prevent the lions dragging it into the nearest thicket. Lions dislike the sun for long periods, but, of course, to take good photographs light is essential. The feeding business is an art. Lions usually kill every third or fourth day; you must provide enough dead animals—gazelle, zebra or eland— to keep up their interest. Timing is all-important. If you wait too long, until they are really hungry, they will make a kill of their own and drag it into the shade. Then they will ignore you and all your allurements.

We were in a quandary. The pride we had seen had obviously made a kill the day before we arrived, so the problem was: when would they next accept food? The following day, of course, they were not interested. Two days later they had moved into new hunting grounds. We searched for them without success. The great plains, dotted with thickets, were ideal for lionesses and their cubs to play and rest, but to search for them was a hopeless task.

We broke camp and moved on through the rain which made travel very difficult indeed. Our vehicles were constantly bogged down and erecting tents was a nightmare. Dry season! This became a joke which quickly palled. Tempers became frayed and, to make matters worse, Texan-garbed Brad let us know that he would like to go off on a private safari with Bill Forsyte to kill for sport.

He was told that neither Armand nor I permitted the killing of wild animals for pleasure, and that was that. But his answer was to stay in camp and devour piles of lurid American paper-back novels, or shampoo his hair and tend his reddish fuzz of beard. After a day's fruitless scouting for lion, we would return to find that Brad had done nothing about organizing dinner, so we had to set about preparing and cooking it ourselves. He even complained about the food and completely ignored rationing. On safari only a certain amount of food can be carried, but this meant nothing to Brad. How many mornings have I watched him pouring out shameless scoopfuls of our precious sugar on his porridge!

It is these small things that show a man's character, and our first doubts of Brad now seemed to be confirmed; but human nature is quite unpredictable; he was later to atone for his bad behaviour by rising to the occasion when he was most needed.

The disappointment over lion forced us to seek for other pictures; and chance, which always plays a large part in wild animal photography, suddenly, after heart-breaking failures, presented us, out of the blue, with the vultures.

They were busy round a carcass left by a lion. Unlovely, repulsive even, they are fascinating to watch. Their outstanding quality is cowardice, but that is almost a condition of their survival. So is their miraculous eyesight which isolates detail on the ground from incredible heights. The dead body of an animal or—in this case—the remains left by a lion of his kill, is enough to call forth tiny black specks high up in the sky. Soon these specks grow larger; then they seem to coalesce and the downward spiral of the vulture column begins. A hundred or more of these gruesome, flapping creatures come down to the trees near the corpse, watching and waiting until they are quite sure the coast is clear. If the lion is still there, they will sit brooding with folded wings, like ghastly women in shawls, drooling in anticipation of the feast. After the lion has departed they still wait until they are quite satisfied that there is no danger. Then one bird will flutter down and approach the carcass.

This is the signal. One after another they flap down with clanking wings, fighting among themselves to get at the meat. When they are not threatening one another, they utter a curious thin piping sound. Bullies of the column stride up and down with outspread wings, with necks sunk into shoulders and heads thrust forward. As I watched I saw one of these bullies preparing to drive off a weaker bird from the feast, when suddenly two jackals ran out of the bushes. In a flash the vultures scattered, but the jackals chased and worried them like dogs among hens, driving them back to the trees. There they watched the usurpers gorging the juicy meat, mournful, brooding, patient.

We watched, too, and saw the lion re-emerge from the thicket. The jackals were so engrossed that they were unaware of the danger. The lion bounded towards them.

71

Like a flash the jackals were off, their craven hindquarters well down. After deep muttering, the lion settled down to the carcass, nonchalantly gnawing the bones. We left silently, but the vultures sat it out, hunched and alert, knowing that sooner or later their turn would come again.

These vultures reminded me of the condors—largest of the vultures—which we had sought in the Andes, in Peru. Large and black, with white ruffs round their necks and the characteristic bald heads of the vulture tribe, they are far larger and heavier than their African relations, more powerful and more aggressive. Condors attack living animals—after making certain that their victims are practically defenceless.

One day Armand and I, after having spent most of a day filming, sat down to eat. Above us the condors were flying high in the sky, circling round and round. Suddenly they dived. High as they were, they had seen the sandwiches we were eating and no doubt had concluded that they could help themselves without serious risk.

We were in a bad spot—a rocky plateau a thousand feet above sea level. All around were crags completely bare of vegetation; they were our only possible cover unless we could reach the narrow ledge by which we had come up. The condors, however, were too quick for us. Down they swept, down so close that the wind of their flight blew back our hair. With great fleshless claws thrust out, and an enormous wing spread of ten feet or more, they headed straight towards us to the attack. Quite defenceless, we did the only thing possible—threw the rest of our sandwiches as far from us as we could. Instantly the condors wheeled away from us and pounced down on the food, seizing it with miraculous sureness and swallowing it in savage gulps.

We had to get away—somehow. Gripping the camera tripod in one hand and me in the other, Armand made for the rocky ledge that hung sickeningly over the thousand-foot drop to the gulf below. Then he stopped. The condors were after us. They swooped barely four feet above our heads, staring into our eyes with such malignity that we both instantly divined their intention. They wanted us to go back to that ledge. Their hard, black eyes were hypnotic, and the constant swish of their beating wings and the clutching movements of their claws filled me with horror. Once driven from the rocky wall to the edge, we might stumble and fall if they pressed home their attack and then be dashed to pieces on the bottom of the gulf. These were the tactics condors used to drive cows and goats over the precipices. Why not us? They could then feed on our broken bodies a thousand feet below.

Armand dragged me away from the edge of the plateau and over to a small heap of boulders. There he slashed at the condors with his tripod. What would have happened to us had not a party of Indians seen our plight, I shudder to think. They bombarded the birds with stones from the loose scree, howling maledictions at them. With a final swoop towards us and a last vengeful stare into our faces, our tormentors wheeled away, rose sharply, and were soon harmless specks in the sky.

It was while tramping back to camp through the African rain that I recalled this South American adventure and almost wished that something as exciting would happen now. I was beginning to learn that breath-taking animal sequences which thrill millions in the world's cinemas, are only the highspots of weeks and even months of routine work, of constant disappointments, back-breaking journeys, and danger.

Danger—real danger—seemed to be rather remote now —so at least I thought. But I need not have worried; the safari was soon to run into it. This is how it came about. Armand and I had for some time wanted to photograph weaver birds at work, so one morning, under a strong sun which dried the sodden plains and hung rainbow lights on the wet thorn trees, we drove off alone into the bush. We parked our truck and walked nearly half a mile before we came on a likely thicket. There, on the undersides of the branches of the trees, were the hanging basket-like nests of the birds we sought.

We made our painful way into the middle of a thorn bush, set up the camera and settled down to wait. We knew we should have to wait until the disturbance we had made had been forgotten and the birds had resumed their normal way of life. For an hour we read; then we saw the busy black and yellow birds sporting themselves in the sun and hopefully building their nests. They flew back and forth with long strands of fibre in their beaks. Back at the nests, they hung on to the branches with their small feet and intertwined the fibres with marvellous skill. The males alone build nests and they are masters; the reward of their skill is a female that will occupy the nest with them.

At last the sky was that deep African blue which seems to burnish the gold of the plains; for endless miles, in such sky conditions, the bright earth lies like an enormous shield in the clear air. After the deadening rains, everything seemed to be springing into life. Swarms of insects chirped in the sunlight and the birds kept up an unbroken cheep and twitter, with an occasional long scream.

We began to film. It was so absorbing that I had no eyes for anything but the scene before the camera. But something prompted me to look away, and I saw two small lion cubs coming in our direction. They may have caught our scent, or perhaps they had been attracted by the whirring of the camera. My first reaction was one of delight. As they moved nearer to our hide-out, they stared straight into the bush with that mixure of wide-eyed curiosity and innocence common to the cat family.

I had overlooked one terrifying possibility.

Armand had not. He stopped the film and gripped my

arm painfully, enjoining silence. He had seen something. Then I saw her, too. It was the lioness, uneasy for her young. She was not more than fifty yards away from the bush. She stopped as if conscious of menace. Her tail lashed back and forth. She looked enormous.

Time seemed to hang suspended. I watched the lioness sniffing, but luckily the wind was not blowing in her direction. For perhaps a score of seconds she stood there, a quivering complex of protective energy. Then she came closer, her eyes on the thicket.

For one agonizing moment I saw the hideous sequel. If the cubs approached nearer to us, she would follow, see us, and spring to the attack. Within a minute we should be mauled to death.

To make for the truck was out of the question. It was half a mile away. Our only chance was to stay here. I froze, scarcely daring to breathe. Horrified, I watched the cubs come into the thicket. Then Armand did the only thing possible. It all happened in a second. As one of the cubs poked its square, furry little nose into our hide-out, it made a surprised little noise. Instantly the lioness crouched, her tail lashing her honey-coloured body. The muscles rippled and bunched.

Armand let out an unearthly scream which caused the cub to leap into the air. Then it turned and rejoined the other cub and both made their way back to their mother. The scream had distracted her from her deadly spring.

What was to be done now? Armand and I backed slowly away from the hide-out, sheltered by the bushes. The lioness, hesitant, stood in front of her young. We forced ourselves to go slowly; for we both knew that a large cat will always pursue a rapidly retreating figure. Once out on the other side, we walked leisurely in the direction of the truck.

We were safe. It seemed incredible. But we were safe!

We had left our precious camera in the thicket, and it was some hours before we thought it safe to return for it. The weaver birds were forgotten. In our hide-out was the tripod laying at a crazy angle against the thorn bush; its legs were scored with teeth and claw marks left by the investigating lioness. The pad marks also told a tale that would hardly bear thinking about. We drove back to the camp in silence.

A few hours later it started to rain again. For four days it went on. Finally Armand decided to give up the project and to return to Nairobi. I was not sorry, for luck definitely seemed against us.

We drove day and night: there could be no thought of pitching tents in the darkness and pelting rain. The mud was appalling. Our five vehicles slithered and skidded along that terrible road at a crawl. Gone were the visions of a simple two hours' run into Narok. The difficulty was for a vehicle to keep in the tracks of the one in front. Our car crashed into a tree. We were bringing up the rear and we saw the rear lights of the truck ahead gradually become fainter.

This was trouble—bad trouble. The car had slithered to a stop at a steep angle and it was out of action; the fan had ground into the radiator. We floundered about, up to our knees in mud. Then somebody asked, "What's that?"

It was the unmistakable noise of a party of lions, hunting.

We stared at each other, speechless. For weeks we had been trying to locate lions, and here we were now, by the side of a wrecked car in the streaming night, listening to them and unable to do anything about it.

Casual introduction to a hunting party of lions is to be avoided. The roars are enough to deter even the most curious and courageous. They were close enough to induce us to get into the car and wait until the pride had passed and until our friends ahead missed us and turned back.

76

We could reconstruct what was happening among the lions. They were driving their quarry towards a lioness who was lying in ambush. She would make the kill. The roaring became louder and increased in tempo. We sat huddled together in the car under the drumming of the rain on the roof—trapped. There was a possibility that the hunting lions would locate us. At one time the roars were so near and so savage that I thought they had done so. The king of beasts in his dominion of the night, out to kill, gains tremendously in majesty and terror. Let all beware.

Out there in the darkness was being re-enacted the oldest drama in the world. We seemed to be right in the middle of the stage, planted there by the irony of unexpected circumstances, our only refuge a broken-down mechanical contraption. No wonder I felt helpless! Outside, for the better part of an hour, lion roars rent the night and reverberated in one's very soul, bringing to the surface of the mind deep-seated primeval emotions.

Finally, however, the pride had passed; soon after we saw through the rain-blurred windscreen two yellow lights. One of our trucks was returning. Armand and the men examined the damage to our car; it could be repaired on the spot, but the power wagon would have to return to haul it out of the mud with the winch.

Every few yards each vehicle in turn would get bogged down in knee-deep mud.

It was now that Brad proved his worth. He had been in charge of one hundred and fifty power wagons when he worked for the oil company up north, and he was used to difficult terrain. Assuming command, he organized both Europeans and Africans to work all through that dreadful night. The dongas, usually dry, were in full flood. For one wild moment Queen Mary tottered on the brink of a donga. Then, miraculously, she righted herself.

We inched along, wading through mud and pushing any truck that was halted. In the vast wet black bubble of the African night the effort seemed futile and endless: we were reduced to helpless creatures of mud, darkness and rain. Twice we had to stop to change tyres. But we sang African songs and remained human, and as we sang our spirits rose above our miserable physical condition. With the first streak of dawn came a feeling of exultation and triumph. We reached the cross-roads near Narok from where we had started so hopefully a month before. It had taken us thirty nightmarish hours.

We dared not pause for sleep. After a cup of tea and a cigarette, we were on the move again, dirty and dishevelled, into the dispirited dawn.

Further along the road a man hailed us cheerfully. "Good morning. What are the roads like to Narok?"

He was one of a party consisting of two adult couples and some children. The adults had the rather pinched faces which seem to be characteristic of many missionaries in Africa. They had pitched tents, and a small, battered Austin car was parked in front of their camp.

Armand gazed at them and then at their car. How could it hold all of them? he was thinking.

"The roads," he replied, scratching some dried mud off his unshaven chin, "are quite strictly definitely impossible. We barely made it with the help of our power wagon."

One of the women caught up a small child as it tried to run by her. She had the dauntless look of a mother on a wet seaside town promenade.

"Oh, what a shame!" she said, brightly. "Never mind, we shall manage it. But it does rather spoil our holiday!"

Off we drove, freezing our smiles, and they waved us out of sight. For days afterwards I kept wondering how they came to be in such an unlikely spot at all, and how they could possibly reach any sort of outpost in that car.

As the morning advanced a pale and watery sun came into view. We came upon a group of Masai, striking people: the men tall and handsome, with long hair in the Morani fashion; the women beautiful in spite of their shaven heads. They were roasting slices of an ox at a huge fire. They politely invited us to eat with them, and I found their roasted meat delicious.

Then the rain came down once more.

We said good-bye to our Masai friends and headed towards Nairobi. Floods forced us to make detours, but finally we climbed the sodden escarpment. An hour later, we were in Nairobi, depressed and exhausted. Two cables were waiting for us. One was from RKO:

"ABSOLUTELY NECESSARY YOU SECURE MORE THRILLS AND EXCITEMENT."

Obviously, the sensational charge of the black rhino, which we had sent off to them a few weeks before, had been lost or delayed in the post. We had to have another climax for *Below the Sahara*. Lions had failed us. What next?

Armand puzzled over the other one, which was signed by one of his scientist friends:

"VERY GRATEFUL IF YOU COULD PROCURE FRESH BLOOD SAMPLE ADULT MALE ARCTOCEPHALUS PUSILLUS THIS SCIENTIFICALLY IMPORTANT DETAILED INSTRUCTIONS FOLLOW."

I said: "Maybe the Coryndon Museum can tell us what this thing is." Armand reached for the phone and talked to the Museum. After a while he put the phone down and said, "It's some kind of sea-lion. One of the fur-seals, to be quite exact. Family of the *Otariidae*. Adult males weigh about eight hundred pounds. On islands off the coast, in South Africa. The Museum does not think anyone has ever caught an adult male. In fact they don't think it can be done. This all sounds excellent to me."

We started at once to make arrangements to fly south and wired to South Africa to expect us. I packed my jewellery in a biscuit box and left it in the hotel safe, changed my clothes and was ready to go.

Next morning we left. We carried some doubts with us, for we were running it fine. Our fruitless month in the Reserve had depleted our resources and we would have to be careful. Our destination was Seal Island, to visit which official permission would have to be obtained in Cape Town. No difficulty in that direction presented itself, the officer in charge gave us all the needed permits and wished us luck with *Otariidae*. I had an idea that we would need it. Memories of the eight hundred pound monsters I had seen off the coast of Peru rose to my mind, many of them half-scalped, for they were capable of inflicting terrible wounds on one another.

Seal Island strides three oceans—the Antarctic, the Atlantic and the Indian. To reach it in rough weather in a small fishing boat put all one's Viking qualities to the test. The currents swelled and heaved, forcing great waves into foamy collisions, ending in salty plumes. Seal Island is merely a rock sticking out of the water. The fishermen with us told us that a landing was impossible; but we persuaded them to allow us to take the dinghy close to the island to investigate.

A landing seemed indeed difficult and dangerous. The island was literally covered with hundreds of sea-lions, but hundreds more were around us in the sea. They kept popping up all round the dinghy with faces full of curiosity. We turned back towards the fishing boat and when Armand was about to leap on board a wave hit us and I was flattened by his sixteen stone. The dinghy came close to capsizing. I clung on desperately, for I could not swim a stroke. I thought of the depths of the sea and felt helpless. It took all my courage to stand up in the rocking dinghy and follow Armand on board.

This exploit finished us with the fishermen. If people were crazy enough to try to film sea-lions, that was their

Armand spent most of the morning getting this picture, which he
calls "Etude"

Women can never leave themselves alone but insist upon improving on Nature

Circumcision dancers. No women may normally see them dance
or see any part of the secret rituals. I wound a scarf round my
head and pretended to be blind, so I saw everything

Kebe-Kebe dancers of French Equatorial Africa

own business; but they had better look after themselves. But we refused to give up. Our permission to film had only a week to run and there was no chance of getting it renewed until the following year. Fortunately, some Cape Town University students volunteered to help us, and they were wonderful.

They were painfully seasick on the way out to Seal Island, but this did not deter them. They were desperately keen to try a landing. Time and time again we took the dinghy right up to the rock, only to be swept off again and again. Looking back, I think it was miraculous that the boat survived those pounding, crushing waves. We were, of course, soon wet to the skin. Equipment was largely saved from the fury of the sea by the students, who held various parts of it above their heads, beyond the reach of the hungry waves.

Tom Stobart was carried away by a wave and lost a camera and tripod before we finally made a landing by using a wave that swept the dinghy directly on to a rock and then gauging the right moment to jump. How we envied the sea-lions their flippers!

We hadn't time to recover our breath before we were plunged in the middle of a stampede of sea-lions—twenty or more full-grown animals, squirming and slithering between us in their panic to get to the sea. One of them heaved a student into a rock pool. The hunt was on with a vengeance! In a moment of wild excitement we netted a young male, but our hands slipped on the wet nylon ropes and in a second he had joined the student in the rock pool. Both sat up with the same astonished expression on their faces; but the sea-lion, with a contemptuous flip of its tail, poured lithely over the rocks and dived off into the waves.

We spread out the nylon net, upon which we based high hopes: Armand had found in Cape Town several hundred yards of parachute shroud lines made of nylon, many times stronger than any manila rope; and had had a nylon net woven to his design by local fishermen.

But our luck had run out. We were left alone on a deserted rock. All around and below us in the sea were hundreds of bewhiskered sea-lion faces, young and old, barking and sporting in the sea. They were waiting for us to go—and they hadn't long to wait. The fishing boat which had brought us over sounded its fog-horn for us to return. The light was fading and a difficult re-embarkation faced us.

No picture. Not that day. All we had got were cuts, bruises and strained muscles. As we climbed into the dinghy to obey the summons of the impatient fog-horn, complete exhaustion overtook me and I hardly knew how we got back.

For days afterwards a gale raged and no one seemed eager to make another attempt in the teeth of the wind. Finally, our permit expired and we had to give up. But we were told of another sea-lion colony on the mainland at Cape Cross, in South-West Africa. We went there as soon as the necessary permits had been obtained. We flew for several hours, via Kimberley, to Windhoek; then, by chartered plane, over large herds of antelope to Swakopmund. This used to be German territory, and Swakopmund had preserved all its German characteristics.

On Sundays a German band played and the young men wore *lederhosen*. In the little square was a marble monument of a German soldier in the arms of an angel. We made contact with Mr. Offen, who had the concession to hunt and kill the sea-lions for their fur. It seemed brutal to massacre such harmless and sociable creatures, but we were in no position to argue this point, and were grateful to Mr. Offen for sending his son-in-law along with us to Cape Cross. We drove along salt roads into the desert. Apart from a few mierkats we saw gambolling in the dunes it was a completely empty and apparently lifeless region; after three hours we arrived at the Offens'

82

small camp and heard the sea-lions barking on the shore.

Armand asked for volunteers to help us capture a large male, and five men came forward, although they looked doubtfully at the nylon net. They had never tried netting a fully grown male. Usually only very young ones were taken alive, for zoos. We knew the net would be strong enough, for we had used nylon nets before, for capturing hyenas, and their teeth are sharp enough. We had a dress rehearsal in which I took the part of the sea-lion, flopping along the beach on my stomach and barking. I entered into the part so completely that I ended up by trying to escape into the sea and was then successfully netted and hauled out amidst shouts of laughter.

After this rehearsal we crept along the beach cautiously in search of our victim. The large bulls were basking in the sun with their wives; each time it was a female who saw us and slid into the water. We were able to edge up to the males, but as we approached them, crawling among the sharp flints on the beach, they sensed danger and followed the females. At last we became more skilful and managed to net a large male. But he somehow managed to slide out of the net and chased us for five or six yards, barking furiously. We dropped the net and ran, for one look at those rows of menacing teeth and that gaping throat was enough.

As soon as we had secured the net once more, there was a shout from Armand. He and the men had run into the midst of a mass of sea-lions, and managed to trap a large, angry eight hundred pounder. Everyone, except Tom Stobart, who was busily filming, had flung themselves on to the net to keep the infuriated animal from heaving and squirming out. Armand gestured to his trousers pocket and I dived my hand in and brought out the bottle for the blood sample. We quickly cut away some of the wet, tough hair on the animal's rump and stuck the needle in. Our job was soon done, the bottle was full of blood, and the sea-lion none the worse. We lifted the

83

corners of the net and he was out in a flash, travelling at great speed on his pliable flippers to the sea. In relief and joy, we waved good-bye to him.

We had accomplished the impossible. Now we could only hope the pictures would turn out right. Suppose the lenses had not been in place, or the film had run out? Tom assured us that everything was fine, so our only worry now was to get the film to New York and hope that it would not be lost on the way.

We rode back in sober mood to Swakopmund, cold and wet, with sand in our clothes and hair, and smelling dreadfully of sea-lion. Mr. Offen's daughter came to meet us with black bread and sausage and other tasty German foods. We needed them. Now the suspense and excitement were over and we had succeeded, we all suffered from the flatness of anti-climax.

But we had no time to rest on our laurels. We were due back in Nairobi to start another safari, this time to Kitchwamba.

CHAPTER FIVE

ELEPHANT COUNTRY

WE HAD planned a safari into Uganda to photograph elephants. After leaving Nairobi we drove for many hours without incident, left Kenya behind and entered a country of lush vegetation. On either side of the narrow road along which we were travelling, elephant grass towered fifteen feet high. I asked Armand to stop the car and plunged eagerly into it. My sense of curiosity was aroused. From the depth of this high waving grass one gets a beetle's eye view of the world. I wallowed in it.

"Come back," Armand called after me, "you might get stepped on by an elephant!"

He has a marvellous sense of country, for shortly after rejoining him in the car, we turned a corner and looked down on an immense natural amphitheatre of open country dotted with small scrubby bushes. Armand stared intently at the scene.

"Elephants," he said suddenly.

Then I saw the herds moving—hundreds of elephants roaming among the tall trees that marked the river course. Some were wandering aimlessly; others were scratching themselves against the trees. I was thrilled by the scene.

Armand and I have always found unequalled happiness in observing wild animals in their natural state. We selected a tall tree, climbed into its branches and constructed a rough platform. Here we settled down for the night. We had with us our camera, food, blankets and a vacuum flask of hot coffee. Here we were safe. Elephants usually do not look up unless they hear a noise from above; so we had to maintain absolute silence if we were to get what we wanted.

"Here we are, in the heart of Africa, full of the wildest and most savage creatures in the world," said Armand, "yet all of them fear man. . . . Do you remember those baboons?"

I did, and I shall never forget the scene.

We had watched them casually indulging in love-play practically under the feet of rhinos.

"Yes," I replied, "and that lion and the antelope."

Normally, the antelope is terrified of a lion, but once we saw one of these timid creatures lying quite near a lion which dozed and took no notice of it. The explanation is that the lion had fed. He kills to eat, not for pleasure.

But you couldn't get an antelope to stay even at a respectful distance from a man; it would rather risk the lion's hunger.

We dozed on and off through the night, listening between naps to the eerie noises of birds, the trumpeting of elephants and the occasional roar of a hunting lion. The dark hours passed in half-dream, half-reality, and when the dawn broke into a pink translucence over the muddy water of the river, we saw our elephants returning to bathe and drink.

The cows were wonderful with their babies. They helped the small, stumpy creatures down the steep and slippery banks of the river by curling trunks round their bodies.

"We're lucky," whispered Armand. "Hand over the camera."

Both cows and the young drank deeply. The babies were being taught to squirt the cooling water from their tiny trunks over their backs; but most of them objected. They preferred to wallow submerged and to roll in the muddy shallows until their mothers righted them with

86

playful slaps and squeals. The bulls formed a protective screen.

We were so engrossed in the scene and the business of getting pictures that we did not notice a bull detach himself from the herd and move in our direction.

Suddenly our tree was shaking and the platform began to rock alarmingly. I gripped Armand's arm and looked down. There was a bull elephant, scratching his back meditatively against our tree.

The vacuum flask slid towards the edge of the platform. I grabbed for it and stifled a cry. Any noise we made might be fatal. Armand held on to the camera, while we dug our toes between the platform laths, hoping for the best.

This was trouble and I visualized the worst. If the bull heard an unusual noise, or caught our wind, he would push the tree over. The fall would probably kill us both. Even if we survived the fall, the angry beast would finish us off with a charge, kneeling on us and mashing us with his tusks.

The tree cracked ominously. For one awful moment I was sure it was going to fold over. The platform was now tilted at a crazy angle. Armand and I looked at each other. This couldn't go on—and we both knew it.

Then suddenly deliverance came. The bull elephant, having relieved his itching skin, lumbered slowly away. When he had rejoined the others, Armand said in a low voice:

"What a pity there wasn't another camera unit here to film *us*! . . . What a thrill for cinema audiences!"

"If we had another camera unit," I whispered back, "it wouldn't have happened—just out of spite."

The next day we chose another vantage point and settled in a scanty cover of bushes. We were not well hidden, but elephants have poor eyesight.

I used an old Masai trick for checking wind direction by dropping a few blades of grass. If they drifted towards the elephants our scent was being carried towards them. The grass, however, drifted back to us, so we were safe—at least for the time being.

We were treated to another elephant bathing scene. The antics of the babies were a sheer joy to watch.

A large grey head appeared over the river bank less than fifty yards away. Instinctively, I checked the wind with blades of grass. It moved towards the elephant. The wind had changed—as it is apt to do during the heat of the day.

Up went the trunk of the bull. We were discovered.

We had to make a split-second decision. The bull advanced, stopped, his ears flapping slowly forward. Again his trunk went up like a periscope. He began the rocking movement from foot to foot which heralds a charge.

"Now!" said Armand, dropping his camera and starting to run.

We dashed away, running sideways into a clump of thicker bushes. Instantly the elephant charged. The earth shook as the great beast gathered speed.

From our position we could not see what was happening. But we knew that the bull had picked up our scent in the place we had recently occupied and was now stamping around. We had left the camera and the lunch-box behind, and our thoughts were on the camera.

We crouched in the bushes, waiting and listening. Then we heard a trumpeted summons to the bathing herd. Time passed slowly, but at last the cows and babies were rounded up and moved off. When we last saw them, they were moving, slowly and ponderously, through the trees into the tall grass, snatching branches here and there as they passed.

As soon as we judged it safe, we returned to our original position; we found the camera undamaged but the metal lunch-box smashed in.

An elephant does not necessarily charge to kill; it will nearly always swerve to one side at the last moment. But fear, both in animals and humans, can provoke normally peaceful creatures to murderous rage. In my opinion, the elephant's charge is often a warning—like a man adopting a threatening attitude with his fists.

Armand and I have several times staked our lives on this opinion.

After this adventure, we set out on an expedition for buffalo pictures. By ourselves, we never carry guns; but the party was getting big, for we had been joined by two young men, Brian Dowling and Godfrey Hopkins, and bigness—and the newness to Africa of some of the members of our party—raised problems. So we asked two friends, Bill Pridham and Temple-Perkins, to accompany us as gun-guards—with strict instructions not to shoot except in extreme emergency.

Not long after we set out, the work of filming began with another elephant incident. We photographed some spectacular scenes with Armand and me in the foreground and the elephants only twenty-five yards away. One great bull scented us, turned in our direction, and displayed himself in all his menacing magnificence.

For a time he watched us with ears thrust out, rocking from side to side. Then he broke into a charge and my heart missed a beat; but before reaching us he suddenly swerved away. Right there we made a picture to prove that Armand and I were right in our opinion—at least on this occasion.

We piled into a small boat and travelled a few miles up the channel. There we unloaded our cameras and other equipment and prepared to follow the elephants on foot. This can be an exhausting business, for elephants move much faster than they appear to do.

Our quarry on this occasion was a herd of nine elephants. They led us a fine dance. Armand and I got separated from the others, and we found to our surprise that the herd had split into two groups, one of which had got between us and the main party.

It was very hot, and Armand was tiring under the burden of the camera and tripod. I thrive on African heat and feel at my best under the caressing sun. We plunged into acres of tall elephant grass and penetrated through tracts of bush and trees.

There was danger in the grass. At any moment an elephant might loom up suddenly from nowhere, for they are adepts at concealment and noiseless movement. Against the background of bird calls and animal cries we might not hear them.

"We seem to be lost," I remarked, after a time.

"Oh, it's not as bad as that," said Armand. "The others will be somewhere along the river bank. . . . We'll find them all right."

As he had the camera and tripod to look after, I volunteered to go in search of them.

"All right," he said, "but don't run into anything."

I set off at a trot, taking advantage of a glade by the water's edge. I felt wonderful. This was the Africa I loved, its untilled earth and natural vegetation, the home of the wild animals that meant so much to me. I jogged along, at peace with myself under the deep blue sky which radiated life-giving heat.

Suddenly a large and grey object blocked my path. I was up to it, almost underneath it, before I realized that it was the backside of an elephant.

I stood still and stared at it, unbelieving. But there could be no doubt about it. Less than three yards from my face was an elephant's behind. I felt no fear. All I was concerned about was the way the animal's loose skin fell in folds from his hips, like baggy pyjama trouser-legs.

Instinct made me drop on all fours and scramble off, crabwise, into the grass. At what I judged to be a safe distance, I got up and ran as hard as I could until I caught up with the main party by the river.

I was told later that a native woman of this region had shortly before been killed in similar circumstances. She was returning to her village in the evening, carrying a load on her back with a strap across her forehead for support, as is the custom in East Africa.

Bent over and with her eyes to the ground, she walked right under the head of an elephant. Instantly, the beast wound its trunk round her neck and broke it. He was frightened at her sudden appearance and smell.

Brian and Godfrey had beginners' luck with us in East Africa. Everything seemed to happen to them. They had experiences of animal life which sometimes come only after years in the country—baboons playing with hippos, the marvellous bird life in Kasinga Channel which lies in what is now the Elizabeth National Park in Uganda.

Some time before the expedition of which I am now writing, Armand, his assistant Duncan, and myself went there to photograph wild pelicans which congregate on a spit of land in the Channel. We built a large blind of the tripod type. But this was elephant country and watch had to be kept.

"I'm going into the blind alone," said Armand. "You and Duncan had better keep your eyes skinned for elephant."

Duncan and I took up positions of vantage. Some time later—towards the end of the morning—we saw three elephants on the island facing the spit of land. Between the island and the land was a water channel about a hundred yards wide.

One of the elephants moved away from the other two towards the water.

"He's going to cross," I said to Duncan.

"My word, so he is!"

"No need to disturb Armand yet. He must be getting some good pictures."

The elephant was now wading across the channel. He carried his trunk raised carefully above the water and held it curved over one of his tusks to keep it dry.

Our pre-arranged danger signal to Armand was a honk on the horn of the truck. As the elephant drew nearer it seemed the time had come to sound it. We honked and waited. On came the elephant, but there was no sign of Armand. I honked again. He was running it very fine.

Presently he slipped out of the blind. Only fifty feet or so separated him from the advancing elephant. I stared at the scene, weighing up the possibilities. The chances were against Armand getting away.

But the blind saved him. It was covered with edible leaves and the elephant stopped before it and started to pluck them off.

Duncan and I leapt into the truck and drove towards Armand as fast as we could. We carried no arms. The only weapon I could think of was an iron attachment to the camera. I fished it out of the back of the truck as we drove and planned to hurl it at the elephant's head to cover our retreat.

I got on to the running board and Duncan cut the motor. The truck rolled past the elephant and we picked up Armand less than thirty yards from the great beast. He slipped into the cab and I followed. Luck was with us. The engine responded instantly to the starter. Its roar drew the elephant's attention to us. I can see him now. He had a branch half-way to his mouth. Suddenly he trumpeted. We didn't wait to see his next reaction.

Photographing wild animals is dangerous business. However careful you may be the unexpected happens.

On this expedition, as I have said, we mainly wanted to get some really unique head-on shots of buffalo, for this was the country for them. We had done well with elephant and now we hoped for some luck with buffalo. After carefully surveying the terrain we began to look for cover and protection against buffalo charges. Finally we chose a bush and settled down to wait.

Strategy had been worked out in advance. Bill Pridham and the others were to take the truck and work the animals slowly towards our bush. We calculated they would pass us on the right side. So we set up a camera to the right of the bush, prepared to lose it if necessary.

The wait seemed interminable. Armand and I chatted of this and that and then relapsed into silence. There was tension in the air and we could both feel it. Distant snortings and snufflings put us on the alert. We strained our ears to catch the direction of the noise. In less than a minute we were left in no doubt. The buffalo were heading straight for us, at a full gallop.

"Can you see anything, Michaela?" asked Armand.

"Not a thing."

But by now we heard the terrific pounding of the buffalo stampede. Thunder and wind! It was thrilling. But where were the buffalo? I strained my eyes to catch sight of them.

"What's happening?" asked Armand.

"There they go!" I cried.

They were stampeding on the wrong—the left—side of the bush, right out of the range of our camera set-up: a magnificent herd, the picture of a lifetime. Lost, irretrievably lost. And there was nothing we could do about it. Eric White, our still cameraman, had managed to get one or two close-ups as the herd flashed past, but they meant nothing.

Bill Pridham and the others were not to blame. Buffalo have some sixth sense where human beings are concerned —quite apart from being camera-shy.

Chance works both ways. Later it was with us in our

search for buffalo pictures. It happened at another time and in a different part of the continent, where hunters are very rare.

So it wasn't altogether chance that drew the buffalo in a circle around us; it was lack of fear. They had never been hunted by man. The result was some really wonderful pictures. They came right up to us and scrutinized us mildly with their pleasant faces outstretched. The cows licked their calves with devoted attention. The bulls, like all herd animals, took up a protective position in front of their families.

The buffalo would stand and watch us for a time, then run. As they ran, tick birds flew from their backs and followed them, flying a few feet above. When the animals stopped, the tick birds swarmed and settled again. These birds are a godsend to buffalo; they pick out ticks from the hides, which cause intense irritation. Their function is similar to that of the crocodile birds which perch inside the open mouths of these monsters and play the part of toothpicks. But the tick birds also give the buffalo valuable warning of approaching danger.

After the affair of the buffalo that stampeded the wrong way, we drove down to Kasinga Channel and ran into what is called the "banana train". In this area bananas are cultivated to make native beer. We passed by long lines of men and women carrying huge bundles of bananas on their heads.

We were busy making a raft of poles lashed across two dugout canoes, with an outboard motor at the back, when we heard the noise of a tremendous shindy coming from one of the native huts on the slope above. Soon we were privileged to see yet another form of wild life.

Presently a woman ran out of one of the huts. Dressed in the prevailing Uganda style—a tunic and a long skirt with a bustle effect—she was handsome and hefty. Anger distorted her face. She was at once surrounded by women

94

from the other huts. These she addressed in loud, hectoring tones and a waving of arms. Our boys, who were enjoying the scene, told us that she was complaining to the other women about her husband.

"Here he comes!" shouted one of the boys.

Out of the handsome woman's hut came a man, obviously enraged and looking for trouble. He ran straight to his wife and gave her a resounding smack on the bottom. The blow appeared to throw her into a fit of hysteria; she shrieked like a mad thing. Then she ran, still raving, into another hut. The boys kept up their running commentary for our benefit.

"She's going to kill him!" cried one of them with delight.

In a moment she emerged from the hut with a pole, at the end of which was a wicked-looking knife. She ran towards her husband screaming, but some of the older women threw themselves on her and wrested the pole out of her grasp.

Then all the life seemed to go out of the poor creature and she walked disconsolately back into her own hut. In a few minutes she came out again with a sleeping mat and a large bundle on her head.

"She's going back to her mother!" jeered a boy.

She was pathetic and her plight wrung my heart. She walked slowly away from her hut, then hesitated. At once the other women hastened to her and obviously tried to persuade her to return. Watching this little human tragedy we had lost all interest in the raft, and we waited to see the end of it. At last the young wife allowed herself to be persuaded and, guided by an old woman, carried her bundle back into her hut.

We pushed off up-channel to continue our work, and when we returned the next day, I asked our boys if they had heard anything more of the young wife.

"No," said one of the boys, grinning, "all right now, Memsahib. She with husband."

The next morning I saw the husband and wife together, happy and smiling, a perfect picture of domestic bliss. I blessed them in my heart.

While we were in the neighbourhood we decided to call on the Fish Warden's wife, or Mrs. Fishy, as she is called. She was a typical attractive Englishwoman and her home was a fragment of England, packed with fine antique furniture. She was in despair. Her boys would not obey her orders and she could do nothing about it.

The reason soon became clear. There had been a plague of small locusts in the district. Africans love locusts. Mrs. Fishy's boys were spending their time catching the insects and eating them as fast as they could. They were nearing a state of drunken frenzy. Locusts really are delicious; we usually fried them in butter, sprinkled salt on them, and ate them with cocktails. They have a queer effect on Africans; a state like that of intoxication follows a feast and then work is out of the question. When we left Mrs. Fishy, however, the madness had passed, and the boys were returning to work.

Our course was now set in the direction of the Sudan. The objective was Murchison Falls, where we wanted to film hippos and crocodiles. Hence the raft. The technique is to cruise very slowly and stop the engine when nearing a group of hippos. It can be dangerous, for they are very inquisitive creatures and strongly resent sudden intrusions into their privacy.

A moving object, such as a raft, will attract their attention. Their first reaction is to pop up and stare at it; then they yawn monstrously. This is probably a nervous reflex action to danger. The thing is to prevent the raft bumping against them and being thrown into the water. If that happens, death can be very near. But hippos are harmless enough if not frightened.

At Butiaba, on the way to Murchison Falls, we met Colonel Reid, an Englishman retired from the Colonial Service. We found much in common with him. He was

A leopard's larder! A leopard, after making a kill, sometimes carries it up a tree and hangs it in a forked branch. This guards it from scavengers. When hungry he goes back to retrieve it

Lions have a highly developed social sense. This young male, panting in the heat of the midday sun, has been left to guard the kill while the other members of the tribe rest

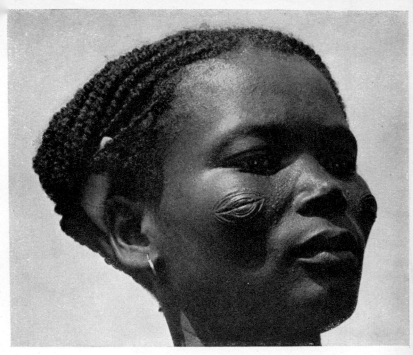

Congo beauty

Our Asongo-Meno "boys". They volunteered to work for Armand and me and wanted to be our "boys" in New York

Anklets of soft native copper in this Congo village represent prestige, wealth. They are the equivalent of a European or American woman's mink coat. Tallest woman is 6 ft. 3½ in.

Filed teeth. Congo

a passionate lover of wild animals and would never kill them. He spent most of his time making solo trips into the wilds in an old car to photograph animals.

We were discussing types of cameras and lenses, when my husband asked Colonel Reid how he managed close-ups.

"Oh," he replied, "I just walk up to the animal and take it. I use an old Bell and Howell camera with a one-inch lens."

We were astonished.

"But why not use a three- or four-inch?" asked Armand.

The colonel looked shocked.

"Oh, come, that's hardly sporting—what? People would think I'd been very much closer to the animal than I actually was, you know."

Here was a man of strict sporting principles, a product of the finest tradition. We were amused at his point of view, but full of admiration for him.

"The risks are increased, of course," I remarked.

"Possibly," answered the colonel, "but we have to give 'em a chance, you know."

"But you're taking photographs, not killing," urged Armand.

"True, quite true, but I feel we must play the game."

He admitted to accidents. Once he had been knocked over by an elephant—"A bad spill, but entirely my own fault, you know."

He delighted us.

Colonel Reid had hired a small boat at Butiaba and planned to go up the river to the Falls to photograph the wild life there. We were able to hire a large boat named *The Murchison* and were intrigued to find that it was the vessel used by John Huston and his company to film *African Queen*.

We joined forces with the colonel and set off together. His small boat could be used for short reconnaissance trips and for inching among the crocodiles. After our first

97

experience with him, we decided that we should have to watch him as carefully as the animals we were filming. He was a great sportsman, but he would suddenly jump up, rocking the boat violently as he focused on the banks of the river.

Armand had bought a large native sheep which was intended partly as food for our boys and partly as bait for the crocodiles. A few hours after leaving Butiaba I was deeply moved by its pathetic face and the harsh fate that was in store for it. It seemed to know what I was feeling, for every time I came near it bleated plaintively. I sat down beside it and stroked its head; it muzzled up to me and bleated again and again, as if begging for its life.

Some time later, I said to Armand as casually as I could:

"Is it absolutely necessary to kill that sheep, darling?"

"Yes, I'm afraid so," he replied.

"Oh, Armand, I'm so unhappy about it. . . . Promise me you won't have it killed."

He looked at me sympathetically, but said nothing. I knew he understood; but he really had no choice in the matter. To spare my feelings he arranged for it to be slaughtered secretly that night. His idea was to save me further pain.

I had a very bad hour when I learned that the sheep was dead. For days its bleating was in my ears.

For my sake the sheep was killed four days before the time fixed for its dispatch. This meant that the carcass had to be kept in the tropic heat for four days, and by the time we were ready to photograph, decomposition had set in. The poor body was swollen like a balloon, with its pathetic match-stick legs stuck up stiffly like legs in a child's drawing.

We decided to tow it at the end of a long rope; it floated like a buoy. Crocodiles like high meat and we knew it would attract them; but we simply could not stand the smell. There was nothing for it but to cut the body adrift and follow it up. It drifted slowly down for perhaps sixty yards. Then suddenly two eyes appeared on the surface of the chocolate-coloured water and a crocodile rose. His grinning jaws opened and snapped on the corpse, which, in a matter of seconds was dragged down to an underwater hole to make a solitary feast.

"Imagine the strength of that crocodile," commented Armand. "It would have taken at least five strong men to pull down that buoyant sheep."

I shuddered and said nothing. I was thinking of the animal that had given me a few hours' happiness while it was alive.

Murchison Falls yielded some fine crocodile pictures and when we were satisfied we moved on to Kioka swamp which had the reputation of being the finest crocodile location in the country. It was, of course, a favourite ground for the hunters, and for a short time after our arrival there we had little luck.

"These areas," Armand told me waving his arm in a half-circle, "must have been shot out. It looks as if we've drawn a blank."

But after a thorough reconnaissance, we found an inlet simply alive with crocodiles. It put Murchison Falls completely in the shade as far as we were concerned. Here was an undisturbed reserve.

We fixed our main base and rowed into the swamp in two canoes for about half an hour. Here we tied and began to photograph. We laid a net to keep our crocodiles corralled in one place, hoping they would crawl to the banks and bask in the reeds.

Crocodile photography eats up film quicker than any other kind, and we had used a tremendous amount of footage. About lunch time Armand said he was running out of film, and off he went to get some more. I was quite happy watching the crocodiles, although it can be a tiring

99

recreation, for their movements are sluggish and monotonous. Now and again they would emerge from the water, with only their nostrils and eyes showing, and float lazily around.

The heat was caressing and I felt drowsy. Tired of watching the crocodiles, I got interested in the birds, of which there was a great variety, ranging from herons to tiny iridescent things that flashed through the air like sudden flames.

I gave myself up entirely to the scene and felt one with all the natural life around me—not merely a witness but an active part of it. In the great African solitudes such moods are never very far away; alone, one falls naturally into them if the mind submits to the magic of nature.

Armand had been gone about twenty minutes when I saw a small crocodile, barely two and a half feet long, floating down-stream. He drew abreast of the net and, as I watched him, I saw one of his forepaws become entangled in it. He was only a baby, and I feared for him for crocodiles are cannibals. I resolved to free him.

I drew near to him, stood up in the canoe and tried to push him back into midstream with my oar. It was not easy. The canoe wobbled as I plied the oar to free him. I tried again and again without success. Then, at full stretch, I managed it. Before I could recover myself, however, the canoe lurched and I was tipped into the water.

As I plunged beneath the surface of the water I tried to scream. I couldn't swim, I couldn't even float on my back. My screams were muffled by the water.

The water seemed to burn my nose and I choked. My mind raced on as I rose to the surface and my hands clutched at nothing. The whole world was eluding me and I could feel death in the dark pit of the water.

Something brushed across my knees. Instantly I was back in the world. It might be a fish or a crocodile—even a crocodile seemed preferable to the horror of the water. Suddenly I felt a violent blow on my shoulder. It swung me round and I saw a tree trunk which had been thrown against me in my struggles.

Here was life within my grasp and I fought for it. I don't know how long my fight to clamber on to the trunk went on, but finally I was astride it and managed to retain my balance. It dipped dangerously under my weight.

The canoe was now about ten feet away, but so far as I was concerned it might have been at the other end of the world. My feet and legs, almost to the knees, were in the water. At any moment a crocodile might snap. The difficulty was to get my legs out of the water and still retain my balance. Then I saw that I could pull the canoe back to me by the rope which was attached to the tree-trunk. In my struggle I had failed to notice this life-line. Half a minute later I scrambled into the canoe and as I did so one foot dipped into the water.

I felt a sudden wrench at the sole of my shoe.

But I was saved. Exhausted, I lay panting and could think of nothing but my escape. For some minutes I lay in this state before I sat up in the canoe to take my bearings with the real world again.

I looked at the shoe and shuddered. The thick rope sole had gone. It had been torn off. Possibly that inch of sole had saved my life. I threw off the horror and when Armand returned I was in a more or less normal frame of mind. He looked astonished at my bedraggled appearance.

"What happened?" he asked.

"Oh, I went for a swim," I said, trying to appear casual.

He looked at me in silence, for he knew I couldn't swim and that the last thing I should do of my own free will was to go into the water.

He had brought back the makings of Martinis with him and having mixed me a stiff one he said:

"Now you'd better tell me all about it."

I did. He listened aghast, gripping my hand and saying

nothing. When I had finished he rose and mixed me another drink.

"Here, take this," he said.

That was very unusual, for Armand knows that I am strictly a one-drink woman.

This adventure befell me because we happened to run out of film; it would never have happened if Armand had been with me.

Film has a habit of running out at inopportune moments, and often with serious or annoying consequences. On one occasion, along the Rutshuru River, in the Belgian Congo, Armand was photographing from the side of a steep bank, and, as it was lunch time, I had gone off for a walk by myself.

I returned to find him frantic. He was out of film and watching a scene we had never witnessed before.

Some hippos were wallowing in a mud pool. Just before I returned, two elephants had lumbered up and one of them had waded in and started slashing the hippos with his trunk. I was just in time to see the sequel.

The hippos, apparently astonished and resentful, began to squeal and scramble farther into the river out of range. But the elephant followed and continued to belabour them across their backs. The screams and snorts of rage were deafening and continued even after the elephant had left to join his companion on the bank, swinging his trunk victoriously.

When it was all over, Armand, who could scarcely control his annoyance at failing to get this scene on film, commented:

"I could kick myself. . . . Imagine running out of film just at that moment. . . . Well, it's a lesson. We must never come out without at least two extra rolls of film handy."

I commiserated with him.

"It was unique—absolutely unique," he said. "I doubt

whether we'll ever see anything like it again. Elephants and hippos always get on perfectly well together—at least, they seem to agree not to take any notice of each other . . . and here we had this strange scene given to us on a plate and—no film!"

Once, in South Africa, Armand, Tom Stobart, and I went after rhino. By a stroke of luck we came across three of the black variety together in a clearing—two adults and one half-grown. They were browsing off the thorns on trees as we drove cautiously upwind towards them.

We got out of the truck and began to move warily on foot with the cameras. Armand took up position, and Tom Stobart stationed himself a short distance away in order to film us filming the rhino.

Whenever you are near them these animals spell danger, and we searched for a line of escape in case of accidents. A climbable tree was selected as the best getaway available.

Shortly after we started to film a really wonderful scene, the noise of the camera apparently disturbed the animals. They stopped feeding, pricked up their ears and began to peer around uneasily, gradually moving closer to us.

Armand, his eye glued to the viewfinder, beckoned to me.

"Warn me when they are too close," he whispered.

Suddenly they picked up our scent. The next instant all three charged, gathering speed every moment. A rhino charge is one of the most awe-inspiring sights in the animal world, but here were three of them bearing down upon us like a panzer column.

I shouted and we made for the tree, leaping into the climb. At such moments one moves with an incredible speed to the order of an emergency. The animals thundered past and suddenly stopped. Once their scent fails them they are shorn Samsons. They moved around puzzled for a time, then turned and ambled off in the other direction.

"What a picture!" cried Armand.

When we came down from the tree, scratched about the hands and legs, Armand ran towards the camera. I noticed that the seat of his trousers was almost torn off and flapped as he ran!

"The camera's all right," he called.

Breathlessly, we hailed Tom.

"Did you get it, Tom?" asked Armand anxiously, as we reached him.

Tom Stobart stood there staring disappointment.

"No, my film ran out just as you scrambled up the tree," he said.

We could have wept.

CHAPTER SIX

THE SORCERESS DANCE

BRAZZAVILLE, capital of French Equatorial Africa, is my favourite African city. It is built in the French colonial style and still retains some old-world charm. The tree-shaded bamboo and wood dwellings in the native quarter possess a dignity of their own and the grace of another century, unlike the waffle-iron-style buildings of Leopoldville.

Brazzaville is linked to Leopoldville by a motor launch service across the broad Congo river, the journey taking half an hour. Charmed with the city, Armand and I walked around admiring its architecture and enjoying the lovely French food in its old-fashioned *bistros*. In one of them we settled down to plan our expedition into the interior to the gorilla country, to photograph the people of Oka.

Food supplies on a journey such as this are always a tricky business. It is essential to lay in a variety of sustaining and palatable foodstuffs. When Robert, our French cameraman, volunteered to make himself responsible for arranging food supplies, we jumped at the chance.

"Nothing like having a man who knows something about good food," said Armand.

But it wasn't until we were actually on the road that I discovered the reason for Robert's generous offer. He had a Frenchman's passion for *pâté de fois gras* and had brought little else. After three meals of this rich but unsuitable fare, Armand and I revolted. We couldn't even bear to watch Robert devouring his beloved delicacy, but we were saved by the discovery of some tins of biscuits in our supplies.

The journey normally takes four days. By driving in relays through the night, we made it in two days. About half-way to our destination we stopped at a village where Robert had friends. They were delighted to see us and they treated us to a banquet of eggs fried in butter, with wonderful home-made French bread, red wine, and coffee. This helped to banish memories of the surfeit of *pâté*.

Oka, the gorilla hunters' village, came into view twenty hours later. Armand knew Oka well. In 1942 he had spent eight lonely months there filming and studying gorillas. His labour was wasted when the ship which was carrying all his films, notebooks and camera equipment back to America was sunk. Fortunately, at the last moment, Armand had decided to fly instead of travelling on the ship.

We lived in a guest hut in Oka village; it was made of bamboo with an over-hanging roof which formed a veranda. The door was a bamboo screen, and there was the usual mud floor. We engaged two brothers, one to cook and the other to work as houseboy.

One morning Armand and I were outside the hut when a small, bouncing figure, wearing a beautifully draped piece of raffia cloth on his hips, came towards us. Armand and the stranger greeted each other with delight.

The visitor was Chief Bamboo, an old friend of Armand. After effusive greetings, I was introduced to him. Armand called the interpreter we had acquired, a native boy who spoke both French and the Oka dialect. I noticed that Chief Bamboo had several fingers missing. It seemed to be a matter of pride with him, for he waved the stumps in Armand's face as he talked.

Armand told me afterwards that the maiming was the result of a gun accident, a frequent occurrence among the natives who use ancient weapons to hunt the gorilla—a kind of blunderbuss. Black gunpowder bought from traders—and often defective—is compressed into the barrel with bits of tin can and old nails. Often the guns blow back, taking off a hand or part of a face.

The Chief gave Armand all the news and some advice before leaving. Then another visitor presented himself— a small, very black-skinned, bearded man with kind sad eyes, who had apparently come for a job. He handed me a letter of recommendation with a smile, showing teeth filed to fine points. The letter was faded, but the signature was legible—Armand Denis, 1942.

I called Armand. "Look, darling, your signature!"

But his eyes were fixed on the visitor, who smiled and hung his head with pleasure and embarrassment.

"Antoine!" cried Armand, seizing the man's hand.

Our interpreter was again called into action and an absorbing adventure story was gradually unfolded as Armand and Antoine recalled the time a gorilla had escaped and was loose in the village. Most of the villagers left and sought safety in an open area nearby. Antoine, Armand, and some other men stayed behind to round the gorilla up.

From what I could gather from the conversation it was a desperate game of hide-and-seek, with death lurking round every corner of the village.

"Then your hut—your hut!" cried Antoine.

For the gorilla took refuge in Armand's hut, where it was finally cornered and caged.

"So many years ago," murmured Antoine when the tale had been told, "so many years ago."

I have seldom seen Armand more affected than he was by Antoine's recital. A dramatic episode from his past was brought vividly to life again by the small, kindly and admiring man.

Among all the friendly villagers there was one solitary African who persistently cold-shouldered us. He was large, shaven and sleek, and grotesquely garbed in cable-knitted golf stockings and heavy brogues. Not for a moment did his icy manner thaw into friendliness.

Robert rebuked him for his churlish attitude.

"I am not as other man. I am a catechist," the African replied.

A catechist is a teacher trained by the Roman Catholic missions. This African seemed to think that that set him apart. And to convince us he assembled some of the villagers in front of our hut and held a prayer meeting. We were not impressed.

When it became known that we wanted to film the ceremonial Gorilla Dance there were uneasy murmurs in the village. Superstitious fears welled up from the souls of these primitive and simple people. They saw it as a thing of evil omen.

"Something's got to be done about this," said Armand. "We must find some way of making them understand that all will be well."

In the next village lived an old Chief; a handsome and muscular man, bearded like all the natives in this part of Africa. We decided to consult him.

The proceedings were conducted with great dignity. The Chief sat down gravely on a big stool and motioned Armand to a smaller one by his side. I, being a woman, sat on the ground at Armand's feet, according to custom.

First there was a big Kebe-Kebe dance.

Only the men actually participate in this dance. The women form a chorus in the background and keep up an unbroken chant.

A dwarf, carrying twin bells shaped like an inverted U, marked the 2/3 rhythm. He stood at the side of the principal drummer as the musicians moved around.

The dancers came into view. Each was completely enveloped in a voluminous cylinder of fine raffia cloth about ten feet high, the top of this cylinder gathered around a stick resembling an elongated neck and bearing a carved and gaudily painted wooden head. As the dancers glided to their positions around us each dancer held his stick upright and aloft over his head; the little grinning wooden heads—one in the unmistakable likeness of General de Gaulle—were only about six inches in diameter, the raffia cloth hung in ten-foot vertical folds, and the effect was one of immense height. But the dancers soon began to revolve, and, as they whirled more rapidly, the cylinders of raffia cloth expanded with centrifugal force, ballooning out to a diameter of ten feet or more. The folds of the raffia cylinders were also gathered at the bottom, leaving only room for the movements of the dancer's feet—as the speed of rotation of each dancer increased he crouched and gradually lowered the stick which he had held over his head—so that soon each dancer had assumed the appearance of a huge madly spinning cushion, ten feet in diameter but no more than four feet high, surmounted by the grotesque little grinning head.

Clouds of dust arose. The drums throbbed. The women's voices rose and fell in eerie cadences.

Next, each revolving cushion began to glide and move into an enormous circular orbit, gravitating around us, occasionally colliding into each other or bouncing off the serried spectators—a dizzying but wonderful sight.

The drums died, the voices trailed, the dust settled slowly on the scene. The Chief, smoking his long curved gorilla pipe, turned to Armand and they talked through the interpreter. After a few minutes, the Chief said:

"Bad luck does not come with you as it does with other white people. All is good. You may speak my words to the people of Oka."

We returned to Oka in high spirits. A serious obstacle to our work had been removed.

"This is wonderful," said Armand, "better than I ever hoped for. If the Chief had turned against us it would have been impossible. We should have gone back empty-handed."

It was night when we reached the village. We had dinner and sat outside of our hut under a full moon of immaculate silver.

"Dance, Michaela," suggested Robert. "Dance one of those Indian dances and sing an Indian song."

The afternoon's experience had, I suppose, left me in a highly emotional state and I wanted to dance more than anything. I had often danced Indian dances to amuse people who did not know them; but to-night I wanted to dance for myself.

As soon as I had uttered the first few notes of Indian music, an answering call seemed to come from the heart of the village. Drums sounded. Presently we saw a group of village maidens coming towards us through the moonbeams which penetrated the thick trees like silver swords.

It was entrancing and unearthly.

They had come to beg me to join them in their own dance.

I glanced at Armand. He nodded acquiescence but told the girls they must bring me back in two hours.

When we reached the clearing in the centre of the village we formed a wide circle, the men on the outside, the girls within. Then the native dancers began to sing and I joined in, humming.

The dance seemed to me to have a ballet quality. It was quite different from the Kebe-Kebe ritual we had seen earlier. It was an altogether more personal dance with a marked individual style. The dancers expressed themselves, freely and joyously.

I quickly picked up the steps and rhythm which are syncopated, and the body movements are very like those of the rhumbas, congas, and mambas of South America.

In spite of the marked individuality of the dance it seemed to fall into a formal pattern and acquire a ritualistic character. There was certainly no improvisation, and when one girl indicated to me with signs that we should dance in the centre of the circle, I was sure that this was a part of the dance's pattern.

As the girl and I performed solos, the villagers shouted expressions of delight. Our dancing was, as it were, the hub of the whirling circle, and I gave myself up completely to its strange and compelling rhythm.

But suddenly angry murmurs arose from parts of the audience. Something was displeasing them. I was at a loss to understand why their mood should have changed in a matter of minutes.

Then I understood. My partner and I, following the pattern of the dance, had performed some secret and symbolic steps. Sections of the audience evidently resented the performance of ancient and mystical movements by a stranger. They were shocked that I should imitate or try to interpret a sacred ritual that I could not possibly understand.

But the muttering died down and the incident was soon forgotten. For the rest of my two hours in the village the dance proceeded without interruption.

I can't hope to give an adequate description of the effect of this dance upon me. The emotional impact was powerful. The senses were sharpened as they might be by a drug. Whenever I have danced with African people I have felt one with them.

Dancing is a vital part of Africa's life. Few Africans I have met were indifferent to it. But the cable-knit stockinged and brogued catechist was violently opposed to dancing. This was all the more strange because the Catholic Missions tolerate it.

One night I watched him as I danced with the native girls. His face was full of disdain as we stamped and swayed to the pagan rhythms. I beckoned him to join us, but he shook his head in scornful silence. Then I thrust a drum into his hands. For a moment he hesitated. Suddenly his newly acquired inhibitions fell away. Hours later he was still beating the drum.

Mosquitoes! How they tormented us! And Robert

had packed *pâté de fois gras* instead of nets! We had no protection against the winged invaders. They injected their poison into our bloodstreams with impunity. All we could do was to dose ourselves with paludrine. Some of our nights were hell.

But the days were lovely. We became one with the slow beat of African life. Our ways were merged with those of the people around us.

Beauty was everywhere. In the animal life, in the vegetation, in the natives. The women were especially beautiful. In some forest clearing a woman would seem suddenly to materialize out of the steamy heat—a sculptured masterpiece in basalt, with broad shoulders and narrow hips, almost masculine in outline. But the limbs were rounded and voluptuous, the breasts richly modelled.

Unlike the women of East Africa, who shave their heads, the Oka beauties take great pride in their long tresses which they dress elaborately in a mass of tiny braids bound with raffia thread. They spend hours on their coiffures.

In the torrid heat I often envied their indifference to clothes. In their presence I felt grotesquely overdressed in my slacks and shirt. The narrow fibre belt they wore supported a strip of cloth passing between the legs and drawn up back and front to hang over the belt—simple, comfortable, and adequate.

For miles the savannah is broken with large tracts of vegetation. Here live the gorillas. The forests we penetrated were not as thick as the jungles of the Amazon or the Ituri in the Belgian Congo. But most of the time we moved about in shadow broken only by streams which reflected the blue of the sky.

There may easily be danger in the areas where the aromatic Ntundulu plant grows, for it is a favourite food with gorillas. By the way I have eaten it and found it excellent.

At night the gorillas break down branches from trees to make sleeping nests. You can hear the sharp cracking of the twigs, the rustle of the leaves, and the chatter and brawl of quarrelling gorillas as the colony makes its preparations for bed. They sleep heavily. But when travelling through the forests it is wise to make plenty of noise.

To stumble on the gorilla in his domestic state, unheralded, may mean death. One must play for safety in those parts of the forest where the male gorilla lords it.

The evening before we left on our expedition into his stronghold there was a ceremonial gorilla dance. It began with the familiar throbbing beat on two tall drums. Then into a circle formed by women and girls two witch doctors leaped. Both were in full regalia, with charms and amulets. One had his head enclosed in a fantastic mask—half-animal and half-human—from which bulbous eyes protruded. High above his head he held the skull of a gorilla.

The other witch doctor carried a bundle of birch twigs —the prevailing symbol of authority in native Africa. As the tempo of the dance quickened he marked the rhythm by striking the gorilla skull with the twigs. Possibly, this was symbolic of banishing the ghost of the dead gorilla, or perhaps it was meant as a re-enactment of the slaying of their ancient jungle enemy.

One can only speculate. Perhaps fear was at the bottom of their revels—a fear flooding over the living from the immemorial past, when the struggle between man and this beast, who is so like man in cunning and ferocity, first began.

One of the objects of our journey was to find and film the strange Circumcision Dance. We had heard that one was to be held and were anxious not to miss it. A request to film it might be refused, but we were resolved to try.

As we made our way towards the village where we understood the dance was to be performed, Armand remarked casually:

"I shouldn't be surprised if we had a little trouble. The Circumcision Dance is supposed to be a secret affair. The Chief warned me there might be objections . . . The dance represents the symbolic entry of boys into manhood."

"How old are the boys?" I asked.

"It varies, but generally the initiation is between four and ten years old, but sometimes not until the age of puberty. A lot depends on the special circumcision witch doctor, who rounds up the boys every four years or so and takes them into the bush where they are left to spend the night alone . . . It goes on all over the Congo."

"What about the actual operation?"

"That takes place by the river. The dancers lead the boys there. In East Africa the women as well as the men take part, but here, I understand, women are barred."

"That seems to put me out," I said.

"Yes, there may be a snag there; but I'll need you to assist me."

The rites of circumcision are in various sections of Africa a living part of the people's lives. Among some of them both males and females undergo it. The missionaries are trying to stamp it out so far as the women are concerned; but the practice has deep roots in tribal life and so, in some cases, is of great social importance. For example, the Kikuyu and the Masai, both of whom practise circumcision on both sexes, will intermarry, but not with the uncircumcised Turkhana.

As we drew near to the village, Armand looked around and said:

"See what I see? There's not a woman anywhere."

"I wonder how they will take to me?"

"Keep your fingers crossed."

We entered the village and reached a place where

114

about a score of men were drawn up on the beaten earth behind the huts. Their bodies, arms and legs were completely covered by a tight-fitting suit of woven raffia palm which had the appearance of crochet work. It was striped black and white; the anklets and bracelets were of natural fringed raffia.

Above the shoulders each dancer wore a circular mask which completely concealed the face; from it protruded two crab-like eyes. The mask was fringed with raffia palm and the whole fringed by black vulture feathers. Each man wore a serval cat's skin as an apron, the tail hanging down in front.

The noise of our truck brought two women out of their huts. Immediately the dancers rang a little bell with one hand and waved a stick with the other, moving almost imperceptibly with one foot striking the ground. The women were chased off and disappeared.

Then the dancers came towards me, tinkling bells and brandishing sticks in a threatening manner. There was no mistaking their purpose. They wanted me out of the way.

Armand tried to make them understand that he needed me to help him make the film. But whenever I came near to the dancers to measure distances for Armand, or to tilt a man's head to catch the light, they stood still and refused to continue the dance.

"We must keep trying," said Armand.

The drummers, squatting with their instruments between their legs, started to clap out the rhythm of the dance with their hands.

Nothing doing. The dancers still stood stock-still.

I went to the truck and listened to the beating of the drums and hoped for the best. After a few minutes, Armand came to fetch me.

"It's no good," he said. "They keep moving out of camera range. I can't do it without your help."

It looked like an impasse. Either we had to be satisfied

with taking a poor undirected picture or stop the dance; for as soon as I showed myself again and approached them, they took offence and stood still.

Suddenly I had an idea.

"I wonder if this will do any good," I said, rummaging among the bags at the back of the truck.

There I found what I was looking for—a silk scarf I sometimes used to protect my hair from the dust during our long hours of driving. It was blue, patterned with navy blue giraffes. I returned with Armand to the dancers with the scarf in my hand.

I then went through a series of pantomimic gestures to Armand to tie the scarf round my eyes. When he had done so I groped my way about, with outstretched hands clawing the air, as if I was blind. I was, in fact, cheating, for I could see quite well through several thicknesses of the scarf, but the dancers could not know that.

Almost at once the drummers struck up and the dancers began to move their feet. The trick had worked. This time there was no warning bell and no waving stick.

"I want them there—there," Armand called, directing me.

I pretended to grope my way towards the dancers and followed his instructions, moving this man's head-dress an inch or two, raising that man's arm a little. They did not resent my touching them now that they thought I couldn't see them. Soon the scene was set to Armand's liking.

Then the dance began—a dance never witnessed before by a woman under pain of death.

It was intensely exciting, with the drums urging the feet of the dancers faster, ever faster until it reached a frenzied tempo. The sun glinted down on their shaking shoulders and swinging feathers. As I stared at them through the folds of my scarf, I felt sure that the crablike eyes had seen through my deception, and I had some bad moments wondering what would happen to me if they had.

But by this time the orgiastic dance had blotted me out of their vision. Under the African sun, surrounded by the primitive forest, the drums beat out the procreative rhythm to a climax where the world was a spurting and spawning vitality. Then the pace slackened as from exhaustion, and finally expired.

Only when the last feeble drum beats had faded away over the jungle, and the clearing was absolutely silent, did I begin my "blind" movements once again. Feeling the empty air around me, I groped my way towards the camera.

"Well done," said Armand, as he undid the scarf.

I blinked my eyes and covered them with my hands as if I had just been thrust out of darkness into the light of day. It was the last precaution against discovery, for the men were already walking into the bush, one by one.

They were going to fetch the boys and take them down to the river.

Armand and I returned to the car and truck and drove to a village about ten miles away. From here I hoped to turn the tables on Armand and watch a dance performed by women, which men are not allowed to see.

I laughed silently to myself. I had a vision of Armand, with my scarf draped over his head, peering into the viewer and pretending he wasn't looking!

There are things that cannot be told, secrets that must not be revealed. I am an initiate. I am under oath. But I can perhaps draw aside a veil that has for centuries hidden all the circumstances of which I am only able to reveal a fragment without being false to my trust.

I cannot be explicit even about the territory, but it is somewhere in Central Africa.

The affair began when I was in camp and had just

117

finished dictating notes on my wire recorder. Armand was away but would be back very soon. I thought I might fill in the time before he returned by sewing some buttons on my shirts.

One of my boys entered the hut.

"Memsahib," he said. "An old woman is here. She want to see you."

"Bring her here."

Visits of this kind were not unusual. Sometimes natives would call upon us for medicine, for they think we carry cures for everything from headaches to leprosy. Occasionally the callers are merely curious or friendly.

In a few minutes my boy returned with a very old woman. The skin of her face was ancient and puckered and she was toothless. Goat skins covered her nakedness. There was nothing remarkable about her except her eyes.

My first impression was that she was blind, for her gaze met mine, fixed and unwavering. A second and closer glance corrected the impression. I felt she saw more than most people, but her eyes, which seemed to hold a thousand secrets, had a distant look, as if scanning far horizons.

I beckoned her to sit down.

"Mother," I said, "what do you want? Can I help you?"

She pointed towards her swollen stomach and then touched her mouth. I assumed that she was hungry and called one of the boys.

"Bring some meat," I told him, "and make some tea."

The meat was cut off a roast joint we had; the tea was a strong brew, very sweet, for the Africans love sugar. The old woman ate the meat and drank the tea with signs of appreciation.

The boy who served was a local fellow, not one of our regulars. The almost exaggerated respect he paid to the old woman struck me as curious. She might have been a royal personage; and there was, indeed, something queenly about her.

I noticed her necklace. It was old because it was made in part of the old Portuguese beads which had come to Africa hundreds of years ago. You can't mistake them. Made of blue glass, they were originally large and round, but wear had flattened them and added to their beautiful quality. There were also one or two white beads which were new to me.

Attached to a cord was an antelope horn with a metal top. I assumed that this must contain snuff. I pointed to it and the old woman turned her eyes full on me. I have never forgotten that look.

Uncertain as to whether she understood Swahili or not, I made an elaborate pantomime. I went through the motions of taking snuff. She smiled and shook her head, saying in laboured Swahili:

"You are good. You are a good woman."

She used the term for a native woman, Mwana Mume, not Memsahib. Then she turned to the boy and talked to him in a language I did not understand. He wriggled with embarrassment as the old woman was obviously urging him to translate.

"What is it?" I asked him.

He was still tongue-tied and I repeated the question. The old woman also urged him on. Unable to resist us both he began haltingly:

"The old lady is a Muganga," he began.

"She is not a Mchout," I said.

Both terms apply to witch doctors, but a Mchout is associated with evil practices.

"No, no," he gasped, his eyes full of fear. "No, Memsahib. She is a good woman, a good sorceress." Then suddenly plucking up his courage, he added boldly: "Memsahib, look into her eyes."

The old woman beckoned me to come nearer to her. I did so and gazed into her eyes. Instantly I felt as if our personalities had merged. The sense of interpenetration was almost physical. My mind was filled with the knowledge that we were no longer strangers, that we could never be strangers again. Then I suddenly felt my head slowly moving from side to side, increasing in pace. I had seen these head movements among the witchcraft initiates.

But what was most remarkable was the change in the old woman herself. In my eyes she was transfigured. Gone was the toothless old ancient. The woman before me now had majesty and power; she had increased in stature; the years had fallen away from her.

The vision—call it hypnotic or what you like—passed and I heard the old woman saying:

"Tonight, tonight, ngoma" (dance).

I was back to mundane existence and thought of Armand and our film-making.

I asked the boy to translate: "May my husband come with me?"

"No, it is for you alone, for you, not for man, for women, not for all women," she said, shaking her head violently.

She rose from her seat and hobbled out of the hut. The boy stared at me with wide eyes.

"Memsahib," he cried, "you are the first European."

"What do you mean," I asked—"the first European? First for what?"

He refused to answer, but kept on repeating, "The first European, the first European."

He was silent for a moment and then added: "No, no, Memsahib, you are not really European, you are African. You have an African soul."

I was in a ferment. Vague fears swept over me. Yet at the same time I was possessed by a curious excitement. When Armand returned, I said to him:

"Are we going to stay in camp tonight?"

"Yes," he replied. "We have a lot to do in the morning. We have to photograph those pets."

"May I go to a dance tonight?"

This was not an unusual request. He nodded and said, "Yes, of course."

The day passed in a dream. I was photographed with the pets and had to direct a small scene. When our work was over time began to drag intolerably and by the time we sat down to dinner, I was too strung up by mingled excitement and apprehension to eat.

There is, I kept thinking, something odd about the whole thing. Should I refuse to go or should I insist that Armand came with me? But I remembered the old woman's words and was certain she bore me no malice. On the contrary, I had felt sympathy and even love in her.

As soon as our meal was over the call came. Three young women came into our camp and stood near the hut. I saw them standing still, waiting. They were dressed for dancing, the upper part of their bodies nude and glistening. Painted white patches, with fringed lines around them, encircled their eyes. Their foreheads were marked with a V in scarlet paint. Attached to their necklaces and hanging almost to the ground was a rope formed of some kind of large seed which reminded me of the conkers that English boys collect in September.

At the end of this rope was a bell.

For one moment I drew back, seized by an inner tumult. Armand looked at me curiously, as if to say, "They are waiting for you." So I said goodbye to him, joined the waiting dancers and took their hands.

I had expected that the dance would be held in the centre of the village, the usual place. But the dancers led me right through the village and its surrounding gardens and plantations to a narrow track which led into the forest.

The sense of mystery increased as we penetrated into

the dense vegetation. We walked in single file, one of the dancers in front of me, leading, the other two following me behind. In the mounting excitement I had one wild moment of panic when I felt I should have to turn and run back to our camp, but I controlled myself and walked on.

We must have gone two miles into the forest when suddenly I heard the throbbing of drums. With every step we took the noise grew in volume, until we found ourselves in a cunningly concealed clearing which was very difficult to enter.

First, we had to cross a small stream; the water was knee-high. I rolled up my trousers, tied my shoes together by the laces and slung them around my neck. The dancers held my hands as we crossed. On the other side of the stream the small track went on into a tangled mass of undergrowth. We made our way through this and suddenly found ourselves in the clearing.

The first impression was a blaze of light; it came from a fire around which were grouped seven tall figures whom at first sight I thought must be men; but I saw they had the full breasts of women. Masked, they looked enormous in their towering headdresses. Each had a rope of the large seeds hanging behind them and they wore several serval cat skins round their waists, which hung down to form skirts.

As my eyes became accustomed to the light, I was able to distinguish individuals. Some of the women were very young, some were of middle age. Then I saw the old woman. She wore a strange cone-like headdress, shaped with feathers at the top, in a great pom-pom. Gone was the poorly dressed old lady who had visited me at the hut. She was obviously wealthy. She wore copper ornaments and at least thirty pounds of charms and amulets on her person. In her hands was a gourd which she shook, muttering incantations.

A loud wild cry went up from the women when I

appeared. I went over to the old lady and, kneeling beside her, clapped my hands in the ceremonial manner common to Africans when they greet an important person or one worthy of respect.

Then a woman approached me. Her hair was painted red with clay. She knelt and signalled to another woman to bring two gourds. Then a circle was formed which enclosed the old woman, the woman with the gourds, and myself. The circle swayed and chanted to the beating of drums.

I looked at the drummers; they were women. The old lady held up the antelope horn, opened it at the top, and shook out some powder. She gestured to me to open my mouth. As I did so the thought that it might be poison flashed through my mind and instantly vanished, leaving me fearless and eager with curiosity. The powder was shaken on to my tongue. I closed my mouth and swallowed. It had a slightly astringent taste.

The women stared at me with unwavering eyes. They seemed to be watching my reactions to the powder. The circle danced and swayed for about five minutes.

One of the women who spoke Swahili told me later that vomiting normally follows the swallowing of the powder. The fact that I did not vomit marked me out as a woman fit to go through with the rest of the ceremony.

For a few minutes I was conscious of nothing but silence and eyes. The drums ceased to throb, but the eyes of the women did not move from me. Then the drums started up again and the eyes were withdrawn.

The old lady signalled.

At once the woman with the gourds shook them above my head. Another woman approached me waving the tail of some animal; she brushed it over my face, across my breasts and between my thighs. Then the tail was passed slowly over my forehead and mouth.

The gourds were again shaken over my head and

passed over me several times. The gourd woman placed them at her feet and painted my forehead with a V. I could feel its wetness and shape. All the time I had kept my eyes open, staring in front of me. This, I learned later, was regarded as a good omen; but at the time I did not want to miss a second of the fascinating ceremony.

After the painting I rose to my feet and shouted from sheer excitement. Again and again I shouted the word which was repeated in their chant. I will not give the word here. It would be meaningless to any except those who had undergone a similar experience; but it burst from me without conscious effort, and the women took it up and shouted it until the whole forest seemed filled with the cry.

A necklace was placed on me. It had one of the long ropes attached to it, and there seemed to be some competition among the women to fasten it on my neck. Then the dance began and I joined in, following their steps.

I was outside my normal mundane self. The world beyond the circle of light had ceased to exist for me. I had lost all sense of identity and was one with the dancers. It was an hour of enchantment, of ecstasy. This is the impression that remains with me, but some of the details stand out vividly.

In one dance, for instance, we formed a tight circle and leaned forward until each girl's head touched the heads of the girls on either side of her. Then the circle was drawn even tighter and two women dancers were held in a ring of close-pressed heads. When my turn came I danced with my head pressed against the woolly hair of one of my African sisters.

We danced until the light of dawn began to filter weakly through the forest trees. This restored my sense of time and I was alarmed. I stopped dancing; the others followed my example and stopped too. I went to the old lady, bowed to her and motioned that I would have to go back and join my husband. Some instinct made me fumble with my necklace at the back to take it off. Women came forward and removed it.

But another curious ceremony began. They dug a small hole in the ground with a stick and, still chanting, buried it and carefully covered it with earth.

As I made my way out of the circle I felt no fatigue after all these hours of dancing. The old woman hobbled in front of me, setting a fast pace. I hadn't the least idea of what was going to happen now, but I felt certain that, like Grettir, the hero of the Icelandic Saga, who had wrestled with the spirit of Glaum, I should never be the same again.

When we approached the outskirts of the village, we stopped and a young woman, acting as interpreter for the old lady, spoke to me and translated what she said, slowly and word for word.

"You are always one of us," I was told. "There are many people in the world, but there are only a few who are of us. We have given you special power and special strength. You will not be bad with that power because you will never misuse it."

I translated this to myself: "I would not abuse the power, whatever it was."

"You will work," the translator went on. "You will work not for your own plantation. You will work not for your children, because you have no children. You will work for all children because all children are your children.

"You will not work for yourself," she repeated, "but you will work for all people. You will not be bad with the power. You will use the power for good."

"I love people," I answered. "I love animals. I love all people."

They seemed pleased. They nodded as if they had known my declaration of faith all the time. I gave my hand to them in the European fashion and shook their hands. My hand was as warm and oily as their own. To the old lady I gave both my hands. Then we parted.

When I arrived at the camp, Armand was still asleep. I tumbled into bed, for exhaustion had now set in. I was too tired even to clean my face. Excitement and a whole night of dancing had left me an empty shell.

I awoke to find Armand already astir. He came over to my bed and looked at me.

"What have you done to your face?" he asked.

Still half-asleep I answered: "I didn't clean it last night."

"I should think not," he said. "Look at yourself." And he handed me a mirror.

I looked into the glass sleepily and was instantly wide awake.

There on my forehead was a slightly blurred scarlet V. Around my eyes were white patches. Then the previous night's fantastic happenings flooded over me. Still suspended between dream and reality, I could hardly have believed in them but for the painted evidence on my face.

Several years have passed since this tremendous experience. I have travelled much in lands far away from Africa; but I could no more forget the old woman's final words to me than I could change my skin.

Sometimes I am conscious of the power of which she spoke—generally in moments of crisis when it gives me calmness and strength. More and more I long to help people and, in small ways, I think I have done so.

The power draws animals to me by banishing all my fears in their presence. Of this I am absolutely convinced. To many who have asked me the secret of my understanding with animals, I have answered, "Love." But it is love fortified by the power.

The power ensures that I shall accomplish my mission in life, whatever form it may take in future years. It has drawn to Armand and me a circle of friends all over the world who seek for something higher than the selfish material values which have done so much to choke the natural idealism of people.

It may seem ridiculous to many that initiation with a group of African women can have any special significance; but from it I have drawn proof of a transcendent reality behind the harsh and contemptuous face of the world. A few African women? But I believe that their faith and approach to the power and, finally, their acquisition of it, is part of a universal striving towards comprehending life in all its beauty and truth. They are one in spirit with the most noble and enlightened men and women who ever lived.

I believe in a world consciousness which Africans call Roho, or soul. From it power for good flows. It expands from century to century, from people to people, and it often manifests itself sharply and positively among people unconfused by the perplexities of civilised life.

This is the way of all spiritual illumination, whatever religious shape it may take. The Sorceress Dance is but one ceremony to extend the power through initiates. But there is a link between it and all other forms of transcendent experience.

A new religion? No, the oldest in the world, I believe.

CHAPTER SEVEN

HUSBANDS À LA CARTE

ARMAND and I had heard of the Asongo-Meno from some of the old hands in Africa. They had the reputation of being an artistically gifted people of great physical beauty. One friend of ours compared them with the Benin folk whose bronzes are sought after by every important museum in Europe.

But the Asongo-Meno live in the Belgian Congo and—we were given to understand—under the special protection of an enlightened administration. The more we heard about them the more anxious we were to visit them; so we eventually found ourselves in a heavily laden safari truck, with Armand's assistant, Duncan, on the way to a mission on the Sankuru river, which was run by a Mr. and Mrs. Warren.

Our first contact with the Asongo-Meno was made in a dense forest. We were dismayed and astonished at their appearance. These people bore no resemblance to the folk who had been described to us in such glowing terms. They had shaven heads and wore European clothes. We could hardly believe our eyes.

This part of the Congo had been described to us as a show place, the special pride of the then Governor, General Jungers, a man who had a sense of mission to preserve the social habits of the people! The mystery was soon cleared up. The regular administrator was on leave, and had been replaced by a bigoted fool who had forced the Asongo-Meno to shave their heads and—as he phrased it—"to dress decently like Christians".

Since they were conscious of their beauty, the people

He would have made a success in any walk of life. He is actually
at the top of his profession, and our personal witch-doctor

Asongo-Meno hunter. Their nets are pinned against the foliage.
The Bassenji dogs, identical with the dogs of ancient Egypt,
drive the game towards the men who are hidden near the nets.
The dog, unable to bark, wears a wooden bell round its throat

felt outraged—especially the girls, who were proud of their long hair. And the result was, in fact, grotesque, for the shaven scalps were several degrees lighter than the faces. In our view it was worse than vandalism at the expense of dead things; it was a violation of living beauty.

We at once sought out the substitute administrator and protested against his order in the strongest possible terms. He went on blandly to explain his action in the name of progress. He was obviously incapable of realizing the nature of his offence against human dignity.

When, later, we returned to Luluabourg, we lodged a complaint with the high administrator there. He exploded.

"That imbecile! That idiot! He should be forcibly circumcised! . . . Progress, indeed!"

He rescinded the order at once; but it seemed to us that the damage had been done. We could only hope that these Asongo-Meno would grow their hair again and cast aside their European garments. It often happens, however, that when old customs are abandoned, even under protest, a return to them is very difficult. Some subtle psychological change seems to take place.

We were still burning with indignation when we reached the Warrens' place. These two missionaries were shocked at the news; for they had a genuine love and respect for the natives; and the natives loved them in return.

The Warrens were really good people, but like so many other missionaries they had their blind spots. For instance, they discouraged the native dances, probably on the ground of their pagan origin; but worse was to come. We were sitting on the verandah, chatting, when Armand and I mentioned the artistic traditions of the Asongo-Meno and asked the Warrens whether they had come across any masks or carvings or other artifacts belonging to them.

"Yes," said Mrs. Warren, smiling. "We burned great

heaps of those heathen idols—big carved figures they were—when we first came here twenty years ago. Masks and all sorts of rubbish."

There was a dead silence, lasting perhaps half a minute. We were struck dumb. Mr. Warren, feeling that something was amiss, looked round and asked: "Why?"

Neither of the others answered; they looked stunned. To break the embarrassing silence I rushed in with another question: "Were they very old?"

"Oh, yes," said Mr. Warren. "Hundreds of years old, I should say. . . . The natives brought them all in to us."

"All," I said, hoping to hear that perhaps some of them had escaped the flames.

"Yes, all."

"Then there's none left?"

"No, they've gone for good," said Mrs. Warren; and as if to cheer us up, she added, brightly, "You should have seen the bonfires we had!"

I tried to keep a hold over my tongue, but the words tumbled out, protestingly:

"Do you realize what you've done? You've burned priceless art treasures. . . . They can never be replaced. . . . Never."

The Warrens were completely taken aback. They looked more puzzled than annoyed.

"Art treasures?" said Mr. Warren with an edge on his voice. "Art treasures? But it was all pagan, the whole lot of it."

So the conversation ran into the blank wall of misunderstanding. But I thought how much better it would be if missionaries were given some sort of training in art and cultural matters before being sent out to the so-called backward areas. Every missionary, I thought, ought to have at least an elementary knowledge of native art and archaeology which would enable him to appreciate and preserve the works of native genius. How much richer the world would be in art treasures if it were so.

Our purpose was to photograph the Asongo-Meno in their natural state. This meant an expedition deep into the forest and a walk of some twenty miles, so we took four tipoyes. These are litter chairs carried by Africans. All three men—for Mr. Warren accompanied us—used the tipoyes, but I preferred to walk with the natives, wearing sneakers and treading exactly in their footprints. Once the marching rhythm is established one can go on for hours without tiring.

It was wonderful in the forest, a time of sheer enchantment. Spangles of light showered through the thick trees and lay in heaps on the small clearings. The spirit soared. When the boys and I were ahead of the other members of the party, they broke into fascinating dance steps which I tried to imitate.

They sang at the top of their voices, making up the songs as they went along, Calypso-style, about members of the party. I wished I could understand the words of the songs. The music was a rhythmical chant.

After three hours we stopped for water and papaya, which were carried by the porters. Here we saw our first Asongo-Menos living unmolested in their original state.

The serenity was profound, the peace almost tangible. This was Africa as it must have been centuries ago. The beauty of these people almost took my breath away. Here was primitive innocence, unstained by the squalid prohibitions of a guilt-ridden civilization.

They stood before us, free and straight, with a piece of raffia cloth hanging down back and front from the waist. They wore their hair long, twisted into braids and treated with resin and palm oil which keeps lice away. Their bodies, which seemed to preserve the formal beauty of black wood carvings, were decorated with *ngula*.

Their general aspect had the hieratic quality one associates with the sculpture of ancient Egypt. The hair-do emphasized the likeness. I pointed it out to Armand.

"Yes," he replied, "there is certainly a connection. Centuries ago there must have been contact between the Egyptians and the remote ancestors of these people. Perhaps they originally drew their artistic inspiration and skill from the Egyptians. It's possible, but who knows?"

He went on to explain the making of *ngula*.

"It comes from a certain type of wood," he said. "They grind the wood on a flat stone, under dripping water, and work on it until a red liquid comes out which later hardens into powder."

This red powder is highly prized and much sought after. We carried some to give as presents to the people who worked for us. We had also brought heavy copper wire for gifts; it was cut into lengths as we needed it.

In a short time we reached the Asongo-Meno village and were well received. The houses are made of bamboo and palm fronds, and decorated with the patterns of natural wood. The roof is peaked; the door is a movable screen hung from the top of a lengthwise pole and attached by pieces of vine which pull it across the entrance.

Inside, herbs hang in each corner, tied to the roof. The floor is stamped earth. All cooking is done outside the huts, not inside as in most African communities. Three logs are placed on the ground, ends facing to the middle, and on this stand they place their clay pots. As the logs burn, so they are pushed in.

I watched the younger Asongo-Meno girls carry the water. They were able to take as many as twenty gourds in a basket over their shoulders. Some of the African baskets are works of art, varying greatly in shape, size and design. One can tell at once from what part of Africa they come by the workmanship. And there are many different ways of carrying them. The Kikuyu women, for example, carry their flat baskets strung from straps across their foreheads. The Asongo-Meno method resembles the rucksack technique.

We had come without our boys, Shabani and Mucharia. They had explained to us that they were not bushmen.

"Memsahib will understand," went on Shabani. "We cannot walk so many, many miles."

So we planned to cook for ourselves, with Warren's boy lending a hand. Armand and I shared a sleeping hut, while Duncan and Mr. Warren had one each. We were comfortable enough, but all the same I wished we had Shabani and Mucharia to help with the chores.

Then two beautiful Asongo-Meno youths presented themselves and asked if they could work for us. They might have strayed from ancient Egypt's Amarna Age, so instinctively cultured and graceful were their movements when they waited upon us at table. They learned fast and soon became devoted to us. We were very attached to them, but, as so often happens, these attachments end in heart-pulls. When we left they wanted to come with us, but we refused to take them, knowing that in Kenya they would soon become homesick for their own forests and people.

We began to investigate the social life of the Asongo-Menos. There are four orders among the men—sorcerers, medicine men, blacksmiths and the Kumisenji. The sorcerers are credited with the power to smell out thieves and cast spells to remove them; the medicine men are herbalists and cure the sick; the blacksmiths smelt copper and other metals.

"Look what an excellent heating system they have," Armand pointed out. "Look at these forges and how cleverly designed the bellows are."

The bellows are made of pots over which goatskins are stretched, with a tube leading to the fire. The blacksmiths beat on the goatskins and the draught thus created fans the flames. Armand was fascinated by these

133

bellows, and told me that a unique and most ingenious principle of physics was used by the Asongo-Meno in their construction.

The Kumisenji are the highest rank in the Asongo-Meno social order. We were never able to find out the exact nature of their duties, but they appeared to be super-sorcerers and were treated with great respect. They wear necklets of ancient Portuguese make, for the Portuguese were the first explorers and traders in this region. The dark blue glass beads which form the necklaces are opaque with age and much treasured; they are strung with the symbolic leopard teeth, three of which hang like a pendant from the centre. We tried to buy one of these necklaces and we were courteously but firmly given to understand that they were not for sale.

The copper smelted by the blacksmiths is made into anklets of solid metal weighing several pounds. We filmed a smelting scene and also one of a father presenting his child with one of these lovely anklets. The old anklet had become tight on the growing child and had to be removed. The child looked straight up in the air and winced slightly every time the metal mallet hit the chisel.

It was rather frightening to watch; one felt the child might be suffering. But the hammering was done with such care that I am sure she experienced little pain. When the old anklet was at last opened, it was slipped off and the new and larger one was hammered on. As soon as she was free, the child ran off, smiling, displaying her new anklet with pride to her friends—like any little European girl after receiving a gift of jewellery on her birthday.

The tribal marks of the Asongo-Meno are formed by cicatrices. The men wear a dotted and curved line on cheekbones and forehead; the women have their foreheads treated with dots and large concentric circles of solid lines on their cheeks. The designs are carved out of flesh.

Armand and I agreed that they added to the beauty of these people; but behind the practice there is possibly a reason other than aesthetic: a moral reason. The pain undergone may be a form of ritualistic trial.

The operation is certainly painful. During our stay among the Asongo-Meno we witnessed the carving of a woman's face and arms. Those who have skill in this are greatly honoured, we learned. A woman performed the operation which we saw; she had a club foot and wonderful manual dexterity. She held a tiny gourd containing a mixture of ashes and water in one hand and painted the design with the other.

Then she began to cut the flesh with a knife; blood poured out of the wounds but the girl bore it stoically. It was while watching this scene that I got a strong impression of a moral test.

The cuts are allowed to heal, then opened again. This process is repeated several times until finally raised weals are formed.

Asongo-Meno means "filed teeth", and all the tribe follow the custom. I have my doubts about the artistic results of the practice, but it seems to suit these people— or at least, it does not detract noticeably from their beauty.

Their instinctive feeling for art finds expression in bodily decoration. Their natural skin colour is copper which again emphasizes their resemblance, already strongly marked in cast of features and dress, to the ancient Egyptians. But both men and women paint themselves black with charcoal mixed with palm oil. The facial patterns executed in *ngula* are very striking.

The Bassenji dogs, which the Asongo-Meno use for hunting, were of course of tremendous interest to us. It was while I was watching two dogs in play that Armand said to me:

"What do those dogs remind you of?"

I thought of the dogs at home. No, not Europe, but Africa—Egypt.

"The strong resemblance they have to the dogs portrayed on the old Egyptian pictures and carvings! This is surely another link with Egypt."

Curious about it, I asked some of the tribe questions with the aid of the boy whom Warren had brought along.

"Where did your father's father's father come from?"

"From the north, when we had to escape from the great plague of ants," came the reply.

This answer would not satisfy a modern ethnologist, but the traditions of native people telescope history and preserve the ancient stories of their race. Further enquiry into the matter has led me to the tentative conclusion that long ago the ancestors of the Asongo-Meno came from the northern part of Africa to find refuge in this forest region.

They have wonderful eyes; in the darkness they could discern objects invisible to me.

I used to wander through the village at night, guided by a small child, to visit the huts. The people never failed to give me a warm and courteous welcome, and I soon began to feel that I could spend the rest of my life among them. They pursued the ancient ways of life with beautiful and healthy bodies and unruffled minds, untouched by the fears which encompass the civilized world in this atomic age.

Deep in their forest they led an almost idyllic existence. Nobody seemed to have grudges against life or his fellows; there was no quarrelling, no noise of strife. Even the babies seldom cried. There was little disease except leprosy, but this scourge was not widespread. The lepers were not isolated; they covered themselves with paint and the sores were difficult to detect. Often the only visible evidence of the disease was a missing toe or finger.

We had to take risks and we took them with our eyes open. After all, you can contract T.B. in London and

New York as easily as leprosy among the Asongo-Menos.

One of the important sorcerers was a leper. He had the characteristic sores round his mouth and he exuded the strange smell of the disease.

But we constantly forgot about his disease and moved him into position for photographing without much thought and certainly very little fear. We always took the precaution of washing our hands in antiseptic after we had handled him. We were told that leprosy was only infectious at a certain stage, but we were always careful.

The witch doctors' and sorcerers' charms fascinated me.

"We must get this chap dancing," said Armand on one occasion, indicating a sorcerer who wore an antelope horn filled with all sorts of charms and covered on the top with a metal lid.

As he moved, more charms on the outside of the horn rattled. When he began his sorcerer's dance, I joined him, and we stepped and swayed to the noise of his charms, while Armand photographed the scene and the Asongo-Meno encouraged us with stamping feet and shouts of approval.

The little copper-coloured babies were wonderful. I suspect that the mothers thought I possessed some special kind of magic, for they all insisted that I should hold their babies for a time. Outside our hut a line of mothers would wait patiently in a queue, each with her child. I would take the first baby in my arms, cuddle and talk to it for a moment, and hand it back to its mother and so on down the line.

We made frequent journeys into the forest and ate the native food, prepared in our own fashion. Manioc was cooked like French fried potatoes; we baked our own bread and used the Asongo-Meno vegetables. After a hunt the men would sell some of their meat to us.

The Asongo-Menos hunt with nets and take their Bassenji dogs with them; large wooden bells with metal clappers are strung round their necks. These dogs cannot bark, but they emit a strange howling noise and drive the game towards the hunters by the tinkling of the bells.

We bought four of the dogs to take with us on our expeditions into the forest, two of the southern type and two of the northern. We took them back to Kenya with us, but the two southern dogs died. Loali and Wangu, the northern dogs, survived to interest and delight all dog-lovers who saw them.

They were magnificent pure specimens, uncrossed by any European breeds. Tawny in colour, they have frown marks on their foreheads, small eyes, upstanding ears and curly tails. The dogs from the southern Belgian Congo are of the same colour though taller and rangier, with tails like greyhounds. I have seen a white Bassenji and another type, black with orange eyebrows and a white line down the nose.

Africans like dogs and are good judges of them. On our travels Loali and Wangu were much admired for their glossy coats and liveliness, for we kept them in top condition. One native offered us the equivalent of fifteen dollars for them—a fabulous amount of money to an African.

We finished our work among the Asongo-Meno and had to go. It was a big wrench for all of us. Armand and I had grown to love these beautiful and gracious people, and they were desolate when we set off.

They followed us for at least an hour into the forest, singing and chanting; some of them joined arms with me to dance to the place of our parting. I had to tear myself away from them. After they had disappeared into the forest, I saw that two small boys were still following us, and I had to send them back to their mothers.

A few months after we had left the Asongo-Meno country we reached Matadi, the furthest point west in the Belgian Congo. There was a letter from Mrs. Warren awaiting us. It contained strange and—to me—disturbing news. A severed human arm had been found in the forest. After examination, the police decided that it had been chopped off.

The Asongo-Menos were once ritualistic cannibals. Perhaps one of them had reverted. These things happen among native people. It may have been a crime of revenge, or one committed in the practice of magic. The news set me thinking and I discussed the matter with Armand. We agreed that the injection of a totally different set of values into an ancient social and religious pattern could not be done without risk, now and then, of moral disequilibrium.

Strangely enough, Mrs. Warren's letter reached us after we had passed through a village which had a very odd story attached to it, and one which struck a note, illustrative of our talk.

The village was well in the interior. Externally, there was nothing unusual about it, but there was something very unusual about the women. They were beautiful, indeed remarkably so; but what attracted our attention was their bold and brazen gestures. Most African women are of a great modesty; on the surface, at least, they give the impression of complete sexual innocence.

But these women were saucy and even lascivious in their gestures. They waggled their hips in conscious sexual provocation.

"I've never seen anything like this before in Africa. . . . What's going on here?" exclaimed Armand.

The women were beautifully dressed in expensive cottons, obviously imported from England or Belgium. There was a definite fashion trend both in colour and pattern. I learned later that the prints changed seasonally, sometimes copying batik, other times following a geometric style in pattern, and sometimes a naturalistic motif.

"Look at them!" Armand went on. "These are not

simple bush women. They are what the French call *évoluées*."

We passed on, wondering. We could find no convincing explanation for the conduct of these women.

"Is it possible that they have been wholly corrupted by some gang of white men?" I asked.

"Impossible — unthinkable," said Armand. "What would their men be doing?"

And there the matter rested until we met a Belgian administrator and asked him to explain the mystery. He had a strange and gruesome story to tell.

"It began a few years ago," he said, "when a tall and handsome young girl married an elderly and soured man. They got on badly together. He nagged her constantly and perhaps ill-treated her. As far as I can make out, she had a very happy disposition and suffered a lot at his hands."

"Did he have other wives?" asked Armand.

"No; it was a Christian village, so he could have no other wives to share the work of the house and take the young wife's mind off her unhappiness. This may seem strange to us, but polygamous peoples, you know, are not jealous and the wives generally get on well together. The trouble starts when the husband begins to look to other women outside his own family circle. That can be serious and may cost him a great deal in goats or copper. And the erring wife is always beaten.

"But this affair is something very different. . . . After some months the elderly husband disappeared. The young wife told her relations and friends that he'd gone to the city to find work."

"Is that usual?" I asked.

"It happens sometimes," said the administrator. "A man will go to Stanleyville or Leopoldville, work for a time and then return to his home. . . . By no means unusual.

"But this young wife seemed to be highly delighted

with her husband's departure. She prepared a large banquet for all her women friends. Then something very strange happened. The women's banquet became a monthly custom when a husband departed for the city. . . And, one by one, off they went."

"Just like that!" interjected Armand.

"Yes, just like that! . . . The trouble arose when the administrator came round to collect the taxes. He found that at least six men—taxpayers—were missing. And since tax-collecting was his business he questioned people here and there about the missing men but could learn nothing of their movements since they left the village. . . . He gave it up."

"Well, what happened?" I asked, eager to hear the end of the story.

"Nothing until the time came round for the administrator to collect the taxes again. He then found that more men were missing; in fact, there was a noticeable scarcity of men in the village. He questioned the grass widows. They vaguely waved hands in the direction of the coast. That was all he could get out of them. Some of the women had even married again. Then there was something furtive about everybody, even the men. . . . He decided to get to the bottom of the matter.

"He tackled the men first and finally concentrated his questions on one who seemed ill at ease and even afraid. He soon got the whole horrible story.

"The women, it seems, had formed a society and once a month each member had to give a feast at which her murdered husband's carcass was served as the main dish. . . . The village had never known such happy times: the women danced and enjoyed themselves all day, for they had no work to do and only themselves and their children to feed."

The Belgian paused for a moment, presumably to let these gruesome facts sink in, and then resumed:

"The administrator called the women together and

cross-examined them. They all denied the charge and demanded the name of the informer. But bit by bit he amassed enough evidence from relations and friends to make his charges stick. Then he ordered a search of the huts.

"In the home of one of the missing men he found a fountain pen stuck in the roof of the hut. The administrator had himself given this very pen as a present to the missing man and knew that he would on no account part with it. He called the women together again and made an open accusation of murder. They gave a complete denial."

Armand said: "Then there was little he could do—I mean apart from locating some of the remains of the murdered men."

"That's apparently what he thought for a time," said the administrator. "But an old man came to him and whispered a suggestion. He decided to act upon it.

"Addressing the watchful circle of women again, he said: 'Although you are Christians, I shall get a witch doctor who has the power of calling back the souls of the dead. They will tell me what I wish to know. They will also haunt the guilty ones.'

"The silence that followed was broken by a wail from one of the women. 'I will tell all I know,' she screamed hysterically, 'if the soul of my husband is kept from me.' Then, one by one, each confessed and the whole crime was laid bare.

"Each of the men had been killed in the night by his wife, usually by a blow on the head. The body was then secretly dismembered, cooked and eaten ceremoniously by the members of the club. . . . It had all begun with the murder of the elderly husband by his young wife."

"What happened to the women?" I asked.

"What could the administrator do?" replied the Belgian. "There were so many women in it . . . he referred the matter to higher authority who decided to send the ringleader to prison and severely reprimand the others. After that there were no more murders and nothing further was heard of the women's crime club."

That had happened some years before we passed through the village; but the women are still different from any other Africans I have met. They are still full of themselves and conscious of their power. The men are still cowed, for the fear of a blow on the head in the night is always with them. They do a fair share of the work, and they buy their wives beautiful costly cotton clothes in which they parade in the village, gesturing lasciviously to strangers. What can the men do? The women's club might be revived any time. Who knows? Women are so unpredictable.

CHAPTER EIGHT

THE DUCK-BILLED WOMEN

EXPEDITION! A thrill every day you may think. But the reality is different: excitement comes suddenly, after weeks of routine work. Then it is that your reactions must be lightning swift—your life may depend on it.

We had left the Asongo-Meno people far behind us, together with about three-quarters of the Belgian Congo. Conditions were perfect and we were moving through hot and desolate savannah country at a steady clip on our way to Tshikapa.

A wonderful feeling of peace, such as I have experienced only in Africa, enfolded me, and I gave myself up to the magic of it. Of course, I should have known that this unconquerable continent is always master.

For suddenly the car broke down, landing us in a position from which escape with our lives seemed improbable. Armand and I looked at each other with the same thought in our minds: *Is this the end of the journey?*

On our way south to the Congo diamond mining area, prior to this trouble, we reached the little town of Bunia, once famous for its duck-billed women. We had the idea of filming here, but the administrator told us that the young women no longer disfigured themselves in the old tribal way. However, he would find some old women with plate lips.

Armand and I had discussed the origin of this

The prima ballerina—her rattles sounding like maracas—sways
with sinuous grace. One side of her face is painted blue, the
other white, and red ngula enhances the cicatrices on her legs

Left: Two of these pygmy men are grandfathers

Below: "Somewhere in the Congo." We travel hundreds of miles like this. In front a man carries a serval cat skin with a bell attached to its tail. This is witchcraft — protection against the forest devils

Right: Congo ballet. I learn a new dance. The girls glisten with palm oil; their anklets are solid copper

Below: I take my turn with the drum. The dance goes on. Among the Bapende, near the Angola border, Belgian Congo

Virile rhythm and
supple young bodies
indicate that it is good
to be alive; it is good
to be African

grotesque practice, for there is no general agreement on the custom among travellers and anthropologists.

"It's possible," said Armand, "that it began as beauty culture, like the cicatrices of the Asongo-Meno women, or the giraffe necks of the Burmese women."

"The most likely explanation," I said, "is that it began as a way to defeat the slave-traders who once operated in the area. For the Bunia women were famous for their beauty and fetched high prices in the slave market; but they lost their market value when plates were inserted into their lips."

So we talked and agreed that in the course of time the practice lost its original purpose and acquired a symbolic value. Perhaps by sacrificing physical beauty the mutilated women were supposed to have achieved beauty of spirit.

The duck-bill was made by first drilling a tiny hole in the upper lip and inserting a small disc after the hole had healed and become firm. Larger discs were inserted at intervals, so that the lip was stretched finally to duck-bill proportions. In Bunia, only the upper lip was distorted, but the Ubangi, in French Equatorial Africa, made a real job of it by doing both the upper and lower lips.

The administrator kept his word. The next day we found some old women with plate lips waiting for us in the village square. They sat in a group, dressed in goat and antelope skins. The sight of them filled me with pity, for their age accentuated the cruel disfigurement.

"We just can't film them," I said to Armand. "It would be too pathetic."

"I agree. We'll take some stills, though."

The old women seemed delighted to be the centre of attraction. We took the photographs and rewarded them for giving up their day to us. I gave one of them a cigarette and the others crowded round as I lighted it for her, but she found smoking difficult with her distended lip. Malformation made talking very difficult for her, but she seemed cheerful enough. I am sure the interpreter understood more from her expressions than her words. To please the women, I asked the interpreter to give me their word for beautiful. Pointing to their clothes I began to praise them, stroking the skins they were wearing.

One old lady nodded and pointed admiringly to my handbag which was made of sisal by the natives of Machakos. She stroked it, thus returning my compliment.

Armand took a magnificent photograph during this session. I felt the old ladies would show a lively interest in anything I did with my own lips. As I applied my lipstick they watched fascinated. The picture which Armand made of this has been reproduced in magazines and newspapers throughout the world.

When they were thoroughly at their ease, the old ladies allowed us to examine their lip plates; some were very ornate but not as impressive as a long-stemmed African pipe which one of them was smoking.

From Bunia we moved on to a small village where only three Europeans lived, the administrator and a married couple who owned three boxers. I listened to these people with disgust while they boasted that their pets were able to kill dogs belonging to the natives. Armand stared disapproval and said bluntly:

"That's nothing to be proud of."

Another day's travel brought us to another remote forest village. Here, we had been told, we would see some of the most beautiful dancing to be found in the entire forest—and of course the local administrator would give us all the necessary co-operation in our work. But we sensed quickly that this was poor advice.

The administrator's quarters consisted of a collection of large huts on the edge of the village. A handsome

146

African woman, with her hair twisted and braided in the local style, and wearing beautiful cotton robes, welcomed us and took us in to meet M. Delbert.

He measured up to tropical sub-standard. Dressed in faded khaki shorts and shirt, he wore a battered sun-helmet on the back of his head and on his chin several days' growth of whiskers. He looked as if he slept in his clothes on an unmade bed. At his elbow was a whisky bottle.

"Have a drink?" he asked.

He seemed surprised when we declined and waved us to a couple of chairs covered with old newspapers. There are a few—very few—minor officials of this old type left in the Belgian Congo; left over from times when it was hard to recruit good men for the colonial service; exiled, usually, with little power, to remote areas. These men are in sharp contrast to the fine type of young official, highly trained in the Belgian Colonial University, idealistic and hardworking, which we met almost everywhere in the Congo.

We knew at once that M. Delbert would be of little use to us in our work with the natives. In the presence of a man of his type, they would be shy, sullen, and unco-operative, and all Armand's and my efforts would be in vain.

M. Delbert listened politely while we explained the purpose of our visit to his area.

"I shall be pleased to assist you in any way I can," he said.

"It's very kind of you," said Armand. "I much appreciate your offer; but we prefer to work alone. You know how it is. Natives are often shy when their administrator is around. I hope you understand."

"Of course."

"But if you'd be kind enough to call the people together so that we can film a dance, I'd be very grateful."

M. Delbert promised to do so, and it was agreed that

we should pay the people for their services in presents of copper and *ngula*.

Armand and I were given a large guest room and our boys, Mucharia and Shabani, were accommodated in the servants' huts. Shabani drew me aside and said he had found out that the comely African woman was M. Delbert's "wife". He was able in no time to discover the secrets of any household we visited, and he always imparted them to me whether I cared to hear or not.

At dinner that night, our host was in a genial and expansive mood. He talked of this and that and then passed on to the subject of his son, who was at a Belgian university. This boy was obviously the most important person in the world for his father. After praising his son's intellectual qualities, and drawing a glowing picture of the lad's future, M. Delbert showed us a photograph.

We looked at the picture of a handsome young man, partly African, taller and much more distinguished in appearance than his father. Shabani was right—as usual.

As I returned the photograph to him I felt the room spinning around me. Armand and I usually drink water at meals, with enough red wine to kill the flat taste of the boiled water. Shabani had just poured water into our glasses when something occurred to me. I asked him to show me the water bottle—an old gin bottle, marked with a cross as neither of our boys could read, filled with boiled water.

Shabani had picked up the wrong bottle and mixed neat gin with the red wine. His apologies and pleas for forgiveness amused M. Delbert, who was hardly a man who could be given a drink in error.

The dancers arrived early next morning. They were led by a dusky ballerina dressed in a costume which looked more Javanese than African. Her upper arms were encased in metal rings and she wore a headdress decorated with fronds of feathery palm. Her skirt was made from the skins of four servals. She was striking and graceful.

Her face was sensational; painted bright blue on one side and dead white on the other.

The rest of the company of dancers, all girls, were dressed in short swaying raffia skirts. Their legs were painted a brilliant vermilion; the exposed parts of their bodies shone with palm oil and coloured clay. Each wore a cord across the bosom to imprison their beautifully moulded breasts. The pendulous rather than uplifted breasts are considered most desirable in many parts of Africa.

I have seldom seen lovelier girls than these with their finely-cut features and lithe figures—narrow hips and broad shoulders. Their hair was brushed up, Fiji-fashion, with a couple of white feathers stuck into it, pointing forward like ears. Each carried a large rattle-shaped dumb-bell made of cane, and the solid copper anklets they wore indicated their prosperity.

Great tropical trees formed the background of the dance, interspersed with native huts. Before the drummers went into action, a dozen or so old men beat time with blocks of wood in each hand. Then the drummers put a central spot of resin on their instruments and held them over a fire, until the resin melted and stretched the skins taut. They tuned up by striking their drums with the palms of their hands, listening raptly to the vibrations until they were quite satisfied.

The dance began with a wide semi-circle of performers. The ballerina, with a girl on either side of her, moved rhythmically. They were excessively graceful and impressive. I have never seen any Asian dancer use her hands more expressively than this African ballerina. Beauty of controlled movement flowed from her wrists and fingers. Behind, the chorus line, as well trained as any *corps de ballet*, bent and swayed to the beat of the drums with a soft insistence. They also used their hands eloquently to give the dance its full meaning.

Africans are born story-tellers and they tell their tales most eloquently in dancing. The theme of the next dance was of a woman sitting on a river bank, catching fish and driving away flies that annoyed her. The dancers sat together in an arc and mimed every action from the moment the woman had caught her fish until she had cleaned and cooked it. It was enchanting as a fairy tale.

We had no cameraman with us, so I helped with the direction while Armand did the photography. I had to measure distances, watch for the unusual among the dancers, and act as watchdog to prevent interruptions from unwelcome visitors.

For the first few hours work flowed smoothly. Then the dancers began to get restless.

"I think we may have trouble," I told Armand.

He ran out of film and had to return to the hut to get another reel. During his absence the ballerina became temperamental. The cooking pot was calling her. She came to me and told me she was hungry and was going home. I tried to keep her amused until Armand returned. I allowed her to examine my nails, touch my hands and hair, but this only detained her for a short time. She began to move away and most of the other girls followed her. Desperate, I snatched a rattle from one of the company and started to dance myself. She looked at me with professional eyes. Then she took the rattle from me and demonstrated the proper movement and steps. So the dance was in full flow again when Armand returned to the scene to find me covered with palm oil and red clay.

We had no further trouble. When the last reel of film had run out we had a magnificent collection of dance sequences.

The performers returned to their village still dancing. A short time before, they had wanted to stop. When they reached their homes, they preferred to go on dancing rather than face the household chores. They danced for the next three days and nights. Which confirmed that African women are as unpredictable as those of any other country, race or colour.

Later, we visited another village, perched on a high hill, isolated. The natives here had seen very few Europeans. They stared at us bewildered, and the women huddled together, pointing at me and talking. I was wearing safari slacks and shirt. They couldn't understand and were trying to sum me up. At last, one of them detached herself from the group, walked up to me and suddenly pinched my breast. Then she hurried back to her companions, nodding delightedly. So I was a woman after all!

This was a tragic village. We hadn't been there long when we noticed the absence of young people and learned of the cause. Venereal disease had killed most of the children and made their parents sterile; only old people were left. They danced for us the same dances as we had filmed at the other village in the same paint and costumes. But how different was the effect here! Instead of the vigour and rapture of the young and healthy there was the grotesque and pitiful caricature trodden out by elderly women in the grip of disease.

In the same territory we visited a witch doctors' dance, deep in the forest. We had never before seen anything like it. Eight witch doctors from places many miles apart had come together to dance before a large gathering of Africans. Each wore a distinctive dress.

The dance began with the killing of a white cock and the sprinkling of its bright red blood over the shoulders of the performers. After a short time each dancer entered into a state of auto-hypnosis; they left their bodies dancing on the soil of Africa, but who knows where their souls were? The drums beat faster and their movements quickened. Into the fine haze of dust which rose from the ground they leapt with outstretched arms.

Mingled with the compulsive rhythm of the drums was the sharp jingle of clashing ornaments and charms. They seemed to be endowed with independent life and added to the barbaric splendour of the scene. One witch doctor, his hair braided like an Asongo-Meno, held a copper-studded ball like an orb in his hand.

Here was the very soul of Africa, the land I loved more than any other in the world. In this scene was encompassed the essence of a mode of ecstatic existence untouched by civilization and out of the reach of the white man.

We resumed our journey to Tshikapa in a dream. Armand and I drove on in silence; we were still under the potent spell of the witch doctors' dance. My imagination was a screen for drums and wild leaping figures in a forest glade. Not until we reached the European colony we had set out for, and entered a new Africa, was the spell broken.

Civilization was planted firmly in this little paradise. We drove along the single broad avenue, lined with mango trees half a century old. Tshikapa is the head-quarters of the Forminière Diamond Mining Company, and a fine example which other mining companies with native labour might well follow. These native employees are organized and provided with free medical care—not only the workers, but their families who live with them.

The men and their families eat in cafeterias provided by the Forminière. In adjacent wash-rooms I watched young wives bathe their gurgling brown babies. A general prosperity, in which the African workers shared, was shown in the gay cottons and jewellery worn by the women.

We relaxed. After our long and arduous journey from

Mombasa across the Congo it was pleasant to loaf. We ate in a large restaurant as guests of the mining company, while our boys lived with the Africans. There was a reading room and a hall for dances, where a cinema show was put on every week. Under a trellis at the far end of the building gleamed the deep blue water of a swimming pool.

Our Bassenji dogs soon made themselves favourites, especially Wangu, who had a way with him. I used to take them for a walk along the central avenue every morning, sit down in the soothing sunshine and watch Wangu and Lehala quarrel over a fallen mango.

We got to know an immensely fat Belgian lady with enormous energy—every day she could be seen riding a bicycle. She had a pet pigeon to whom she would whistle and call:

"Gamin, Gamin—attack, attack!"

And the pigeon would at once respond, swivelling round until his chest swelled enormously. Then he would dart for the feet of the lady's husband and peck until he was called off.

The civilized attractions of Tshikapa failed to hold us. Inevitably, the day came when Armand and I looked at each other and knew it was time to move on. There was much to be filmed, and time was passing all too quickly.

We wanted to get going. We wanted new faces to photograph. News had reached us of native dancers who used huge masks with fringes which covered the whole of their bodies, so that it seemed as if the heads alone were dancing. We drove after them, with Duncan and the boys, all day until nightfall. Then we ran into trouble.

Our route passed along a sandy road stretching across apparently endless flat, grassy country. We drove on in dim moonlight. Suddenly a storm broke and down came

153

torrential rain. Very soon the grassland was transformed into a series of great lakes. Then our truck bogged down and failed to start up. We got out and pushed. Soaked to the skin, we heaved and struggled until finally we reached a large brick building which we assumed must be the house of a Belgian government official.

It looked unoccupied; but when we passed on to the verandah and through a door, we saw a man dining in solitary state. We knocked, but he didn't even look up. At last a servant let us in and we walked into the room, leaving puddles behind us. We had stood there perhaps half a minute when the solitary diner suddenly swung round to us, scowling, and snapped:

"Well, what do you want?"

Armand and I were speechless. In Africa there is an unwritten law that is honoured in the wildest parts— a stranger is always to be welcomed within one's gates. I was furious.

"We're very sorry to disturb your dinner," I said, sarcastically.

He was neither amused nor angry; he was just indifferent. He merely resumed work with his knife and fork.

I could see that Armand was having difficulty in restraining his anger, but he said courteously:

"We really are sorry to disturb you, but we've been caught in a storm in a bogged-down truck which we've managed to push here."

No comment from the diner; not even a glance at Armand.

"We're in this territory to do some filming," my husband went on.

At that the man at the table jumped up and glared at us.

"A film!" he yelled. "Film people! I hate them! I had film people here three years ago and was fool enough to believe their promises. They said they would

154

send photographs. They promised to mention my name . . ."

He waved his arms excitedly, spluttering with rage.

"I don't know what they weren't going to do. But they did nothing—absolutely nothing! That's film people for you . . . As far as I'm concerned you can get moving at once!"

"That will be a pleasure," retorted Armand, taking me by the arm. "Come, let's leave this lout to his swill-tub."

That really stung the official. He moved away from the table, faced us and shouted:

"If you haven't got permission to film I'll report you to headquarters. In any case, I'll not allow you to use a camera in my territory."

Armand and I both rapped back that we had all the permissions we needed.

Dignified exit from the room was difficult in our drenched condition, but we did the best we could. At the door I turned to fire the last shot.

"Please don't trouble to open the door for me."

To my surprise he moved quickly from the table and swung the door open. I walked past him and we exchanged a look of mutual hatred.

Outside, Duncan hailed us cheerfully:

"Well, where do we sleep?"

"Rough, I expect," said Armand, and he went on to tell Duncan of the reception we had had from the official.

Our best hope was for the rain to slacken and enable us to put up a couple of tents for the night. We got the truck moving and drove away from the house into the wet darkness. It was not long before we came across another brick house. We approached the door doubt-fully and knocked. It was opened by a young man who welcomed us cheerfully.

He was in the midst of packing and the room was

155

littered with his possessions. Over a drink we related what had happened at the other house.

"Ah, you must have met Vanderdahl! He's a madman!" exclaimed the young man.

He went on to tell us that for the last three years, he and Vanderdahl and the priests at the mission nearby had been the only white men in the district. Vanderdahl had never spoken to anybody.

Our host was leaving the next day and we thought it unfair to park ourselves upon him for the night and interrupt his packing. He protested, but we insisted and returned to our truck. Halfway up a steep hill, we were passed by a motor cyclist. He stopped and returned. To our surprise and pleasure we had met him in Tshikapa, during his visits there for supplies.

He guided us to the mission where we were able to change into dry clothes and sit down to a meal in the company of two priests, cultured and erudite men, fully informed of what was happening in the great world outside their forest domain. Their conversation was a delight.

In bed, I fell asleep at once. But a loud crash awakened me. Only half awake, I formed the unpleasant impression that Vanderdahl was outside, looking for us with a gun.

I rushed to the door and flung it open. Armand had awakened at the noise. He got out of bed and moved towards the window.

"Be careful!" I warned. "Somebody may be shooting."

He looked out of the window and said he could see nothing. Just as he spoke there was another sound like a muffled explosion. Armand persuaded me that there was nothing to worry about, but all through the rest of the night I was awakened by those bangs.

Armand and I joined the priests at the breakfast table. I mentioned the noises in the night and asked:

"Do you think it's possible that M. Vanderdahl was prowling around with a shot-gun?"

They laughed and explained that under our bedroom window were some empty petrol tins. The over-ripe mangoes fell upon them, making a noise like a rifle shot.

But Vanderdahl won. He was, officially, the monarch of all he surveyed in these parts, and he wrecked our plans to search for and photograph the masked dancers. We asked the advice of the priests, but they held out little hope for us.

So there was nothing to do but to return to Tshikapa.

The Vanderdahl episode was a lesson for us. When we started, a week later, on another safari, we made sure before we left of the sort of reception we were likely to receive from the administrator of the territory we proposed to visit.

When we arrived at his village we found both him and his wife waiting to welcome us. They were a young Flemish couple, recently out from Belgium. They were eager and full of enthusiasm for their work. They wore the briefest shorts I have ever seen.

Mme. Lippens had courage of an unspectacular kind. After dinner, I saw that she was terrified of animals and insects. As we talked about our plans to visit a native chief in the area, I noticed that she had to steel her nerves against the insects that flew in swarms round the lamp and settled on our hair and clothes. She must have been in a state of nervous agony; but she stuck it without comment. I thought how brave she was to accompany her husband, feeling as she did about wild creatures.

Next morning I watched the astonishing spectacle of their new truck being loaded for our joint journey. The callow young bride was piling in an iron bath, pots, pans, clothes, provisions, and bedding sufficient for a six-month safari. When the truck began to sag, I advised her what to leave behind. Armand explained that if the truck got into difficulties in a strange and lonely place it would be impossible to move because of its great weight.

We reached the big chief's village at nightfall. We had left the boys behind, so Mme. Lippens and I did the cooking. The kitchen contained a fire but no outlet for the smoke. Over a dozen Africans were trying to cook or sleep there; we stumbled around in smoke dense as a fog, tripping over prone bodies. Mme. Lippens managed to turn out a chocolate mousse from powdered milk and chocolate mixture, while I struggled with soup and fried croutons.

A boy took the plates and I followed with the soup and croutons, but in the darkness I must have gone astray. Suddenly I fell into a pit, landing on my hands and knees but still clutching the soup container; the croutons disappeared.

As my eyes became accustomed to the darkness I was able to see that I was in a pit about seven feet deep. Above me was the velvety African sky. How to get out of the pit was a problem. I shouted for help. It was some time before I heard Armand's voice.

"Where are you, Michaela?" he shouted.

"Here—here—in a pit," I yelled back. "Be careful you don't fall in."

I could hear him moving around and then I saw his head silhouetted against the sky.

"I'm here!" I shouted again.

He saw me and disappeared in search of a torch. He was soon back, hauling me out of the pit. I was in a mess, dirty and bespattered with soup. I had stumbled into a newly-dug outdoor lavatory—luckily unused.

Falling into holes seems to be a weakness of mine. I recall another occasion when I really had a narrow escape.

In the elephant country of the Congo, the Africans set traps for marauding elephants which rob and damage the plantations. Their usual method is to dig a pit, between nine and twelve feet deep, and to plant a

158

sharpened stake in the middle to impale the intruder. The pit is carefully camouflaged with branches, leaves and grass.

One late evening, Armand was asleep in his cot; I, in mine, was turning over in my mind the events of the day. We had been filming all day on the edge of a native plantation. I now remembered that I had left my note-book underneath a tree where we had been working. If it were left out all night, the heavy dew would destroy it.

I dressed hastily and crept out of our hut. I was walking along in the moonlight towards the tree when suddenly the earth gave way under me. I fell into blackness, too surprised to cry out. Then I heard the back of my shirt being ripped and I was pulled up with a spine-shattering jerk. I was the victim—not the expected elephant!

I felt around gingerly. I stretched my toes down. To my great relief I felt the ground beneath my toes. I bunched my shoulders together and pulled hard. The shirt ripped apart and I dropped to the bottom of the pit.

Above my head were the stars. The walls of the pit had unfortunately been hollowed out only too well and were perfectly smooth. There was no foothold anywhere.

I shouted several times, but I knew this was a forlorn hope. No one would be likely to hear me in the village; it was too far away. There was nothing to be done but wait for the daylight.

During the night I heard the trumpeting of elephants. Some time later they passed silently, their ghostly bulk moving on either side of the pit. I lay flat on the bottom. If they suspected my presence they would reach in with their trunks, pull me out, and trample me. I could hear them feeding in the plantation to a cracking of branches.

All through the night I remained tense and ready to duck. My eyes never left the circle of sky above me, as it gradually paled into dawn. Time passed; one by one the stars faded. The cold was almost unbearable and I was drenched with dew. How long could I stand the cold?

Then, in the half-light, I heard the song of a bird. My heart leapt with joy. Very soon came the sound of African voices approaching the plantation. At once I was galvanized into action. Standing up I shouted at the top of my voice.

The danger was that the Africans, seeing that the plantation had been trampled, would rush to the pit and hurl their spears into the impaled animal—that is, into me.

Soon the top of the pit was fringed with a score of spears. Surprised faces, with rolling eyes, gazed down at me.

I gesticulated wildly, showing my torn shirt and making signs appealing for help. But the men ran away shouting. Soon they were back with Armand. He looked at me with astonishment for a moment and then made a typical comment before reaching down to haul me out.

He said: "You are up early, aren't you?"

But to return, as it were, to my tumble into the village lavatory, after dinner we were sitting round the fire, trying to forget our lost dinner, when the chief came to see M. Lippens. He was tall and broad-shouldered and draped in a blanket of leopard skin pattern which, he told us, he had picked up during a recent visit to Stanleyville.

It was not the only thing he had picked up on that visit. He had left eleven happy and contented wives at home when he departed for the city; after he returned they fell ill, one by one. By the time the medical officer paid his routine six-monthly visit, all eleven were infected with syphilis. Since it was in the primary stage, however, they were cured.

Next day, on the chief's invitation, we visited his compound to film a dance which he promised to arrange for us. The wives' huts surrounded that occupied by the chief, which was much larger than theirs; it had a high-pointed sloping roof whose eaves swept down to within

Much of our photography is done from trees, in which we often
spend the night to take advantage of the first daylight hours

Elephant training at Gangalan-a-Bodio, the elephant station of the Belgian Congo, only place in the world where the African elephant goes to school

Elephants, like lions, have a highly developed social sense. Surprised by the sound of the camera, they face about, the large bulls in front, females and children behind them

about three feet of the ground. The walls were made of mud and in between there was a small verandah under which one of the chief's wives preferred to cook. This was a risky business, for there was always a danger of fire; in fact, the hut had been alight several times. The African character is curiously fatalistic in such matters.

Inside, the walls of the hut were covered with white clay, on which designs and pictures were painted. The chief laid out his treasures on the ground for our benefit —bead necklaces that had belonged to remote ancestors, a beautiful leopard skin, carved ornaments, masks, and a silver spoon brought from his Stanleyville jaunt.

From Stanleyville, also, he had brought a spectacular arrangement of lightning rods and installed them on his hut. However, he had not connected them with the ground, and we concluded that his hut would be certain to catch fire when the first thunderstorm broke.

While the chief was displaying his possessions, the dance was being prepared—drums heated, bodies smeared with a reddish brown clay and palm oil, and painted. As soon as they were ready, the dancers took two long staves each, moved into the circle of drums, and began.

It was a mourning dance for a close relative—the only one of its kind I have ever seen in Africa. Holding a stave in each hand and half-leaning on them, the dancers rocked gently to and fro, murmuring a melancholy lullaby. When it was over, other men and women joined the dancers, and even the children clapped and stamped and waggled around after their parents.

In order to ensure complete naturalness and to prevent them looking at the camera, I danced first with one group and then another. They soon forgot they were being filmed and we got some fine sequences. We said farewell to the chief and his people and returned with the Lippens to their home. After dinner we took our leave of them and returned to Tshikapa.

My memory holds a tender picture of our farewell to

OCP/865—F   161

these two charming young Flemish people—a dark young man and his pretty golden-haired wife, in their absurd shorts and with arms entwined—alone outside their thatched house in the heart of Africa. I can see them now under the dark trees, waving until they lost sight of us.

Finally, we had to admit defeat in our search for the masked dancers. We had come too late.

"If only," said Armand, "we could step back into the last century, with a movie camera and unlimited film— what wonderful things we might have recorded!"

In those almost forgotten days every village had its own tribal customs and dress; but that was a thing of the past. Now only here and there did one come across vestiges of the ancient Africa.

We drew up new plans. Duncan was to drive our two boys, Mucharia and Shabani, back to Nairobi, taking with him the provisions and camping equipment. Armand and I intended to visit Loanda in Portuguese West Africa. We decided to shorten the journey by taking a lonely route through the savannah country, uninhabited because of lack of water. A two-day supply of food and water, we thought, would suffice for the trip.

It was after four hours of driving that our car broke down, as related at the beginning of this chapter. Armand made a thorough check of the car and located the trouble: a burned-out coil. We had no spare.

We looked at each other. We were stranded under a blazing sun, sixty miles from the nearest outpost, with only a two days' supply of provisions. I began to feel a little uneasy.

Armand got out his map and studied it for some time.

"We could walk the rest of the way," he said. "It would mean a three-day trek, and this isn't walking country. But we might do it."

I worked out our prospects in my mind. "There's just a chance of some truck coming along."

We both smiled a little thinly at this desperate hope, but it helped.

I checked the stores. There were five bottles of boiled water, two of wine, a tin of corned beef, four of chipolata sausages, two tins of sardines, three oranges, and some water biscuits.

We shared a tin of sardines, drank a tooth mug of water and wine mixed, and decided to sleep on the problem. We awoke to the chirp of insects and the lifeless savannah. Our prospects hadn't changed while we slept.

We banished the thought of food and chewed on our dilemma. The question was: should we both go, or should only one of us risk the three-day tramp for help, and, if so, which one?

I tried to persuade Armand that I was a tough and tireless walker. Hadn't I kept up with Africans when we legged it through the jungle, covering twenty miles a day for days on end? But he wouldn't hear of it. He just pointed to the car with a grin which indicated that that was where I was to serve. It was no good arguing with him further.

We had to split up the supplies. Armand took three oranges and a couple of tins of sausages: the rest we divided equally.

The parting was a wrench—to say the least. He has never been nearer and dearer to me than in that last moment together in the car. Every inflection of his voice, every gesture of his hand, and the lock of hair that fell over his forehead took on a new significance. I simply could not bear to see him go and I held on his arm to detain him.

We embraced and he opened the door of the car and stepped out. As much affected by our parting as I, he forgot to look where he was stepping. He fell out of my view and I heard him groan. I found him sitting on the ground, clutching his ankle. He had tripped on a stone as he stepped out of the car and had fallen heavily.

It was a bad wrench; the foot was already puffed. I sprinkled a little of our precious water on a handkerchief and bound up the ankle.

"Now," I said, "you see I was right. I was meant to go. I knew it all the time."

I grabbed the pack from his back and put an old battered bush hat on my head. Then I bent down and kissed him and moved off.

"See you soon!" I called.

But I dared not look back. Tears were running down my cheeks. I hated the thought of leaving him there alone, in this waterless African waste, with a damaged ankle; but it had to be done.

I walked on, not trusting myself to turn round until I thought the car was out of sight. When I did so, I saw that Armand had managed to hoist himself on to the roof to wave to me. He must have watched me until I was swallowed up in that dry, burning wilderness.

For miles, on each side of the road, the bush stretched away—dusty, treeless, ever-dying. I walked on, emptying my mind of possibilities and consequences, thinking only of each step I made and the need to cover distance. Then I became conscious of aching calves and the caking dust in my shoes.

The sun became unbearably fierce; its heat on my back was as paralysing as a spear thrust. I crawled under a low bush to eat an orange, letting the juice trickle slowly down my parched throat. It was the sweetest relief I have ever known. As I emptied the dust from the sneakers, I knew that next day my leg muscles would be more or less free of aches.

When I began to walk again, I tried to imitate the African style of walking, breaking into the little dancing step which seemed to banish their fatigue. The trick worked and I made good progress. When I looked back again there was no sign of life anywhere—nothing but the ribbon of the road and the motionless scrub.

I looked at my watch and saw I had been walking five hours. By this time I was well into my stride, but I decided that at high noon I would get into shade, eat and rest. At last I came across a boulder and sat down in its shadow, my back resting against the hard rock.

My food plan had been worked out in advance—I knew just what I could afford to eat. The two oranges I kept in reserve and took a few sips of wine and water and opened a tin of sausages. As I ate a coolness enveloped me and I must have dozed. When I came to myself I turned instinctively to speak to Armand. A sense of loneliness swept over me, but I threw it off and began to walk again.

The sun had lost its burning intensity; the shadows had lengthened; and I tramped on through a slight haze. To drive away morbid thoughts, I played all kinds of games with myself, counting bushes, kicking stones out of my path; but all the time my eyes probed into the now misty landscape for a sign of some living creature or hut. There was none. I was alone in emptiness and silence.

I tried to sing but no words came. Dusk thickened into night. The stars came out. A faint breeze began to move and it refreshed me like cool water. I broke into a trot, free of the searing chains of the sun. But I was weary and soon my legs failed to respond to my will. Down I went beside a large bush and, with an effort, ringed myself in with smaller bushes, like an animal seeking shelter.

I finished the sausages, ate a biscuit, and drank alternate sips of wine and water. After cleaning out my shoes, I threw a blanket over me and sank into the dreamless depths of sleep.

The call of some bird awoke me at dawn. Through half-opened eyes I saw its grey shape sail across the sky. Then memories of the previous day's happenings flooded my mind. I wondered what Armand was doing and whether I should ever get out of this awful solitude.

165

Half an orange restored me and I began to count my blessings. Chief among them was the wonderful pair of shoes I was wearing (how many times had my friends told me that they were unsuitable for Africa!). With my mind full of thoughts of Armand, I began to walk. I imagined him at work on the car, dragging himself around on his damaged ankle. I had been walking for perhaps an hour when I saw something that stopped me dead in my tracks.

High up in the deep blue sky black specks were gathering. As I watched them they formed into a column of vultures preparing to spiral down to earth. Their evolutions told me that in the burning waterless bush, perhaps miles away, some poor animal was dying or dead. If I fell, I, too, should become food for these ravenous creatures with evil eyes and rending beaks. The thought drove me on.

My first stop on this second day was under the scanty shade of a stunted tree. Here I drank a little water. If our reckoning was correct, I should reach a small village by the following night. I had to reach it, for by then I should be out of food and water.

Up again and on the road. The vultures had gone; but after half an hour's walking I heard the sound of what seemed to be an aeroplane engine—a mechanical heartbeat in the body of this vast primitive wilderness. I wondered how I could let the pilot know of the presence of a tired woman, walking her feet into the ground.

My eyes searched the dazzling blue of the sky. There was no aeroplane to be seen. The sound moved and seemed to come from the road behind me. I looked back. There was nothing to be seen there either, except dust. Then my heart leapt. Although not a breath of air stirred, the dust seemed to be moving.

This is a desert hallucination, I told myself. Perhaps I've got a touch of the sun. My brains are boiling in this heat. I walked on, but the noise continued to pursue me.

I had an impulse to run. For one wild moment I thought I had gone crazy.

Then I stopped walking and turned round again.

A car was racing towards me—a car! It was going so fast and threw up so much dust that its shape was hidden. I stared into the dust-cloud, trying to see what sort of car it was and to halt the driver, I sprang into the middle of the road. The driver might pass without seeing me! Then suddenly out of the dust-cloud loomed a familiar shape. I waved and shouted. As it drew nearer, I recognized the driver. He was Armand. The car came to a grinding stop. I rushed towards it and saw my husband getting out of the cab and limping towards me. We embraced.

"Get in, darling," he said, "and I'll tell you how I managed to get the car going after messing about with it ever since you left."

He handed me a mug of wine and we drank to each other and to Providence. As Armand let in the clutch to continue the journey, the sun seemed friendlier, the dust less choking, and the road a perfect highway through a savannah now free of danger.

CHAPTER NINE

CHIMBU PARADISE

"I CAN'T believe it," Armand said to me, as he shaved on the verandah before an audience of fifty fascinated Chimbu tribesmen. "It's like living in a fairy tale. But if we were children and reading about this sort of life, we'd long for it—and yet not believe it possible."

I thoroughly agreed. We were in a camp reminiscent of an African village. The houses were made of cane matting with thatched roofs. But we were far from Africa. This was a clearing in the primeval forest, seven thousand feet up, in the remote highlands of New Guinea.

The crowd of people that stared fascinated at every movement Armand made were painted and decorated in styles that had not changed since the Stone Age. They had only been known to the white man since 1933, when the Leahy brothers first flew over their territory.

We had been working night and day in New York, rough-cutting the film *Below the Sahara*. At the same time we were to take part in three other films in New Guinea, the Great Barrier Reef, and Australia. We were going to make two pictures also for the Chrysler corporation, *Wheels Across Australia* and *Land of the Kangaroo*.

In preparation was a joint expedition to New Guinea with the American Museum of National History, under Armand's leadership, for the purpose of filming the fabulous birds of paradise and the Chimbu people. Armand was financing the Museum effort and they were lending a scientific staff.

For three weeks we worked in New York—eighteen

hours a day. Finally, the film was ready to show RKO. Their executives who saw it were enthusiastic. We listened, relieved. Then Armand said:

"Thank you. May we go now?"

"Yes, but go where?"

"New Guinea."

"Oh! And when?"

"Tomorrow."

We left the next day, flying to Australia and from there to Lae in New Guinea. Tropical and surrounded by magnificent jungle, Lae is surprisingly lacking in fauna. The gardener in the Quantas Air Line guest house told me that all the fruit trees have to be pollinated by hand, as there are no bees.

Here I saw my first outrigger canoes, pushing off from the black sandy beaches where the water is so deep that large freighters can come right up to the shore. It was a heavenly place, ideal for beachcombing. A hot sun, a burning blue sea under a sky of the same colour—this was the natural setting. We were there for four days, waiting for a plane to fly us into the Central Highlands. Before our chartered plane arrived, I sprained my ankle and had to hobble aboard.

It was an uneasy journey. We flew with about a forty-foot clearance over the tall forests that surrounded Lae, and then followed the Markham river inland. There were breath-taking moments as we passed over deeply carved valleys and over the 12,000-foot Bismarck range, trying to thread through the cloud-shrouded peaks. As the pilot turned and twisted his plane, a mountain would suddenly loom up and it seemed that we must crash into it; but the machine always cleared it. Half-way over the range, the engine suddenly cut out.

"It must be ice forming in the carburettor," said Armand.

I nodded and hung on to my seat as the plane lurched, missing a needle-pointed peak ahead.

"Wahgi valley down below—Chimbu country ahead!" the pilot called back encouragingly, as the motor spluttered into life once more.

I looked at my watch. The journey had taken two hours —two hours from the mainland which belonged to the modern age and its mechanized marvels; but below us was a civilization that went back two hundred centuries. Michael Leahy and his brother must have felt they had discovered a new world when, only a couple of decades ago, they looked down as we were looking now.

Ten thousand feet below us, through the tatters of mist, we saw the Chimbu river twisting south to the Kubor ranges, under a scarf of fog. We were now through the mountain walls that had shut off the Chimbu people for so long, flying easily above a fertile valley towards a plateau about seven thousand feet up.

Casuarina trees grew in clumps on the jutting mountain slopes. Ancient thread-like tracks were visible from the plane, and we could see a lot of land under cultivation, criss-crossed by drainage ditches, where sweet potatoes and corn crops stretched as far as we could see, with colourful strips of garden between.

"There's Kup!" shouted the pilot.

We made towards a narrow green bumpy slope in the middle of this plateau on the top of this new—or very old—world. Down we dived. It looked like a difficult landing, but the pilot brought down his plane lightly as a bird settles.

Before we could congratulate him on his remarkable handling of the machine, we were rushed by a crowd of brightly painted Chimbu. Clad only in woven aprons, with bunches of leaves at the back, they surrounded us and gestured excitedly. They had long slivers of shell through their noses and hanging round their necks. It was like stepping into another planet.

The Chimbu were accustomed to seeing planes land there, for the airstrip was kept by a Catholic missionary,

Father Mike Bodnar, himself a fearless airman. Further to the north, at Hagen airstrip, however, we were told that the people were horrified to see the pilot step out of a plane—and then step back into it again. They imagined that a large fierce bird had swallowed him.

Kup was to be our headquarters. Some weeks earlier, advance members of our expedition had set up camp and contacted Mai-ma, the Kubor chief. With his help we could look forward to finding and filming the rarest birds of paradise in the high, unexplored plateau.

The camp was a large one; sixteen long huts had been built, the walls of cane matting topped by thatched roofs. These housed our expensive equipment and were our sleeping quarters, dining-rooms, workshops, kitchens, aviaries, and storehouses for kina shells.

We were greeted at the camp by Bob Doyle, the Australian explorer, Robert Carmet, French cameraman, and the American ornithologists, Tom and Margaret Gillard. Robert was especially pleased to see us; for weeks he had been virtually cut off, as no one in the party could speak French.

News of our arrival spread quickly, and crowds of magnificently painted Chimbu came to the camp. Mai-ma, the chief, was the most splendid of them all. He wore on his head the fabulous Greater Bird of Paradise feathers, which leapt and wavered in the air like flames.

I could scarcely believe that the bird from which these astonishing feathers came was a cousin of our homely black crow. It seemed incredible, but there it was. Mai-ma's impressive appearance was enhanced by a brass medal bound round his forehead and bestowed on him by the Australian Government, to show that he was a tul-tul, responsible for the maintenance of peace and order in New Guinea. He had with him about a hundred followers, their parrot feathers and cassowary and paradise plumes waving. Shells hung about their chests on woven lengths of string. These shells came from the Torres Strait, between Australia and New Guinea, and served both as currency and jewellery; they were giant mother-of-pearl gold-lip shells, and one of them represented a man's wage for fifty days' work. The natives polished and cut them into the desired shape, then threaded them through their noses (which were pierced at infancy and kept open with twigs) or hung them as face or chest guards.

I noticed one young girl with about a dozen shells round her neck and wearing the breast of a Superb bird of paradise on her head. Her father, I guessed, was a wealthy man, probably a sub-chief. Both women and men were smeared with pig grease and some had charcoal rubbed into their faces. The faces of some were decorated with intricate painted curves and patterns of dots with red and yellow powder.

As the chief made his speech of welcome, it was translated, first into pidgin, then into English. While he spoke the presents piled up before us. Among them were bundles of firewood, sugar cane, bananas, onions, Indian corn, and squashes. Two young white cockatoos and some familiar-looking hens were brought in. I coaxed the cockatoos over to me and they seemed very tame.

Then I saw forks being placed on the ground to support the posts on which live pigs were hung upside down by their legs. They were suffering under the hot sun and looked pitiful. I could only hope they would be killed quickly.

We shook hands and thanked the chief and gave our presents in return—beads, shells, sheets of newspaper, in which the Chimbu would roll their long cigarettes, made of crumbled stick tobacco. I marvelled at the little they seemed to need from us; everything was here at hand in their unspoilt paradise.

As the ceremony drew to a close, we heard sounds of another party approaching. Green and blue and red plumes tossed in the dazzling air, flashing against the deep blue sky. Mai-ma drew back, obviously displeased, murmuring angrily to the men around him.

Into the camp strode the most bizarre and self-satisfied figure of a man I had ever seen in all my travels. He, too, wore the brass medal of authority. Through his nose, decorated with red and yellow stripes, were no fewer than seven slivers of gold-lip shell. From them hung, on thin tambu threads, more pearly shells. Round his neck were whole shells. On his head burned short red feathers like a fringe; above them was a cowrie-sewn cap, with a band of iridescent green beetles encased in orchid fibre; higher still, tossing in an almost conscious vanity, were cassowary feathers, cockatoo wings, and the red and yellow plumes of several birds of paradise. Other astonishing plumes, those of the King of Saxony bird of paradise, ran from holes pierced in his nostrils to his head-dress, like quills hung with little transparent blue pennants, and seemed to illumine the chieftain's face.

He came forward, clearly pleased at the impression he had made, and motioned to his followers to bring the gifts: more onions, peanuts, sweet potatoes, squashes, bananas, pigs on poles, and—good heavens!—a long, writhing yellow tree python, tied to a post.

We learned that the overpowering newcomer was called Bo-mai, and that he was a chieftain equal in importance to Mai-ma. He invited us to attend a sing-sing at Katambagh. These sing-sings, we heard later, were held every week. There were also walk-about days, when whole families trailed over the hills at random, chasing the brilliant butterflies and beetles and picking orchids and sprays of fern. These people never tired of decking themselves; it seemed to me as if they competed with their tiny birds whose crests and plumes filled the forest with flashes of fire.

The sound of an approaching plane brought the speeches to an end. At once the tribesmen tore across the plateau to meet it. We followed, I with a white cockatoo on my shoulder and escorted by brilliantly crowned and painted tribesmen.

Two priests stepped from the small white plane and were rapturously greeted by the people. One of the priests (the taller of the two) seemed to be well known. I found myself looking at him with interest; he radiated authority and kindliness. This solid, black-haired man with the humorous mouth was, I felt sure, the Father Mike Bodnar I had heard so much about. He had been at Kup for many years and had built a large thatched roof church out of native materials.

His companion, Father Hoff, was tall, blond and good-looking and later proved to be an excellent pilot; in fact, one of the best with whom I have ever flown.

We walked up to their house, which was built in native fashion, and watched while they paid the natives for timber and firewood.

"I should think," I said to Father Hoff, "that salt and steel axes are about the only two things the outside world could usefully offer to these people."

He laughed, raised his eyebrows and motioned towards the beautiful little church.

"Ah," I said, "but to teach a native, you have to be one."

"The blind leading the blind?" he queried with a half-smile.

"No, but how can one predict how our European thought will be interpreted?" I asked, watching a young girl, gorgeously beaded and be-shelled and painted, cross herself as she passed a crucifix hanging on the wall. "Look at that young girl. Crossing herself merely means a sign of appeasement to a strange God."

I wondered whether I had gone too far and hastily turned to Father Mike Bodnar.

"How did these people manage for salt before the white man came?" I asked.

But he had overheard my last words to Father Hoff and he let my question go unanswered. With a tolerance I have come to expect of Catholic priests, he said gently:

"Come to church tomorrow—it's Corpus Christi—then you will see how they worship God."

I nodded. Then he briskly returned to the subject of salt.

"It took them three months to make a pound," he told me. "It was very highly prized because in this area only one tribe was permitted to make it. Bundles of *kunai* grass were soaked in salt water springs and then burnt. More and more bundles were then thrown on to the fire, until there, in the ashes, were thin wafers of salt. These were rolled into flat cakes. It was a long job."

Out of respect for Father Mike we went to church the next day. The people sang their native songs, to new words, and I was surprised at the European ring of their voices; there was hardly a trace of the Asiatic.

I glanced from the rapt face of Father Mike to the woman sitting next to me. A shaft of sunlight picked out the little silver cross on her breast; it swung in company with a screw-nut from an acroplane and a piece of polished shell. Protection plus decoration. All history displayed on one woman's breast, from the Stone to the Atomic Age.

Obviously the people enjoyed singing; they liked their church and I believe they loved Father Mike, who respected their ancient customs and was content to lead, and not to push.

In the weeks that followed I came to love and respect these people, too. They were as open and as natural as children and quite without guile; their thoughts could be read in their faces as they spoke.

Mai-ma and his wife visited me as I rested my sprained ankle in the hut. They were amused to see the white cockatoo, that had adopted me, gently push my nose away from my coffee cup, so that he could have the first sip.

I assumed their visit was an informal one, for Mai-ma had put away his ceremonial feathers and came dressed only in shells and paint and woven strip. We sat in the living-room which was built up on a platform; the roof was supported by columns of wood.

The view from all sides was theatrically beautiful. From our plateau we could see the valleys and gorges descending to lower ground level, sometimes shrouded in mist, sometimes clearly etched. Across the valley the mountains soared into the clouds.

Rain fell every night. After misty mornings the sun came out like a sparkling jewel, hanging rainbows on the wet casuarinas and orchids.

The injury to my ankle kept me in camp for the first week or so, but I was not bored. There was a constant stream of visitors bringing food and various kinds of birds of paradise, alive and drooping, three kangaroos and green snakes for us to photograph. One little boy brought two dead rats for our birds in exchange for a pinch of beads.

I saw my first New Guinea toy in this boy's hair. When I made signs that I was interested, he took it out to let me see. It was a small pointed stick with an acorn-like object at one end, hollow, and pierced on one side. He threw it in the air and caught it in the palm of his hand. It spun like a top and made a sweet whistling noise.

The captive birds of paradise brought to our camp for the ornithologists and photographers caused me much pain. They cried harshly all the time and I longed to release them. The ornithologists were building blinds in the trees on the surrounding crags to watch the birds during their wonderful courtship dances. But things were going badly. The damp corroded vital parts of the equipment, the camera lens misted over, and the darkness of the dense forests, where the elusive birds courted, sometimes made photography impossible. When reflectors were used, the birds became frightened and left their usual haunts.

Birds of paradise—what a wonderfully apt name, I mused, thinking of the feathers the warriors were wearing on our arrival. Then I remembered that the first explorers in these waters were Magellan and his men. They took back with them skins of the Greater Bird of Paradise, shot by native hunters. For some reason the natives removed the legs and feet of the birds, so the naturalists of the day concluded that the birds were blown from great heights—from Paradise itself. So they were called *Paradisaea apoda*, meaning the Footless from Paradise. The fabulous appearance of the feathers startled Europe and, like the Chimbu people, fashionable women wished to deck themselves out in the brilliant plumes.

The hunt was on. New Guinea villagers lived by the sale of plumes to traders, and such was the massacre of these lovely creatures that in the 1920's the law stepped in with a protective hand—just in time to prevent their annihilation. Luckily, across the Chimbu gorges, up in the deep clefts of the rocky canyons, at least twenty separate species of ornamented birds of paradise remained, many of them never yet seen by the white man. Hunted in the depths of the dark forest with bow and arrow, these small creatures—about the size of our thrush—had at least a chance of survival.

The male depends on his vivid colouring to attract a mate. He selects a branch for his display dance; he preens, jumping up and down and uttering coarse cries of amorous invitation.

Sooner or later a dowdy female hops down beside him. He is breathless and trembling. She pecks at him half-heartedly at first, gradually giving herself up to love play until she finally mates with him. Afterwards they go off to feed together, and she builds herself an inconspicuous nest high up in a tree in which she later lays her eggs.

There the romance ends. The polygamous male bird then seeks other females, repeating his performance on the branch, shining in the dimness of the forest like a halo.

The ornithologists managed to film about a dozen species: the red type, the Magnificent, the Superb, the Majestic, the Greater, the Lesser, the Princess Stephanie, the Queen Carola, the King of Saxony, the Sickle-bill, the Loria, and the Macgregor. This last one was, ornithologically speaking, in the no-man's land between bower-bird and bird of paradise; but the Macgregor was finally established as a bird of paradise. It did not build a nest to attract its mate, like the sombre bower-bird, but neither did it perform the love dance in the manner of its exhibitionistic brothers; it lived quietly in the upper branches of a tree.

As soon as my ankle mended, I went with Armand and Robert to a blind they had built thirty feet up a giant casuarina tree. The bamboo platform was slippery and unsafe, and, as we shivered in the grey dawn, I wondered how these fantastically beautiful creatures could live in such a damp world. The forest was full of shadows and strange glinting insects; something mewed like a kitten in the trees to our left, and I grasped Armand's arm. "What's that?" I asked. "It surely can't be a cat up a tree!"

"No," Armand laughed softly, "no. Listen again, and watch carefully. . . . Look—quickly—through there!"

My eyes followed his pointing finger and saw a flash of emerald, through the trees. At that moment the sun came out. Long black tail feathers swept after the green flash, and were gone. A moment later came a mocking, long-drawn-out mew.

"That's the Princess Stephanie bird of paradise," said Armand.

From our left came a sudden machine-gun-like chatter. Then silence. Again, as if in reply, we heard the fast deep note, like a stammer this time, followed by a whirring sound like that made by disturbed grouse.

"I think that's the Sickle-Bill," said Armand. "Ah, they're coming! Are you ready, Robert?"

Robert's eyes were on his viewfinder. Armand watched him. A hundred yards away, across a grove, a bird of breathtaking beauty had landed on the branch of a tree. He walked carefully down the branch, raised his wings and thumped them together behind his back; we could hear the vibrations from where we crouched. His head was yellow, his plumage red as a flaming torch when he shook it; then his plumes flew up, the feathers spraying out like sparks from the torch of his body.

Two male birds flew down to join him, but he chased them away and they stayed nearby as spectators. Then four little drab females came flying towards him; one of them, as if intoxicated by his beauty, landed beside him. He fluted with excitement, his body quivering. He pecked at her and they mated. Presently all flew off, leaving the forest in darkness, as if the lights had been switched off.

So we made the first moving picture of the "footless one from paradise".

I had seen the fabulous courtship dance. It seemed to me, as we trudged the hilly miles back to Kup, that this was yet another example of the finesse and subtlety that Nature puts into her creations. There was that flamboyant little bird, lost in the contemplation of his own beauty and the erotic ectasy of his dance: an ideal target for a hunter. His function was to draw off the enemy and make sure of the continuance of his species; hence his exhibitionistic colouring and polygamous habits. The female, with her dowdy protective colouring, had another function—to guard the eggs and rear the next generation.

Armand and I discussed the subject on the way back.

"If we're lucky enough to get pictures of bower-birds,"

179

he said, "you'll see the same sort of thing. Only the bower-bird doesn't display. He attracts the female by building a large sort of dance platform and decorating it with bright berries, leaves and stones. They don't live in it, though. The female builds a safer nest, high up, and has her family in peace."

"Well," interjected Robert, "what self-respecting female would raise her family in a dance hall!"

We stopped. Armand was suddenly quiet.

"Wait a moment," he said. "Look at that enormous spider. Michaela, can you——?"

I nodded. I was used to this sort of request. Digging my spiked golf shoes into the wet mud, I crawled and wriggled up the bank towards the spider. It was sitting motionless on a banana leaf.

Armand quickly got his camera into action.

Carefully, I detached the leaf. Still the spider did not move. It was glistening gold, with black and yellow legs; on either side of its head were scarlet fangs which I watched carefully.

When the picture had been taken, I laid the leaf down. The spider instantly scuttled away out of sight behind a brilliant orchid.

"What an obliging spider!" exclaimed Armand. "This makes up for the wretched tambou trick that fellow played on me yesterday."

He had been unlucky the previous day.

We relied a great deal on information brought to us by the Chimbu people concerning the habitat of birds we wanted to film. We paid them well and they were always ready to put their knowledge of bird and animal life at our disposal. One man came to Robert and told him that a certain tree, which he owned, was a favourite with the Princess Stephanie.

The tree was mossy green, with long flat branches, and in a state of decay. Orchids and vivid spongy growths ornamented its trunk and limbs. It certainly looked a likely place; but there was a snag. The tree was too deep in the shade for a photographer to work.

Robert tried to explain this to the man, and moved away to another tree in a better position. The man became excited.

"No good grass-belong-dewai. Tambou!" he exclaimed time and again. "No good grass-belong-dewai. Tambou too!"

He drew from the branches a split piece of cane with a leaf stuck in it. This was the bad-luck Tambou. He was trying to explain that the branches and roots of the chosen tree were cursed.

Next day Armand went to the tree which Robert had picked out and, disregarding the tambou, put his hand lightly on it. A heavy branch crashed down on his head. Bleeding from the nose, he examined the branch. It had been half-sawn through in two places.

Obviously, the owner of the rejected tree was giving magic a little human help.

We arrived back in camp just as a downpour started. We prayed that the next day would be fine and sunny, for we were making the promised journey to Katambagh, Chief Bo-mai's territory, for the great sing-sing.

CHAPTER TEN

OFF TO KATAMBAGH

As soon as the mist looked like lifting we were off. With two hundred porters we formed a long line. Up and down gorges we went, digging our spiked shoes and sticks into the hard ground to prevent ourselves slipping a hundred feet or more down the muddy, treacherous slopes.

Our destination was Katambagh. There Chief Bo-mai was putting on a ceremonial sing-sing for our benefit—an affair not to be missed.

We passed through pockets of forest. The dense trees were alive with birds and animal life whose whistlings and mewings provided music for our journey. Once we heard a crow-like cawing; we had disturbed a courtship dance of the Greater Bird of Paradise.

A river lay across our path, and we bathed our feet in its cool, crocodile-free water, ate lunch, and pushed ahead. We topped a mountain rise; far below us, in the valley, lay Bo-mai's land.

Our boys stopped. Throwing aside their burdens, they raised their hands to their mouths and began to yodel. Melodious notes bounced from peak to peak and finally died away in the valley. From very far away, came answering notes like a long-drawn-out sigh.

I asked Tai, one of our boys, why they did this. It was to tell Bo-mai's people that we were coming, he said, and to let them know that we were friendly. As we drew nearer to Katambagh, the track widened. It was planted on each side with coloured leaves. The Chimbu are the only native people we have come across who plant ornamental flowers or hedges to border their plantations.

Then we came upon an amazing thing. I caught up with Armand, who had been ahead and now waited for me. He said, "We are over a mile still from the village. And look at the trail." The trail had been covered with flowers, as a welcome to us. We walked on towards the village on a thick carpet of red and yellow flower petals.

I noticed some women hiding shyly behind trees at the side of the trail. When I smiled to them they rushed forward embracing our knees, a ceremonial form of welcome. But we touched the tops of their heads with our hands, in affectionate greeting—and their shyness vanished. Shouting, men rushed forward and surrounded Armand, picking him up bodily, while a band of women did the same to me. They carried us into the village at a wild run.

We were hot, tired and muddy. My cockatoo still sat clinging to my shoulder, but now he was flapping his wings excitedly and squawking, "Hello! Hello!"

Now from all directions tall, painted and plumed men converged on the village. Bo-mai, even more magnificently decorated than before, greeted us. Among the gifts he had received from members of the expedition were some pieces of coloured cellophane; these he had wound round his head.

One of our gifts to his wife was a mirror. Bo-mai had tucked it into his headgear. His spouse stood by, rather disconsolate, I thought. One of her eyes was half-closed. We drew our own conclusions.

Mai-ma and his wife, Ondouk, were also there, beaming, full of eager greetings. We tried to show our appreciation of the honours done us; but we were shown a two-room hut, placed at our disposal for as long as we remained in Katambagh. On the floor a circle of bare earth was placed on the woven bamboo covering; here we could make a fire, if we wished. What meant more to me was that the hut, too, had been decorated with flowers for us, the stems of the flowers pushed between the wall slats of bamboo.

We had supper—a little of the mountains of food brought to us as gifts. Then Tai was brought in on a stretcher; he had suddenly collapsed with high fever, so we treated him for malaria and hoped it was nothing worse. But one of the other boys told us that he had probably been poisoned, because he had been sleeping with a young girl who had another man's mark on her. This is considered improper, as a "marked" or "engaged" girl is not free like a "young fella Mary".

As we had just heard of the Chimbu methods of getting rid of dangerous rivals, we feared for Tai. Their favourite murder weapon is a long thin bamboo sliver which the murderer inserts into the rectum of his sleeping enemy. Days later, the victim develops peritonitis; the chances of recovery are slight. Meanwhile, the murderer has vanished.

Next morning, as I came sleepily out of the hut, brushing my hair, the first rays of the sun were struggling to penetrate the dense early morning mist. A crowd of men were already in the clearing, waiting for the sing-sing to begin. They were painted and greased and topped by every kind of feather, from the tail feathers of barn-yard fowls to King of Saxony plumes. They carried three-foot ceremonial drums shaped like elongated hour-glasses and covered with taut python skin.

As I brushed my hair, they watched me with as much interest as I watched them. They were silent; but suddenly the sun shone through a rift in the clouds and "spotted" me like a limelight. Exclamations and excited chatter broke out. One of the warriors pointed to his paradise plumes and made a speech in pidgin comparing the tawny red of the feathers to my hair.

They marvelled at everything we did. We might have

been people from the moon, so strange did we seem to them. Apart from a rare misisonary, perhaps, white people were unknown to them. Their delight in watching Armand shaving or cleaning his teeth was unbounded.

The cameras were set up to film the great dance. Old people and children moved from warrior to warrior admiring and criticizing and comparing decoration and feathers.

The sun came out in full splendour, and into the dance arena strode the decorated men, four abreast. They shouted twice to draw attention to themselves, then stamped. As I watched their proud movements I was irresistibly reminded of the birds of paradise on their dance platforms.

Drum beats began. Four of the men stepped forward and the dance opened. It proceeded to the chants of the crowd. The whole scene was a mass of colour. Sunlight lay hot on vermilion and blue, struck fire from gold, shimmered on green. The plumes waved like a forest to the hypnotic beat of the drums. Feet alternately shuffled, and pounded the earth. Hollow palm-nuts clicked as they swung from the men's shoulders. Long aprons, worn in front, and made of the woven inner bark of the casuarina tree, swung rhythmically, and the bunches of fresh leaves stuck in the backs of the belts waggled and flirted like tails.

Staring at the scene I began to pick out more details of the adornments. I noticed the woven anklets and arm-bands worn by the men, and the little woven caps of the painted and bejewelled women, which were sewn with tambou and cowrie shells.

I recognized two of our houseboys. Some days before Armand had recorded their voices—plangent, high-pitched, seductive. At the time I had not seen whose voices he was recording. I had thought women were singing. I was astonished when I saw two broad-

185

shouldered, hefty young men walk out of the hut, arm-in-arm.

Now I watched one of them with hardly less astonishment. He was dressed as a woman, with two lemons slung across his chest, playing softly on a small bamboo instrument like a jew's harp, called a tambass. He was casting enticing eyes at his much decorated partner who stood erect and proud, with the wings of an owl, and tufts of cockatoo and paradise plumes stuck into his gold-coloured kapul fur cap.

The dancing went on all day. Food for the feast that was to follow piled up in the shade of neighbouring trees. I was horror struck at finding a number of pigs strung up, hanging by the legs from poles, half-dead from the sun and thirst. At once I had them untied and watered. Their last hours would at least be free of suffering.

As the shadows grew longer and the brilliant sky clouded over, a few drops of rain began to fall. The ranks of the dancers broke at once and the warriors dashed to the huts. There they carefully removed their plumes and laid them inside long pods of the pandanus; for these plumes were treasured possessions and jealously guarded.

The sit-down sing-sing—the boy and girl sing-sing—was to be held in the evening. While it poured with rain, we sat around the fire in our huts, roasting steaks on sticks. When we had eaten we moved towards the sing-sing hut to watch the proceedings.

On the way, we saw two groups of men in a fierce argument. Between them was a plump young girl, her arms held firmly by the disputants. She wore a cassowary wing quill through her nose, and she was crying bitterly.

One of the boys explained to me that she was Tai's girl; but she had been engaged to be married; and the bridegroom-to-be, as well as her own family, had come to claim her, for she had been paid for with kina shells

186

and pigs. Now the pigs, of course, had been eaten long ago and were beyond recovery; the girl must therefore go with them. But Tai's friends were trying to detain her. Tai had presumably promised to refund the dowry; but how he could do this with a wife of his own whom he could scarcely support, our boy did not know. He shrugged as the girl was dragged off triumphantly by the bridegroom-to-be, and left me to give the bad news to Tai.

Young Chimbu girls are very free; freer than the girls in many African communities I have visited. Until they are married, or promised in marriage, they do no work and can "sing-sing" with any of the men, and, if they so desire, indulge in sexual relations.

An unmarried girl, however, never has an illegitimate child. The birth-control methods of the Chimbu are certainly effective. They are polygamous, some of the men having as many as eight wives; but families are limited to three children per wife. The food resources of the Wahgi valley, an area of twenty by sixty miles, in which seventy-five thousand people live, are not inexhaustible; and this makes some form of birth-control necessary, if the population is not to be reduced to poverty, and the control of its numbers left to starvation or disease.

The danger of missionary interference with this control system is great, and evident. Overbreeding would bring about a state of affairs as deplorable as that which exists in great areas of Asia and even in Europe and the United States. These so-called primitive Chimbu people have at least one important lesson to teach to civilized people.

The period of courtship is long enough to enable the bride to satisfy herself that she can accept the man who buys her. Prices vary according to the social status of the girls, but payment is usually made up of four "things" —pigs, ceremonial axes, tree-climbing kus-kus, fine sets of plumes, and so on. If a bride is unhappy with her husband, she can return to her family provided the dowry is repaid.

Stooping low, we entered the long sing-sing hut, lit by two flickering fires. When our eyes had become accustomed to the dim light and to the smoke which at first made them smart, we could see a platform, about a foot high, along the two long walls of the hut. On this platform girls sat cross-legged, like Buddhas, their hands clasped in their laps. They were richly decorated with caps embroidered with tambou shells and with kina shell hung around their necks, and they wore woven bracelets on their arms.

The men entered, ducking low to avoid disarranging their gorgeous head-dresses. They were even more heavily painted than for the previous dance. They stepped on to the platform and sat, facing the wall and the girls, each man between two girls, his knees touching the knees of two girls.

A high-pitched chant gradually rose from the men. The women remained silent but began to sway slightly. This slow, rhythmic swaying, in time to the wavering, high-pitched, whiny chant, went on with little change for maybe thirty minutes. The fires flickered and burned lower—my smarting eyes involuntarily closed—then I shook myself awake. The swaying of men and girls had become more pronounced. I watched the girls with curiosity: about half of them were visibly in a state of tense excitement, their lips parted, their breathing hurried, their entwined fingers convulsive. One girl swayed so far she almost fell towards the man on her left. She opened her eyes and seemed to become conscious again of her surroundings. Then she put out her left hand and rested it on the man's left shoulder, clasping and kneading jerkily the knotted muscles. The man, without interrupting his swaying, leant forward and laid his face against that of the girl and, face to face, they swayed together. Then I noticed that all the men had done this. Now, still swaying, men and girls were rolling their faces together: some with effort, in deadly earnest, breathing in short gasps, their faces sweaty; some dreamily and ecstatically—paint and grease being transferred from cheek to cheek, carefully painted patterns melting, ornaments swinging and tinkling, savage head-dresses sweeping by each other, bodies gleaming in the firelight.

"This is what they call 'roll 'em face'," I whispered to Armand. "They told me about it this morning."

Now with snake-like speed the girls withdrew their faces and began to rub noses with the man on the other side. With a hand on the man's shoulder, the girl rubbed right, rubbed left, her fingers beating out the mounting ecstasy as the chant quickened. The nose ornament clinked and swung but did not interfere with the movement. With ever increasing ardour they crushed their noses together until the noses seemed boneless, splattered lumps of flesh, savagely kneaded and mauled in cruel perversion.

Then the beat slackened and at last the noses rested together for longer and longer periods. There was no other bodily contact between the girls and the men. Eyes closed in paint-blurred faces covered with amorous sweat. Thus the second movement of the dance finished. This was "cook 'em nose".

The third and last movement, "shoot 'em leg", began. And this was a strange interlude, which did not seem to follow logically upon the obviously erotic stimulations attendant upon "cook 'em nose". For the men now got up; each turned around, sat himself chummily next to the girl whose nose he had so recently and so passionately belaboured with his own, held her hands in his—in full view of all present—and proceeded to entertain her with humorous anecdote and witty quip. This is exactly what took place. True, each girl's legs were clasped between

189

her partner's, and her hands imprisoned in his; and true, the girls' giggles hinted that some of the story-telling verged a little on the *risqué*; but this whole performance was so gay, innocent and above board, and so obviously based on sane tradition and convention as to have a positively Victorian flavour.

At this point Armand and I, feeling tired, left the hut; dancing was still going on, and continued happily for three days and nights.

On a subsequent occasion two of our party, Bob Doyle and Henry Kaltenthaler, painted themselves like Chimbu to join in a sing-sing. The face paint was most becoming to them. They returned very late, rather shaken at having discovered for themselves that "cook 'em nose" had indeed had a disturbing effect upon the balance of their emotions.

Our problem was to film the sit-down sing-sing. We had no lights with us; Armand could only hope to persuade the people to do it during the daylight hours, after removing the roof of the hut. At first they were exceedingly self-conscious about this, then amused, then completely carried away as soon as the sing-sing chanting began.

Chief Bo-mai chose one of the comeliest "young fella Marys", not more than thirteen years old, with whom he had been flirting all morning, and settled down happily to the sing-sing, with her as his partner.

But here I came up against a curious taboo. While getting the dancers into position, I tried to arrange the women so that those with the best-looking breasts would be nearest the camera. I chose a girl with a lovely figure and put her next to Chief Mai-ma, moving his partner down a few paces.

Excited talk broke out. I could feel something was wrong and I looked questioningly at those near me. Consternation showed on all faces. Tai—fully recovered, by the way—dashed up and whispered something to the effect that I was practically signing the chief's death-warrant. Any man who sing-sings with his own daughter, he said, was doomed to die within a year.

I apologized to the chief, complimenting him on his daughter's beauty and moving her away from him. He forgave me without hesitation, and the filming began.

For three noisy days the dances went on. By that time our boys were dragging themselves around as if drugged, with half-shut eyes and slack mouths. Robert teased Tai, saying that his nose must be worn out after so much sing-sing.

"Me strong nose too much," replied Tai indignantly. "Me strong nose all the same master."

The ornithologists of course wanted as much information as possible about the birds of paradise, especially the rare and less-known species. To make it easier for the Chimbu to identify correctly the different species which interested the Museum, they had brought with them from the Museum a trunkful of bird skins and mounted specimens to show the people. As Tom held up each mounted bird before them, the Chimbu would shout its native name. The King of Saxony, for example, they called *kisaba*—a word which sounds like the long hissing noise made by the male when displaying.

As each mounted bird was held up, Tom told the people how many shells would be given for news of its living counterpart and for guidance to its courtship sites. We filmed this sequence, with the invaluable help of Tai. In the middle of it his girl appeared again, and there was a touching reunion between them. It seems that Tai had managed to borrow money from the other boys to pay off the bridegroom, and so was once more in possession.

We planned to film the cooking of the feast. Before going off to see how it could best be done, I warned the boys not to allow anyone to touch the "bockus-he-talk"—the recording machine.

Twenty or thirty pigs were being sliced up at the back of the huts. Men carved swiftly with sharp knives of bamboo. Hollowed-out hardwood tree trunks, some four or five feet high, served as cooking pots; into them went the carved meat after being wrapped in the young leaves of the giant breadfruit and alternate layers of Kau-Kau and a spinach-like vegetable.

Meanwhile at some distance from the cooking pots, great fires had been lighted; and in these the cooking stones—round stones the size of a child's head—were being heated. Into the pots now went a layer of the almost red-hot cooking stones, swiftly plucked out of the fires with long wooden tongs—and then more carved meat, more vegetables, more hot stones—until the pots were full. Finally, water was poured on and great clouds of steam billowed out. Now the pots were covered with thick layers of banana leaves, wrapped round with vines and grasses and left unattended for some hours. When the outer covering of this crude but effective fireless cooker was eventually removed, the food was perfectly cooked and ready to serve on banana leaves. Pork cooked in this way is delicious.

Poor Tai was in trouble again. Long ago a man belonging to the Katambagh people had killed one of his ancestors. He could not, therefore, eat pig provided and killed by them. He was a picture of misery as he watched us eat. We promised to give him a special feast of pork when we returned to Kup, but I doubt whether his watering mouth was appeased.

After the feast four chiefs in turn expressed their thanks for the presents—pigs and gold-lipped shells—which we had given them. Mai-ma began; when the next chief had said his piece, Mai-ma would sandwich in another speech before the next chief had a chance to get going; he made two speeches to everyone else's one, in an incredibly loud and earnest voice.

Armand responded, and Tai translated into Chimbu

One of the flying foxes (fruit-eating bats)

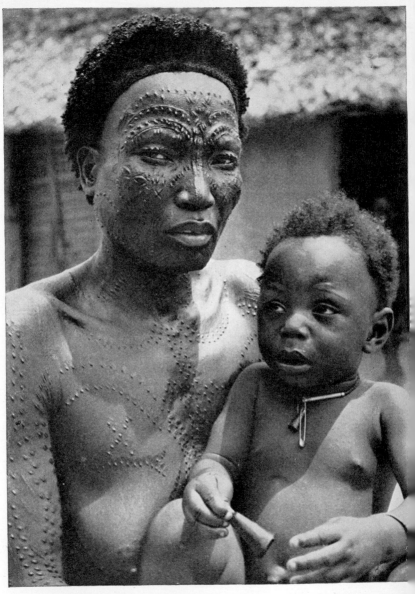

Sculpture on flesh. One soon gets used to this and finds it beautiful. Congo

with such fluency and force that Armand looked astonished.

"Did I really say all that?" he whispered, spellbound at Tai's oratory and gestures.

All around us were warriors, crowned with plumes, fiery in the sun—rank upon rank of nodding head-dresses outlined against the cobalt sky. As I took in the whole scene, I had the feeling of living out of time in a fantastic waking dream.

Armand unobtrusively started the bockus-he-talk, which the Chimbu had not yet heard, and played back to them the speeches just made by their chiefs and which we had recorded. For a while there was near-panic, then endless exclamations of wonder and delight.

Among the crowd were several Chimbu who had made a five-day journey from uncontrolled territory—territory not yet entered by the Australian authorities, and not under official control. They had never seen white people before. One old man, who had travelled with his son, stared at me in amazement, touching my hands and hair as if to assure himself that they were real. In return I admired his necklace. He wore an unusual decoration on each breast—the paw of some reptile with three large claws. He pointed to the distant peaks to indicate the extent of their journey. I concluded that the decoration he was wearing must be the feet of the iguana, said to live in uncontrolled territory.

A crowd of Chimbu gathered round us and indicated that the old gentleman was a medicine man, and when I repeated the word in their own language, they nodded and smiled.

Next morning I awoke early. Something was nudging my cheek; it smelt strongly of shaving cream. It could not be Armand, for he was already up and about. We were leaving to-day and he had a lot to do.

I opened my eyes and saw Wahgi, my white cockatoo, balancing back and forth on my pillow, crooning and holding out his head to be scratched. As I stroked him my fingers came into contact with a white paste. It was Armand's shaving cream.

I sprang out of bed to see what fresh mischief Wahgi had been up to. A few days before he had broken off the tops of two three-pronged ceremonial spears, and we had had to console their owners with presents. Now I saw on the box that served as dressing table and writing desk a pierced tube of shaving cream. Our tubes of toothpaste had suffered the same fate.

Wahgi watched me, crooning with delight. I could not be angry with him; but he was not always popular with the men. He was death on hats; if anyone left a hat lying around, the cockatoo would delightedly snip holes out of it. Soon there were no hats left.

Wahgi shared the living quarters of our chickens, and quickly picked up all the sounds made by hens and young roosters. In the morning, when the chickens would be let out, Wahgi would waddle forth with them, clucking and crowing, triumphantly announcing to the world the laying of entirely imaginary eggs, interspersing all this with cheerful calls to us of "Hallo! Hallo!"

We said good-bye to the assembled Chimbu, telling them that we would return one day. We said this because we knew that, following an ancient custom, they were apt to chop off a finger to show grief at a friend's departure. The younger men and women promised to visit us at Kup.

My ankle hurt, for I had wrenched it again; but I managed the twelve-mile walk back. It had been a rewarding visit, for we had captured these virtually unknown and completely happy people on film for the first time in their history.

That night we shivered under blankets at our evening meal, and I noticed that the Chimbu gathered round fires in their huts. But we saw the full moon through a heavy fog and hoped that, as Father Mike assured us, it heralded a change in the weather. We wanted to film a bridge-building sequence on the Wahgi river.

Father Mike was right; the weather changed with the full moon and next day the sun shone. It was Independence Day and we treated ourselves to a rest which we needed badly, for the visit to Katambagh had tired us out. After the farewell sing-sing the Chimbu boys slept all day.

I had a visit from Father Mike who was taking a hand in arrangements for the river expedition. He brought with him a Kodachrome reproduction of a beautiful view, which had been torn from a magazine. He had apparently not noticed another coloured reproduction on the back— a blonde pin-up, clad in pink wool combinations, with a neckline plunging to her waist. Later I learned that the girl was Marilyn Monroe. While the good priest proudly pointed out the beauties of the view, some members of our party, who saw the other side of the picture, began to giggle. One of the Chimbu boys saw the Monroe and joined in the fun.

"Ka-wee! Ka-wee!" (Good, good.) He grinned and pursed his lips. "Ka-wee! Ka-wee!" he repeated in the exact cadence of a wolf-whistle.

Then, to make matters worse, he pointed to me and nodded sagely, saying: "Missus, missus. Ka-wee!"

Armand had a few days of fever, aftermath perhaps of the tick typhus which he had contracted in Africa some months before. No doubt the dampness brought it on; our clothes were seldom dry and every night we slept in wet beds. But he recovered in a few days and we then set out for the bridge-building location.

Over a hundred painted and feathered Chimbu came with us to work on the bridge and on the picture. Young wives accompanied them, walking behind their husbands, with their babies riding in a net slung over their heads and resting on their backs. This custom seems to be universal in primitive communities; the husband walks in front with a spear to protect his wife and child.

It was a steep climb down to the river. The Chimbu wanted to carry me, but I have a complex about being carried and refused. When we reached the Numandi river, however, I had to submit, for the water, although not deep, flowed very swiftly. Four of the men carried me across; one had a nose painted a vivid green with a shell in it, another was a leper. I had my arms round the necks of two of them and two held my feet, while a film man supported my back.

Armand was also carried across by five men—a really remarkable achievement considering his size and weight. Father Mike's dog, Judy, would not wait to be carried but swam after us in spite of the strong current.

We approached the Wahgi river along a trail worn by thousands of feet over the years. An old bridge, spanning the wide and chocolate-coloured water for perhaps a hundred and twenty feet, was sagging badly. The new one would be built in a few days.

The art of building these suspension bridges has been handed down from generation to generation. Many of the men still used the hand-ground stone axes, almost as efficient for splitting the casuarina logs as modern steel axes. To a Chimbu a stone axe is precious: each stone axe takes three months to make; old men grind the stone and polish it on wet sandstone, with infinite patience. But a Chimbu gladly exchanges his beautiful stone axe for one, cheaply machine-made, of the white man's steel.

Fewer hand-made axes are being made every year, for steel axes are somehow trickling into the country; but the craftsmanship that goes into the making of Chimbu tools remains admirable. Especially fine are the ceremonial axes, made of softer stone, bound to the hardwood shaft with woven casuarina bark.

Father Bodnar had collected several artifacts from an

earlier age. Some of them resembled those I had seen in South America—the Inca maces, star-shaped, with a round hole at the end, in which the stick is inserted. I understand that the American Museum of Natural History confirmed this resemblance when they received the Chimbu specimens.

A bird-shaped object also struck me as being similar to an Inca design. Had they come from the same source, or was it a case of parallel evolution? No one can tell. All the Chimbu could say was that they "were the work of the people who lived before us, long ago". Here is a fascinating problem for the archaeologist.

Not a single nail was used in the construction of the bridge. Bamboo abutments were erected on either side of the bank, all components fastened to each other with vines; then one of the men climbed up and took a position with bow and arrow. To the arrow was fastened a long vine, which was shot across the river. As soon as it was secured, heavier vine cables followed, and were hauled into position.

On three successive days we returned to film the building process. Wahgi, the cockatoo, rode on my shoulder to see the river after which he was named, and we crossed the old bridge to get a better view of the men completing the flooring with staves bound by vines. The crossing of the old bridge was precarious, as many of the wooden slats had come out, and the rushing river seemed dangerously near. The bridge swayed and creaked as we walked over in our spiked shoes, all wrong for such an adventure.

Clutching the rocking rails on either side, I could still admire the lovely country plains which stretched away in gentle inclines and grassy slopes, dipping into vivid green swamp lands.

I stood on the swaying bridge full of regret; Armand and I were soon to leave it all. We were expected at the Great Barrier Reef, and later in Australia. Our packing was already well under way, and we had many farewell calls to make.

I had asked for a kina shell belt to be made for me. Two men brought it into the camp and I watched them polish it. The shells are pierced and hung on a cord, varying from three to six inches in length, and they rattle when you dance. I performed the men's dance while trying it on, much to the amusement of the Chimbu warriors.

Among those who came to say good-bye to us was the leprous old man who had helped to carry me across the river. Leprosy is not uncommon in the Wahgi valley, but it is seldom detected until its final stages, when toes begin to shrink. I had always been careful to wash after touching the old man, but I could not bear to hurt and dishonour him in the eyes of his own people by refusing to shake his hand. As we said good-bye, I saw that the hard nodules on his arms were spreading and that his right foot was bandaged.

It was a wrench to part with our many pets. Several chickens had been hatched from eggs which Bob Doyle had brought into the camp, and one of them was a favourite of mine. He lost his tail feathers to a Chimbu boy who wore them on his head. Now, for the last time, I consoled the chicken with peanuts when he flew into my lap with Wahgi, who was under a cloud as far as Armand was concerned.

For the cockatoo's crowning escapade was the destruction of two hundred yards of precious shielded microphone cable. He committed this act of sabotage while we were busy packing. I noticed he was missing and eventually found him in the hut where we kept our sound recording, lighting and camera equipment. The heavy rubber cable had been pierced at distances of three-quarters of a yard along its total length, the connectors carefully detached. When I entered the hut, Wahgi was holding a connector in one claw and nibbling at it daintily.

All the same, we arranged for him to be sent to our home in Africa. The two green snakes, given to me by Armand, I took with me, hoping to get them into Papua where there were no quarantine restrictions on reptiles. These, finally, were left at Nondugl.

We set off in a July dawn for Nondugl, the flora and fauna research station founded by Sir Edward Halstrom. From there we intended to fly to Lae.

Our party, together with two hundred and fifty carriers, struck the narrow, tortuous path over which we walked in single file. From time to time I looked back to see our camp, with a crowd of waving Chimbu, grow smaller.

Kup — the Chimbu name is Googhilaminou — lay already in the past. One day we would try to return; but it seemed unlikely, for we seemed to be the children of a wandering fate, always on the move towards something new and strange.

"Heavenly place!" I said to Armand. "I hope it never gets spoilt."

"Luckily for them—it's a difficult place to get at," he replied. "But I agree—it is a paradise on earth. I shall never forget it. . . . But cheer up. You have a reminder in all those reels of film."

But Kup would not let us go. As we approached the first small river we looked back—and there were Mai-ma and his wife, with a group of friends, still following us. As we crossed the river, a small dog broke away from them, dashed down the slope into the water, and started to swim across. It was the intrepid Judy, Father Mike's dog, who loved us. We had to put a lead on her, and send her back to Father Mike with a boy.

Once more we turned our backs on these good friends and trudged doggedly along the narrow ridges, dropping down into densely forested valleys. On across a grassy plateau, through woods where we saw the largest pigs we had come across in New Guinea—Asiatic pigs with long snouts. We had to cross a river by suspension bridge. As the handrails were only as high as Armand's knees, we had to creep over practically on all fours. That swaying bridge gave us a thrill.

Then Nondugl. We stayed only a few days to photograph the birds and a few charming children. Armand advised me to leave the two green snakes behind and he photographed the green python coiling round my arm like a jewelled bracelet.

A creaky, overloaded little plane took us on towards Port Moresby in Papua. The journey out was as bad as—or worse than—the journey in. Aboard the plane was a missionary family, and two of the three children were soon air sick. We set them down at a desolate place about twenty miles from Lae, picked up more passengers, and then tried to take off again. The plane hovered for a moment, then her tail came down and the pilot braked hard. After unloading some nondescript baggage, she tried again. She became airborne and flew off like a drunken eagle, with wings vertical to the ground, one wing tip almost scraping the tree tops. It was a narrow squeak, but the aircraft—as the pilot rather grandiosely referred to her—righted itself and we were off into the yellow and gold and red of the sky over deep gorges touched with flame: an appropriate farewell to the home of the birds of paradise.

Then real flames came into view, heralded by dense smoke. The New Guinea people were setting fire to their grasslands, driving game into the open where it could be killed.

We touched down at Lae as darkness came. Next day we flew to Port Moresby.

CHAPTER ELEVEN

AUSTRALIAN ADVENTURE

AUSTRALIA extended a dry welcome to us. The wild country of the North was our objective. There rain had not fallen for two years. The heat was like the breath of a blast furnace; it baked the sand to brittle particles that penetrated into food, hair, equipment and bedding.

Man was an outcast in this region. The monarchs were mosquitoes and sandflies and we their tormented subjects. When the sun went down they unleashed their tortures and we were soon covered with bites.

Tom Stobart, who had flown out to join us in New Guinea, was with us for three brief weeks in Northern Australia. Then he was smitten by a wasting disease that did not respond to treatment; he lost twenty-five pounds in twenty-five days, and had to be flown home to England. There his illness was correctly diagnosed and treated. He made an extraordinary recovery and later proved to be fit enough to produce the wonderful film of the successful Everest expedition. We were lucky, and escaped serious illness.

We set off with Des Bartlett, a cook, a mechanic, and three Dodge vehicles on what turned out to be a tough and punishing trip across Australia. We had a Power Wagon, a truck and a sedan car, identical equipment to that we use in Africa. The Power Wagon is built like a wartime Bren gun carrier with a four-wheel drive and a winch on the front. The sedan carries delicate equipment, cameras and sound recorders. Bulky provisions— food, tents, bedding, film supplies, and all the para-phernalia of a scientific film expedition—go into the three-ton truck. Bulk supplies of petrol in forty-gallon drums, chains, ropes, heavy pulleys, shovels and tools, generator and lights, go into the Power Wagon. In this dry country we also had to carry enough water to last us for a week or more. We relied on tinned food, extra supplies of which were to be flown in from one of the cities to selected airstrips on our route.

Once a week we made contact with the chartered plane, but often there was nothing for us; some emergency had occurred and to save weight the food had been off-loaded somewhere on the route. Then, for weeks on end, we would live in that desert country on rice and dried apples. No wonder I developed scurvy.

As we made our way north through the flat country, our wheels pulverized the dry earth into fine choking dust. The crushing monotony of the country was broken by the ghostly white bark of eucalyptus trees and by billabongs—water holes—where we came across sweet-scented ti-trees. We passed whole groves of sandalwood trees with black bark and narrow trunks.

My birthday came along. I have celebrated it all over the world, and rarely in the same place twice. I remember one in Lima, Peru, where a special cake was baked. Too late, I asked for the candles as a memento; only two were left—the Indians had eaten the others!

This time, Armand had brought a special birthday cake as a surprise for me and we decided to stop for the day on a settler's farm. We got the cake ready for slicing, but a tame kangaroo, unobserved, licked off some of the icing and tried to climb on to the table to finish it off. At lunch time she deftly whipped a pork chop off my plate with her long slender tongue. I imagine she ate as well as any of us on my birthday, but I did not let her share the beautiful shell necklace and bracelet which were given to me by members of the expedition.

Next morning I awoke to hear strange chewing noises by my sleeping bag, for we slept on the ground between the trucks. The kangaroo again. She had found a piece of cake and was contentedly eating it. After breakfast we took some pictures of charming koala bears, which are protected against hunters in Australia.

Then a freak storm hit us. For the short time it lasted—about two hours—it was terrific; but when it was over the earth seemed to be newly-born, cool and sweet smelling. I was walking a little way from our truck when I nearly stumbled over a tiny shivering animal which made no attempt to get away from me. It was a baby wallaby, his fur all draggled with the rain. There was no sign of his mother and, left alone, he would soon die of exposure, or be carried off by an eagle. So I carried him back to the camp with me.

Armand and all the members of the expedition were delighted with him. We arranged a triangular paddock for him with chicken wire fastened round three trees, and scattered corn flakes on the ground near his water dish. He was very timid and at first refused to eat, but after a while he nibbled a little food and began to nose round his enclosure. Then an idea occurred to me.

Wallabies are marsupials. I leant over the paddock wire very carefully and unzipped my jacket. At once he looked interested, observing me with bright intelligent eyes. After a moment's hesitation, he hopped over to me. First he explored inside the unzipped jacket with his head, then suddenly leapt inside, turning over on his back with his forepaws folded. He had accepted me as his foster-mother.

After that I made an apron with a large pocket. Whenever I was near he would jump straight into it. Armand christened him Jumpy and when we set off the next day he, of course, came with us. He was a joy and everybody adored him. As the weeks went by he became so used to the apron pocket that he would even jump into it when it hung over the back of a chair. At breakfast he always sat in my lap and drank milk from a saucer.

We also adopted a dingo puppy and two opossums: these are not the true opossums but were thus named by the early Australian settlers. They are strange little animals, and one of them, Nosey, was so greedy for milk that he could never wait until feeding time. Wherever he saw a chance, he would climb on to the table and nose around for the milk jug; we often found him upended on it.

In the evenings, when we had made camp in the desolate bush, I took Dingo out for walks. He behaved exactly like a dog, wagging his tail from side to side with pleasure. Australians told me that the dingo never holds his tail upright like a domesticated dog, but Dingo did. He held his tail well curled above his back when he was enjoying himself. He would smell trees, and I wondered why he got more pleasure from one than another, since there were no other dingos around.

Nosey sometimes accompanied us on our walks, following at my heels and begging to be taken on my shoulder when he was tired. Mike, the "blue heeler" dog which belonged to our mechanic, George, got on very well with Dingo, but the sight of any other dog raised his hackles. He was an animal of character. When we were well into the desert, he looked round for a tree. There was none in sight—nothing but miles of sand and stunted bushes. Down would go his tail in despair. He couldn't understand; this had never happened to him before. I hit upon a scheme to raise his spirits. I stuck a pelican feather upright in the sand. Mike bounded towards it with a joyous bark and, after sniffing, instantly used it. The feather was ruined, but who could regret its loss in such a good cause?

Mike covered all his food with dead leaves or straw as soon as he got it, littering the camp sites with these mounds. Only when one of the mounds stank to high heaven did Mike uncover it and make a good meal. Once he buried under vegetable refuse all the pancakes that the cook had laid aside after cooking. As we searched around, trying to solve the mystery, Mike sat on a mound wagging his tail with delight.

The care of so many pets mitigated the discomfort and irritation of the heat and sand and travel. We were always moving on, driving many miles a day, past giant ant-hills which loomed up on either side of us, sometimes as high as twenty feet. Some of the smaller ones—around eight feet in height—were built differently; they were flat and wide, the broad sides facing east and west and the narrow sides north and south. To lost travellers in that desolate, uninhabited region, these "magnetic" ant-hills could have been the only means of guidance.

The silence of the country was almost absolute. Only the high blue sky above and, on the earth, lizards looking like miniature dinosaurs darting soundlessly from one rock to another. Snakes and frilled lizards, their protective colouring so highly developed that when they froze into immobility they became instantly invisible, lived among the rocks and the sparse vegetation.

Occasionally, we would see the jagged silhouette of an abandoned hut, its shingle roof warped and fallen in. As we passed one of these ruins, Armand expressed the thoughts that were passing through my mind, when he remarked:

"I wonder what man tried to make a life here, in the outback? What was his story? Was he after gold, or just disgusted with civilization?"

"Who knows?" I said. "And where is he now?"

His bones may have rested among those of the desert animals, or he may have gone back to the city, overcome by the timeless, brooding quality of the desert.

In the distance we saw signs of a strange commotion. Great flocks of birds, looking like moving clouds, were flying directly before us.

"This means water," said Armand.

To us it was a miracle, for we were running short of water. And, sure enough, we found a billabong full of it. As we drove nearer we could see that the ti-trees were laden with white corellas. Flocks of the spectacular black cockatoos flew above; brolgas walked in the sand near the water.

We stopped and decided to camp there. I sat by the side of the billabong and poured handfuls of water over my dusty face. Then I began to bathe my feet. A shout from Armand pulled me up.

"Careful, crocodiles!"

I snatched my feet away. At once there was a splash not two yards from the shore and a long grinning snout with two watchful eyes appeared. Quickly I beat a retreat. After that I carried out my ablutions some distance from the billabong, pouring the chocolate-coloured water over myself out of reach of crocodiles.

We made a film of the birds; they congregated in great numbers, probably because the drought had driven them from their usual watering holes. Apart from the cockatoos, there were gelahs, delicately coloured in soft grey and rose shades, and blue mountain parrots in profusion. That night hundreds of wallabies came down to drink.

A new member joined the expedition—a small bat that Armand found hanging on a tree. He called it Squeaky and christened it with a saucer of milk.

Next day we left the billabong and moved towards Normanton. Soon the oasis of coolness and colour was left behind and we plunged into the world of heat and sand again. Wallabies loped through the bushes; small gum trees appeared; and we caught sight of our first emus.

Driving on, we struck a wide dusty deserted road, with abandoned corrugated iron shacks and diggings scattered around. These deserted works of men looked the loneliest things in the world, baking there, without purpose or meaning, in the sun. As we approached the town itself, I was reminded of the ghost towns of western America.

This place was a relic of gold-rush days. One of the old street lamps bore the date 1898. The shacks had been hurriedly thrown together while the mines were being worked. Only a handful of people in a wilderness of corrugated iron is left of the thousands that swept towards the place, driven by the frenzy for gold. The few people that are left live by trading and fishing. Their houses are hotter than ovens, but they have a swimming pool.

We visited a cattle farm nearby, in a well-watered valley, full of bird life. The surrounding ranch land was overgrown by gum trees and grass, and here we saw many different kinds of animals. The pigs imported by the early settlers escaped and now run wild. Buffalo, and wild horses called brombies, roam vast areas of the outback. Wild cats are numerous. In appearance they are like our own domestic types, but very savage and quite untamable.

The early settlers' imports of foreign fauna undermined disastrously the native wild life of Australia. Even to-day there are some of the cattle farmers who declare that the sooner wild life is wiped out the better. Happily, not all are as ruthless as this. One rancher we met had a pelican rookery on his place which he intended to keep as a bird sanctuary. He told us that one day a man turned up and said he would like to smash all the eggs because pelicans polluted the water; but when he saw the breeding colony, and the thousands of young fledglings, he changed his mind.

We pushed on to Normanton and met Norman Smith, a crocodile expert. A born bushman, he was an adept at catching fish, netting crocodiles, climbing trees, and fixing broken-down trucks; in fact, he was a jack of all trades—and good at all. Armand was delighted at his accepting the offer to join us.

The giant marine crocodile frequents the estuaries and

rivers of North Australia, and Norman agreed to help Armand capture one. First, he caught a shark and laid a piece of its flesh on the bank of the river to tempt the crocodile out of the water. The shark flesh was attached to a rope which operated a complicated mechanism, built out of a log fastened in a tree, and numerous lengths of rope. When the bait was tugged towards the river, the trap would spring.

For three days nothing happened. By that time the shark smelt very high indeed—but the higher the smell the more the crocodile's juices run. On the fourth day we found a nineteen-foot monster writhing and lashing in the water, securely held by the noose.

Now we had to haul him out of the river, and load him on the truck. Too big for us to deal with in any other way, he had to be hoisted by the block and tackle method. He was halfway aboard when the tree we were using to haul him up broke, and one of its branches struck me on the head. I was lucky to escape with a bruised forehead and a deep scratch.

Round one to the crocodile. I scrambled to my feet, tied my face up in a handkerchief, and we started again. We got him on the truck. But now our problem was to feed him. He seemed to be ravenous and kept us all busy catching fish to keep him quiet. We had a good film of the capture now and there seemed to be no chance of transporting him to Sydney as we had originally planned; so after a few days we set him free to hunt his own dinners.

Life in this camp was far from easy. We were on the edge of the mangrove swamps and eaten alive by flies and mosquitoes. To make matters worse, we had run out of American mosquito repellent and were driven to use an Australian brand which dissolved any plastic material with which it came into contact. My fountain pen, sun glasses and wrist-watch glass were all damaged.

The pests attacked in force at sunset. We all had to wear two pairs of trousers and two shirts, for the

The koala, which eats only
four kinds of eucalptus leaves

Tshui, my leopard, always
enjoyed a romp

Squawky and a friend.
Sulphur-crested cockatoos

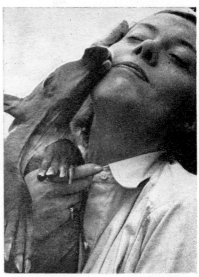

A kiss from an anteater. The
ungainly aardvark is loving

Catscradles. The Aborigines, like most primitive peoples, tell stories as they manipulate string into many ingenious designs

Two old Aborigine women eating. The meat has been more or less cooked by being covered by hot ashes on the ground

This richly ornamented Chimbu is a leper. He wears the rare
King of Saxony feathers between nose and forehead. Tambou
shells are laced underneath the Kina nose ornaments and hang
to his chest. A coronet of iridescent green beetles, Kapoul fur
and birds of paradise surmount the Assyrian-looking headdress

Above: A successful day's haul

Left: The anthills of Australia are renowned for their weird shapes and enormous height. The architecture of this white anthill suggests some exotic castle

mosquitoes bit with ease through one layer of clothes. Mosquito netting food safes—circular hoops—protected our heads and shoulders effectively. It was amusing to see one of the party, thus encased, trying to smoke a pipe. But although our faces and a part of our shoulders were protected, every other available square inch of our bodies was red and swollen with bites.

These mangrove swamps were home to thousands of flying foxes. They made an excellent subject for photography, and we worked in the swamps, up to the hips in soft, oozing grey mud, passing the camera on its heavy tripod back and forth to each other as we went along.

"Heavens, how hot it is!" Armand muttered, as the sweat dropped from his face like rain.

The mangrove roots were a trial. They seemed to be deliberately laid in hoops to trip us up. It seemed hours before we got into position for some wonderful photographs of the thousands of large fruit-eating bats.

Des Bartlett caught one and used Scotch tape to fix it to a tree for a close-up. I offered it a piece of paw-paw; it extended its pointed fox-like face and took the fruit very gently. As it nibbled, I stroked its head and body, and it made no attempt to bite me. I wanted very much to keep it for a pet, but it would not be allowed in Africa, in Europe or in America when we returned there, so I let it go.

It seemed as reluctant to part from me as I was to part from it. Using the hooks on its wings, it climbed on to my shoulder and had to be coaxed to fly to a tree. As we started back towards our camp, it hung and watched us. When I last saw the bat it was in flight towards the swamp.

An Australian friend had asked us to bring him back thirty or forty crocodiles for a crocodile farm he wanted to start as a tourist attraction. Armand, always ready to oblige, had promised that we would do our best; we consulted Norman Smith.

"Yes, it can be done," he said, "but it will be a pretty risky job. Do you mind?"

"Not at all," replied Armand. "We're fairly well used to a few risks now and then."

"It's a goodish way off, you know. But I know a couple of good spots." His blue eyes twinkled as he spoke.

"Never mind, let's go."

So the following day we closed camp and struck inland. Normanton was soon left behind and we moved across arid country through clouds of cinnamon-coloured dust which covered us. Ahead lay the bed of a river. It was dry except for a ribbon of water in the middle. Armand and I were in the sedan, in front of the others. The car slowed down as we bumped on to the sandy bed; we chugged awkwardly along for a few yards and then stopped, stuck.

We tried to dig out the car, but it was no good. Deflating the tyres got us nowhere. We had to wait for the Power Wagon to pull us out. It took two hours for all to get across. If the Power Wagon had stuck, the whole party would have been immobilized.

Some hours later, still driving, I heard a groan from Armand sitting beside me.

"What's wrong?" I asked.

"Look there—river ahead."

It proved to be narrower than the last one. This was not sand; it was dried mud. The mud proved to have a deceptively hard crust. As soon as we were on it, I experienced that awful sinking feeling. The crust cracked and we were in the mud—up to the bonnet.

Again we used the winch and hauled on the cable like a tug-of-war. Gradually, foot by foot, the car came free, then fell in again. After four hours we were on the other side of the river. The effort had exhausted us. To make things worse, Des had a high fever; so we decided to camp on the spot and go after the crocodiles next day.

In the morning, Des seemed a little better; the paludrine had worked. Bumping over the dusty road, we passed many water holes, all dried up, with the bodies of animals strewn around. They told a tale of death from thirst.

The drive seemed endless in that intolerable heat; but at last, just ahead, we saw a clump of trees with parakeets and white cockatoos on the branches.

"Water," I said.

"I wonder how much?" replied Armand.

Our luck was in. Norman found his billabong, and it was a wide one. We drew up alongside, the birds flew up into the air in a great circle and then alighted with deafening screeches. From the chocolate-coloured water and the mud arose an obscene stench. When we reached the edge of the billabong we saw the cause. A dozen cows had been trapped in the thick ooze of the shore and had slowly starved and thirsted to death. Out of their decomposing carcasses their bones stuck up as a warning to travellers like ourselves.

The billabong was literally swarming with crocodiles. Their long wicked mouths, crowded with sharp teeth, opened and closed with a snap as they splashed or basked in the hot sun. In the middle of the billabong they floated motionless, eyes and nostrils above the water level.

Norman's first suggestion was to capture at night, by lassooing. We overhauled the small leaky boat we had with us and rigged torches, nooses and nets. The sun went down. When the darkness had settled, we got into the boat which lurched perilously. The water was not deep, but it was alive with lashing tails and snapping snouts as we pushed off and rowed our tiny overloaded craft into the middle of the billabong.

We tried many times to drop a noose over an inquisitive crocodile's head without success. Then one poked up attracted by the light. In a flash the noose was round it.

Its tail lashed furiously against the side of the boat. We clung on, expecting to be tipped into the water. Water, quite a lot of it, got in over the side of the boat.

Des, trying to get pictures, overbalanced and slumped down heavily, clasping the camera to his chest. Armand and Norman hauled on the rope and the great grinning head came level with the side of the boat.

It was a nightmare of darkness, slapping water and the winking light of torches which lit up hundreds of scaly monsters.

It looked to me a hopeless job. How could we possibly share the boat with a crocodile of this size? And we were after thirty of the murderous creatures. What chance had we?

Thoughts like this were flashing through my mind as the boat again threatened to capsize.

"Steady!" shouted Norman. "I think we had better let him go."

He released the noose. Instantly the slashing teeth grazed his arm; then the infuriated crocodile plunged back into his own element, drenching us with water.

"We had better think this over," said Norman. "Let's get back."

We rowed to the shore and, wading through thick mud up to our thighs, dragged the boat after us. By the light of the torches we saw an evil-looking crowd of bulbous eyes and grinning mouths following us.

We then drew up plans for daylight operations with nets. This seemed to be a more prudent proceeding, for danger could be seen. The nets were laid in an arc, with the boat floating near. When they were in position, Armand, Glen, Norman and I waded into the stinking mud, wallowing like sea-lions.

We tried the technique of half-lying in it, so that we did not sink so deeply; in this position we could use all our strength to pull on the ropes.

It was an amazing haul. The nets were alive with

heaving grey bodies, lashing tails, grasping claws and snapping teeth. We pulled on the ropes, closing the nets like an immense bag. Then the three men grappled with the crocodiles, manhandling them, one by one, into the boat. It was dangerous work.

I saw Armand topple over backwards and disappear at the blow of a scaly tail. I held my breath. He came up, however, in a rage because he had lost his spectacles in the mud. Oblivious of the crocodiles he started searching for them, shouted with triumph as he found them, washed them clean of mud, and went into the battle again. Des Bartlett took wonderful moving pictures of this incident.

Pulling in the nets was back-breaking work and we were getting tired. Norman moved among the haul, counting.

"We've got thirty-six," he announced.

The boat would have to make many trips to our camp, each time almost settling down under their weight. A few escaped over the top of the net and glided towards us. We threw mud at them to beat them off, but they were persistent and we had to keep a sharp look out for the razor-sharp teeth that protruded from the top jaws, even when their snouts were shut.

Norman and Armand would work in the mud, tying up the crocodiles' muzzles. Fascinated by their skill and courage, I perched in the bows and used the dipper to pour water constantly over their backs to keep them cool, and also over the backs of the crocodiles in the boat to keep them from sunburn.

Their shifting bodies were a constant menace and I was careful to keep my feet free of them. When we landed our enraged and still fighting cargo, we tied them by one leg to the stunted trees around our camp. Then we returned for another load.

After six hours' work we were badly scratched and bleeding, for the mud was full of small pieces of mussel shell, sharp as razor blades, and none of us had succeeded in fully avoiding the teeth and tails of our quarry. Armand had a bad gash on his left arm.

Armand lost a shoe in the mud and we nearly lost him when he insisted on retrieving it. His arms were at once engulfed by mud to the shoulder. Time and time again I had fallen full length into the ooze and had to be dragged out; now I looked like a plaster statuette.

Norman shouted: "I think we have got the lot. What about calling it a day."

The final count was sixty-eight crocodiles—a magnificent haul. But first you catch your crocodile—and then keep him. That was the next problem. We bedded down that night on the ground near them, huddled under mosquito nets with all our pets. An alarm was raised when one of our reluctant guests escaped. We went off in pursuit and headed him off in the darkness with torches, for he might have starved to death before the rope round his muzzle rotted off.

While I stood across the path of his retreat to the billabong, the other three scouted around in the scrub and trees. I heard a cry from Armand.

"Here he is!"

The crocodile had slapped his legs with its tail. We ran towards him. It is no joke to hold a torch in one hand and the foreleg of a crocodile with the other; and this monster flung its scaly body from side to side like a coiled spring. At last the four of us took a leg each and carried the beast back to a tree, where we tied it up securely.

How to feed them was the next problem. After breakfast Norman went fishing and caught some small fish like graylings. We untied the crocodiles' muzzles, one at a time, gave them a fish each, then tied them up again. But could we do this all the way across Australia? How could we manage to feed them in the desert?

We loaded about half of them on to the truck. Even then they were packed tight.

"They'll never make the journey," said Armand. "We'll soon have a load of dead crocodiles on our hands."

Norman agreed, and in the end we decided that we should have to release them. The prospect of carrying a load of crocodiles across the desert was too cruel and pointless. Our friend would be disappointed, but that couldn't be helped.

So we began to untie them from the trees—a business almost as dangerous as catching them. For as soon as their snouts were free, they snapped at us as we tried to untie their legs. If we untied their feet first, they had to be chased and caught, while we cut the ropes loose from their snouts.

As we moved among them their tails lashed continually. More than once we were all mown down by blows on our legs. Free at last, they all moved off to the water of the billabong. The only satisfaction we had got out of this terrific hand-to-snout battle was the film that had been made of the proceedings.

I toyed with the idea of keeping two little ones as pets; they were only two feet long. But as they showed a disposition to snap at my fingers, ignoring the fish I offered them, I sent them after their elders.

Armand and I had formed a plan to strike out into the desolate, eroded country far into the Northern Territory. Before beginning the journey we drove to an isolated airstrip, where we took in supplies and saw Norman Smith on to the plane.

The object of the trip was to meet aboriginal Australians. Anthropologists call them the most primitive people left on earth. We first caught up with them as we drove slowly through arid bush country and saw signs of digging in a dried-up river bed. Here, quite recently, somebody had been trying to locate water.

We drove on, full of hope, and soon came across a newish camping sight, with the bones of a brolga—which

Australians call "native companion"—among the cold ashes of a fire.

"We're on the right track," said Armand, pointing to several turtle shells.

But after that—nothing. The shy bush people had, no doubt, heard the noise of our cars and were keeping out of sight. Then, after another day's driving, we saw something that made us brake hard.

Slung between two stakes, some seven feet above the ground, was a straw-strapped bundle. Underneath it a fire was smouldering.

Armand got out to investigate. I followed him. He inspected the swinging bundle.

"There's been a funeral ceremony here," he said at last. "It is the body of an aboriginal child."

It is an aboriginal custom to wrap up dead bodies and smoke them—perhaps to prevent them from being eaten by birds or animals.

I stood by the pathetic bundle, thinking of the time when I was in Ecuador, remembering the solemn funeral procession of a child I had seen there. The father had carried the little white coffin; before him walked a young man playing mournful Inca airs on a violin. This simple straw bundle, slung between two poles, affected me less. Somehow it seemed fitting for the dead body to be in the land of its birth, under the sky. Nevertheless, Armand and I walked back to the car in silence.

A few days later we saw them. In the distance, four naked figures carrying spears, marching in single file, near a billabong. Armand ran towards them, calling and making friendly gestures; but after one look, they ran off in panic, swiftly and silently.

Shortly afterwards, we were breakfasting by the side of a billabong. Jumpy was on my lap and Nosey, the opossum, was trying to steal Squeaky's milk. Armand was sitting near me.

Suddenly he motioned me to be still. He had seen

something move in the bushes. I looked round as he got
to his feet and moved away. There stood three aboriginal
men, stark naked, in between the bushes. One of them
held something white in his arms.

Armand approached them. I watched as the little
white bundle was handed over to Armand. He came back
to me, looking grave, carrying it carefully in his arms.
I jumped to my feet.

It was a child, not more than three years old, smeared
with white clay and scarcely breathing. I looked at the
aborigines.

"They must be pretty desperate," said Armand.
"They've probably been following us for days. They
wanted us to cure this baby."

I made a bed out of boxes and blankets and laid the
little girl child down. Then I washed off the clay and
washed her all over. I could find no injury except a deep
scratch on her nose. Primitive people always smear their
sick with some kind of earth because they believe in its
healing power. The child was in a high fever, and I gave
her penicillin. As I tucked her up in the shade of a
stretched tarpaulin, I felt that invisible eyes were
watching me from the bush. Perhaps the child's mother
was hidden there.

For three days and nights I never left her side. Each
morning we found some offering left near the camp—dead
flying foxes, a speared wallaby, a bundle of fish.

On the fourth day I saw the child's eyelids flutter. Her
forehead was cooler; the high temperature was subsiding.
She managed to drink a little milk. I washed her in tepid
water, as I had done every morning, and she gave me a
faint smile. Then she snuggled back into the blankets
and had her first deep healing sleep. Her breathing was
normal at last.

Relieved, I ran to the edge of the camp and clapped
my hands in joy. I was sure that the watchers would
understand.

217

The next day two wallabies lay beside our truck as a gift. A few hours later little Toowoona sat up for the first time. She drank a whole mug of milk and ate some cereal. For another twenty-four hours she slept soundly; the fever must have left her very weak. When she had slept off her weakness, she was already on the way to recovery.

Two days later an aboriginal woman came shyly to the bushes and stood before me, holding out her hands; in them was a gift of shells. Gently I led her to her daughter, and she bent down and clasped the child in her arms. I made the mother understand that Toowoona was not yet well enough to leave, and she left happily. To cheer and interest the child, I began to shampoo my hair by her cot; she watched me, enthralled. Later, she saw me do my nails and put out her little hand for the same treatment.

This incident was important. As the result of the curing of Toowoona, these aboriginal people accepted us as friends, and we were able to learn a great deal about them.

The men taught Armand to use the woomera, an ingenious spear-throwing device which gives the weapon added momentum and enables it to be thrown much farther. It is a piece of wood with a hook into which the spear is inserted and then released at great speed.

Armand went with them on a wallaby hunt and he returned full of admiration for their skill.

"I've never seen anything like it," he told me. "They are so accurate that they can spear a wallaby in midjump."

They also tried to make Armand proficient in the throwing of a boomerang, but, although he was an interested pupil, he never mastered the art. He explained the principles of the boomerang to me.

"The men work the wood into a curving smoothness which ensures a delicate balance in flight. An engineer trained in aerodynamics would envy them. . . . And the only tool they have is the edge of a mussel shell. They seem to work with instinctive knowledge. Of course, they have generations of craftsmen behind them."

Squatting with the old men, Armand tried to follow the stories they told him. Their dark blunt fingers traced out old legends, relating to their origin, in the soft sand—far back to before the time when the great lakes dried up. Animals were represented by pad marks, rocks and rivers were sketched in, telling of times when water was plentiful and hunting good.

Meanwhile, little Toowoona haunted the camp. She took me to see the women and children, and there I learned some of the secrets of their astonishing survival in a land that looks too bare to support life.

I went with the women to gather food. Walking over that scrubby, sandy waste, where flies seemed to be the only living creatures, they would suddenly stop and start digging in the powdery soil with their hands. Up would come various roots. One—a great favourite—looked like a radish; others resembled peanuts.

Sometimes we went on grub-gathering expeditions; grubs are great delicacies and much practice is needed to locate them. The women tap the stems of certain twiggy bushes to find out if they are hollow. If they are, they break them open to reveal long white maggots; these are cooked in hot ashes.

Another favourite is the honey ant. This is a uniquely specialized kind of ant in which one caste is fed by the workers, in times of plenty, until their bodies become enormously distended with sugar solution. They look like dark shining marbles with little helpless legs—living reservoirs of food for the ant colony. The young girls dig for these in the sand and scoop up the ants in shallow wooden troughs. The girls eat them straightaway—popping them in their mouths as we might eat sweets.

For fruit, there is the pandanus, the root and seed pods

of the lily, or something resembling a new potato growing on trees. I was offered one by an old aboriginal woman and before she could stop me, I had bitten into it. The girls looked aghast—and no wonder. My mouth and tongue felt as though they had sprouted stiff hairs, so astringent was the fruit. Later I was shown how it should be eaten: the fruit is dried, pounded, and then cooked.

We would squat and do complicated cat's cradle patterns, which fascinate primitive peoples all over the world. The women and children sat for hours telling stories by means of these patterns. A favourite tale told of women gathering lily roots and being chased by crocodiles. I would show them cat's cradle stories taught me by the Central Africans.

Or we would bathe in the billabong, for there were no crocodiles here. The boys made mud slides down the bank and the girls dived off the trees. Once they did a water dance for me, a graceful affair of splashing water and weaving hand-movements.

Although the Australian aboriginals are primitive people, we found them full of natural dignity, full of gaiety and humour. They have no culture to speak of; among the women, their arts and crafts seem to be limited to the making of string baskets; and they possessed nothing that would pass for wealth in the modern world.

Nude, they painted themselves with clay and wore leaves for corroborees. Their implements were exceedingly crude; their stone tools lacked the beauty of the stone axes of New Guinea, being merely pieces of unshaped stone bound on to a wooden handle with beeswax and leather thongs. But, as I have already indicated, fine skill goes into the making of boomerangs and woomeras.

The Australian aboriginals, however, have a gift for music. Chants take the place of the drums of Africa. And their dances were quite different from anything we had seen in other parts of the world. Many of the performers could mimic animals vividly—frogs, wallabies, and the totem animals of their tribe.

The men danced with their legs apart, knees bent, the heels moving up and down and the chest and arms in tremulous motion. The dances sometimes portrayed the sacred origins of the tribe, and for these the performers painted themselves in striking designs with ochre, charcoal, and white clay. Tufts of eagle down were stuck into the clay.

Each tribe, they believe, is descended from some kind of animal which is its totem and may not be eaten by any member of the tribe. An aboriginal marrying outside his own tribe must choose a woman whose tribal totem is compatible with his own, or else the marriage is taboo.

Armand and I shared a feast to celebrate a successful wallaby hunt, and I watched the women cooking turtles they had caught. Hot ashes were heaped over them and they were left for hours to bake slowly. Flying foxes, another delicacy, were cooked in the same way. Whole wallabies were split down the middle by a sharp shell and laid in hot ashes. This is the only method of cooking the aborigines seem to know. Inevitably, a lot of charcoal and ash gets mixed with their food and in time their teeth are ground down to stumps.

At the feast, grubs and honey ants were served as *hor d'oeuvres*. Everything served was good, but the turtle especially had a delicious flavour.

After the feast came dancing. Some of the men, smeared with clay and decorated with leaves, mimed the hunted wallaby, peering about and leaping high in the air. As the hunters closed in, the wallaby dancers twisted and leapt desperately to elude them. The climax of the dance came when the hunters pretended to throw their spears. Then the wallabies made great death leaps and collapsed on the ground so realistically that the children stared at the scene apprehensively before they burst into laughter.

The time came for us to leave our friends. One of the

young girls brought me a tiny sulphur-crested cockatoo as a parting gift. He had fallen out of the nest and I fell in love with him at once and reared him by hand. He would make pathetic squawking noises whenever he saw me and run to be fed, his beak gaping open. Even after he could feed himself, he always waited for me to put the food into his beak. I had to make him a bib, he dropped so much food on his chest and his chest feathers got so sticky.

Another gift was Hoppity, a baby wallaby. He was beautiful, with soft eyes and long black eyelashes; but Jumpy was so jealous that he kicked him on sight and never stopped biting and bullying him for the rest of the journey. I finally left Hoppity at a wild life sanctuary we came across on our homeward trip.

I kept our departure a secret from little Toowoona. But I gave her a shampoo as a special treat the day before we left. The dark little face with its merry smile and trusting eyes peering at me from its frame of white bubbles, moved me so much that I longed to take her with us. I had grown completely devoted to her; but she belonged to her family and her own world.

So we set off, heading back in the direction of the Mitchell river, many days' journey away. When at last we arrived, out of food and tired, we restored ourselves in our camp pitched under a mango tree, eating eggs and drinking milk once more.

There was a mission at this place; it was efficiently run and no doubt did good work; but some of the effects of detribalization on the aboriginals we saw were at least doubtful. They were grotesquely dressed, the men in cowboy hats and tight jodhpurs, the women in ugly Mother Hubbards, shorn of their hair.

We did a sound recording and asked the aboriginals to sing their native songs: instead, they started a Maori song, and then Christian hymns, thinking to please us; but with some encouragement from us, they sang their own songs and we made some splendid recordings.

The missionaries suggested that we should make a film of them. Armand and I looked at each other, horror-stricken at the idea. . . . Those hats, those Mother Hubbards!

I turned away, remembering my little Toowoona and her tribe, happy in their untouched wilderness. It seemed to me, as I thought of their freedom, that civilization had come a long, long way to—nowhere.

CHAPTER TWELVE

CANNIBALS, PANTS AND SHARKS

"WHILE WE'RE here," said Robert, looking out of the hotel windows at the swaying heads of palm trees beneath, "why not fly over to Yule Island? I saw some films in Paris made by the Bishop of Yule, and it looked like good country and interesting people."

Armand and I agreed. We were due on the Barrier Reef within a few days, but we had just enough time to spare for the visit.

Early next morning we embarked on a flying boat to the island. Spray blurred the windows of the flying boat and obscured the view as we took off. The flying boat was an enormous plane with two or three decks inside. For two hours we flew low over the deep blue waves. We saw sea birds scattering along the line of our flight and caught glimpses, later, of the island ahead.

Native canoes with bamboo platforms built across them came to meet the plane. They reminded me of the rafts we used for photographing hippos in Africa.

On shore a priest took us to the Sisters' quarters where we were given breakfast. Then we called on Bishop Seurin, who lived in an attractive two-storey house, painted white, surrounded by fine large trees. He greeted us in a room containing Polynesian works of art and wooden objects decorated with incised patterns.

We discussed the best places for filming. The bishop, an enthusiastic movie photographer himself, recommended the interior of the mainland, but we had no time for a foot safari. After hearing some of his stories, we almost cancelled all our plans. It was bitterly

224

Chimbu woman

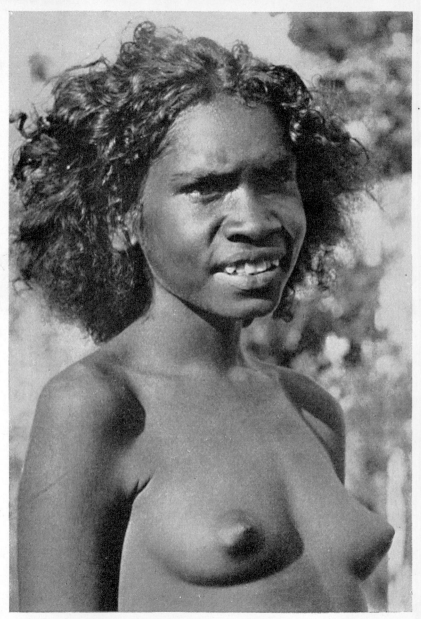

Australian Aborigine girl

disappointing not to be able to make the trip into the interior.

I remember Bishop Seurin's account of a gruesome burial custom of one of the tribes. When a man dies they hang his corpse up in a tree until it is dry and rotten. Then the man's widow cuts the body down, takes it to the river and scrapes the bones clean of flesh. She carries the bones in a bag around her neck, as a symbol of widowhood and sorrow.

The bishop teased me by asking what I should do in similar circumstances.

"It would take me years to scrape Armand's bones," I said. "He is so large."

There were no quarters for married people, and Armand was accommodated in the bishop's house while I was given a room in the convent. The bishop and I struck up a very real and pleasant friendship. We talked a great deal about faith, religion, the celibate life, and God. I loved talking to him. He presented me with a carved crocodile and a beautifully ornamented bottle for holding charms. It had been given to him, he told me, by a famous sorcerer on the island, who became converted to Christianity before he died. It was corked with a leaf. When the bishop uncorked it hundreds of little flies flew up in his face. He jammed in the cork again—quickly. Although empty, the bottle still rattled. It was shaped like a fish and, when it was held upside down, the pattern upon it assumed the form of a human face.

We remarked on the sad fact that the indigenous arts and crafts were disappearing all over the world. The bishop assured us that Papal instructions discouraged interference with any customs that were not anti-social, and insisted on preserving the native way of life, whenever possible.

There had been an exhibition of native arts in Rome, he said, at which Papua was well represented. He favoured decorating churches with native art, on the ground that native people must feel more at home in a traditional setting than in pseudo-Gothic. We remembered churches in the Congo where this Papal order had been carried out with magnificent results.

Sister Marie-Félix was the bishop's sister; she was a vivacious and attractive woman. I was amused to find that the other Sisters were a little jealous of her; they said that as she was the bishop's sister, she got more blessings from him than the others. It was Sister Marie-Félix who told me of a custom, rapidly dying out, but still occasionally practised in the Kunimaipar mountains.

There tradition demands that a mother kill her firstborn and nurse a young pig instead. On the birth of the second child the pig is killed and eaten.

We asked about cannibalism. The bishop shook his kindly head.

"Wait," he said, "let me tell you a story against myself. I had given a strict order that human flesh was not to be eaten on the island. My own villagers obeyed and I had no trouble at all with them.

"Then they were given a present of a human arm—a princely gift—by their neighbours from a village nearby. They were in a dilemma. What were they to do? Eat it and offend me, or not eat it and offend their good neighbours?"

The bishop glanced at his sister. She smiled and shook her head.

"They did neither. They gave the arm to their children to eat."

There was a pause and the bishop added:

"You see, they reasoned that the children knew nothing about my order, so they were disobeying nobody."

The next day we went by launch to visit some of the fishing villages. The old-type houses of palm fronds and wood, with high curved roofs, were built on stilts; a ladder gave access to the veranda and living quarters.

Coconut palms edged down to the sandy beaches. The fishing nets, weighted with shells, were spread over outrigger boats, or laid to dry on the fine sand. The lithe brown bodies of the fishermen gleamed in the sun as they hauled in the sails.

We landed to film the tattooing of a young girl. The custom is to do parts of the tattooing at different periods of the girl's life, and her origin and history can be read at a glance by those who understand the distinctive local patterns.

The girl's mother did the tattooing. The design was painted on the skin, and then the mother, with a thorn-tipped stick and a mallet, pierced the skin in rows of little dots to cover the pattern. The pain must have been intense, but the girl bore it stoically. Blood ran down her arm in streams on to the large leaf she held in her lap to protect her kiva from bloodstains.

I was attracted to a little girl playing cat's cradle. From the Esquimos of the North to the Bantus of Africa—the Australian aborigines and the Papuans—all tell stories by means of intricate designs in string. I held the string while the child made complicated patterns of a crab, and —according to our interpreter—of a palm tree with a "fat belly". No doubt the child's mother had told stories in this way, and her grandmother and great-grandmother too, right back into the remote past.

Nearby a young man was making fire with a friction stick. He used a special wood which smoked after a time and started to glow. This he set to the outer fibrous coating of the coconut and soon had a clear flame and a roaring fire. Near him a beautiful girl sat kneading clay and shaping a wide pot.

"What a lot these people can teach us," I said to Sister Marie-Félix. "Look at the serenity of that girl's face— and contrast it with the strained and hunted expressions seen on women's faces in any big capital anywhere in the world."

"I don't believe you belong to our century at all," said one of the Sisters, smiling. "Would you be happy living here, do you think? Wouldn't you get tired of the sun and sand and sea—until in desperation you would be driven to tattoo yourself all over from sheer boredom?"

I laughed. It was a quaint idea.

"No," I replied, "not here. Africa is my real home. I sleep on the ground there quite happily; I could face life with very few possessions. I sit for hours under one of those high-spreading trees and feel peace and strength flowing into me."

Her smile faded. She nodded as if to herself and looked serious.

"I can see that you mean it," she said, quietly. "Last night we spoke jokingly of you as a pagan. From our Catholic standpoint, I suppose you are. But I think you practise more positive Christianity than many Catholics I know."

Armand called us from the shore and we said no more on the subject.

I have always enjoyed religious discussions. I am deeply religious myself, and I am intensely interested in other people's views on religion. Different beliefs do not worry me. Many Catholic priests I have met liked to discuss religion with me, though they knew that I was not of their faith. They seemed to be conscious of the fact that I have experienced direct communication and strength from some Power.

When I told the Sister of the spiritual fulfilment I get in Africa, sitting alone under a tree in the open air, I think she knew, to some extent, what I meant; but I find it quite impossible to describe fully the natural power that animates all around me and the unity I feel with the earth and with all living creatures. It is a feeling of agelessness, of well-being, goodness, and kindness. I feel myself to be part of the miracle of life, part of the Divine Plan which has existed for all time and will outlast man on this planet.

Even when I have been desperately ill, or facing great danger, I have had no fear of death. Certainly I should be sorry to die, as I feel I have much to do in the world; but the thought of a physical ending of my life means nothing to me. Concerning death itself, I feel immense calmness and trust.

This faith of mine is the secret of my fearlessness in face of physical danger. I can meet it calmly, knowing that death will come in its own good time and is not a matter of fear. If we pass each day as well as it can be passed, without causing sorrow to others, then our life will be worth living.

I have the feeling that every moment of life is precious and must be used to the best advantage. There is a great deal to be done in our life-span, and it is essential to do it to the best of our ability.

For instance, I will fight to the last to prevent the brutal extermination of animals, the senseless chopping down of trees, the spoliation of native peoples and the waste of the world's wealth. To bring happiness to the very old and the sick, to give children confidence in real values, is life to me. These are the important things. Money is unimportant. It cannot purchase freedom or happiness, for these are attributes stemming from spiritual sources within ourselves.

Stupidity—especially official stupidity—has always maddened me.

After we returned to the mainland from Yule Island, we drove from Port Moresby to a fishing village built entirely on stilts. But its Papuan inhabitants were dressed in a sordid mixture of European odds and ends—dirty white ducks, old vests, yellowish blouses, plimsolls and so on.

I asked why. The reply was that the missionaries here

had forbidden the people to dance or to wear their decorative costumes or even flowers in their hair. Their ancient native songs were banned.

To some Papuans, who understood a little English, I made a speech, saying, as they crowded round me:

"These people who tell you that you must not dance or sing are working for the devil and are sent by the devil. They are wicked people pretending to be good. In America we dance and sing, in England and Australia —all over the world. The birds dance and sing. That is how God wished things to be. Otherwise, everything in the world would be dull and unhappy. Because it pleases God, he has made all creatures to express joy at the gift of life."

They listened in wonder and gave us an ovation when we left.

That evening we packed for our flight next day to Australia.

Armand and I had our usual disagreements. We never quarrel at any other time, but the ordeal of packing gets on our nerves and we are apt to bicker with each other.

Armand asked me if there was anything I could throw out. Since I hadn't been allowed to bring my safari clothes from Nairobi, I became mean and said:

"What about these things I bought in Lae? They don't fit me—they never will. These safari pants weren't made for me and I'll always feel uncomfortable in them."

He looked at the brand-new pants and asked: "You aren't going to wear them?"

"No."

"I'll throw them out, then," he said.

Out they shot through the window before I could intervene. I had secretly thought that I might wear them if I had to work in water or mud; they really were not too bad; but how could I admit that now? The pants stayed where they were—down in the dark street below. As far as I knew, they were still there when we boarded the plane the next morning—and I was awfully short of pants.

At the moment the plane took off, we looked at each other and burst out laughing. We were both thinking of the pants. Our sense of humour, thank heavens, always gets the better of us once we are free of the strain of packing.

Across the Pacific by air—what a flight!

We looked down on the green wrinkled skin of the sea and were just able to make out the shadows beneath the surface that were the islands of the future: the indefatigable coral islands, forming over hundreds of years, had at last traced their signatures on the water.

Thousands of feet below, breaking the surface of the glinting ocean and urged upwards by myriads of tiny living organisms that lived and died in their coral honey-combs, we could see the birth of new land.

Some of these nurslings of coral and sea were already crowned by palm trees. The shifting currents of the restless ocean had brought from far-off shores a harvest of seeds. The life cycle had begun. The miracle of a seed! Infinitesimal life, the nucleus, the spark within its guardian husk, ready to stir into growth when the summons reached it.

"We're nearing the Great Barrier Reef now," said Armand, peering out of the window.

Below us, in ever-shifting designs, delicate as Japanese paintings, stretched more coral reefs. They twisted beneath the surface, endlessly intricate, under water which at this height had a glacier transparence.

I could imagine the enchanted drowned sea-gardens, the submerged pools, that lay beneath us. I was eager to get down and explore, although I knew that what would be to me one of the greatest tests I had ever faced loomed ahead.

I would have to learn to swim.

For some reason—perhaps because my grandmother had such a fear of water that she forbade me to go near it—I have always been afraid of water. Whenever I tried to swim, I sank like a plummet—to come up spluttering and furious. Why the water refused to sustain me, I don't know. If I had been thrown into a duckpond as a check on witchcraft, I know I should have sunk to the bottom and earned an unblemished—if posthumous—reputation.

So it was with mixed feelings that I left the plane at Cairns and went with Armand to greet Noel Monkman and his wife.

Noel is an Australian film producer and one of the best underwater cameramen. His wife, Kitty, acted as his assistant, and a very able assistant she was. Both of them had started their careers as professional musicians; but Noel was fascinated by micro-photography in which he soon excelled. The time came when he finally exchanged his hobby for his profession and his profession for his hobby.

They had been working for some months on the small islands in and around the Great Barrier Reef with a team of Australians. Now we were to join this expert team.

We took a boat out to one of the islands off the coast, an islet of about thirty acres, covered with coconut palms, nutmeg trees, and pandanus. The sea around the shores was so clear that we could see the fish swimming in the depths below. Barely a half mile off shore, whales played leaping and rolling, graceful in spite of their bulk. We had timed this portion of our journey to the lowest tides of the year: huge fields of coral emerged. We went to explore the pools left in the coral and the rocks—fantastic marine gardens, endless in variety of design, pattern, and colour!—mauve, blue, green, pink, dark red; coral like delicate lace, coral like branching trees, coral like convoluted brains, coral like castles, castellated and intricate.

I had never realized that it could be both hard and soft, until I tried to break off a piece and felt it rubbery and yielding to the touch.

It was difficult to realize that this beauty was full of hidden dangers. Hands had to be washed after touching it, for it had an irritant quality. Noel fell and scratched his leg; the inflammation became so serious and malignant that we feared that amputation might become necessary. Coral scratches seem to infect the bones.

In addition, there were many killers lurking in those beguiling blue waters. The stone fish, for example, which looks exactly like its name, is one of the most dangerous creatures in this transparent and beautiful underworld. It lies on the bottom, perfectly camouflaged. Woe to the incautious bather! If trodden on, the stone fish does not trouble to move away. It merely discharges a virulent poison through its dorsal spines, connected with poison sacs. Unless medical attention is available within a matter of minutes, the unfortunate bather has had his last dip.

Less deadly than the stone fish, but also venomous, is the lovely butterfly cod which enchants with its graceful motion. Some species of box fish will not harm intentionally but take their revenge after their own death; for they hold an internal secretion that becomes violently toxic when the flesh is eaten.

There were also many harmless creatures—the shiny dark *bêches de mer* (sea cucumbers) which eject a macaroni-like substance when handled; starfish of many sizes and colours—green, ultramarine, black, orange, grey; some sturdily built, others as slim and graceful as lace.

Apart from the sting-rays, poisonous sea-anemones and octopi, there were always the unexpected shark and giant clam to be faced.

One morning, Armand and I were walking on the outer reefs which dipped abruptly into deep water. He stopped suddenly and caught my arm. He had spotted what he thought was the tail of a shark protruding from behind a rock. He made a swift grab and dragged out a baby shark.

Then a struggle began. We tried to photograph it, but it lashed about, turned and twisted and tried to bite his hand, revealing the wicked-looking U-shaped mouth of the killer-to-be. The sun shone on its white belly and grey-brown back. For some minutes Armand and the shark wrestled by the side of the deep water. Then he let it go and it thrashed its tail so violently that he was nearly thrown off his balance. I was ten feet away, and to avoid the splash I stepped back without looking where I was putting my foot.

Noel shouted and I looked down.

Within inches of my heel, a razor-edged giant clam snapped shut like a mantrap. A jet of sea water was flung into the air and shot over my knees.

Armand ran towards me, slipped and scratched his arm on the coral, and at once started to suck out the minute pieces.

"For heaven's sake, Michaela," he said, spitting out a mouthful of blood, "that clam could have had your foot off!"

We started to pick our way back with immense caution. But I was curious. I wanted to find out why the clam had closed up so suddenly when my foot had not, in fact, touched it.

I glanced around the translucent coral shelves and saw another, nearly a foot across. It lay half-open by a sharp rock, its shining yellow mantle fringed with green. As I approached, cautiously, my shadow fell across it. Instantly it closed as if steel-hinged. A jet of water shot a foot into the air. The mantle was withdrawn and only the oblong bluish shell remained to be seen.

"You see," I said triumphantly, "they're sensitive to light as well as to touch. That's why my foot was saved.

234

If the sun had been shining from behind, instead of in front of me——"

I shuddered at the thought of how nearly I had left a foot behind on that jagged outcrop.

I began to understand the hazards divers faced. The shadow of a man descending those deceptively quiet waters would trigger off these live mantraps; they could hold a man's foot long enough to drown him unless he could manage to cut the hinging muscle, or tear himself free and come to the surface, minus a foot.

In spite of the dangers, the expeditions over the coral were delightful, and new underwater worlds were revealed to us hourly. But I could not for ever put off the business of learning to swim.

One morning I went into the water of the sandy beach of a small island and watched a group of children playing in the sea. One little girl, not more than seven years old, was puffing along on waterwings.

"Hello," she called, "come and see me swim!"

I waded over to her and watched.

"My name is Ann," she said. "I can do it without wings. Can you?"

I shook my head.

"I'm learning as well," I told her. "Do you think I'll ever manage it?"

Ann broke into a peal of laughter. Running out of the water, she threw her wings on to the sand and then swam back to me slowly.

"There," she said, proudly. "Now you try!"

How could I fail her? Surely if Ann could swim, I could also. I remembered suddenly how a child had taught me to ride a bicycle in one day, and I felt that if anyone could give me confidence it was Ann.

So I tried. To my surprise I did not this time instantly sink like a stone, but kept up for a few strokes, although I made no headway.

"My mother will help you to-morrow," said Ann, importantly. "She's a wonderful swimmer."

Everybody on this idyllic coast seemed to be a wonderful swimmer. Even a one-legged man made progress against a stiff nor-easter that blew up in the days that followed. All the children who came from the mainland to watch us filming seemed as much at home in the water as on the land.

With the help of Ann's mother I made a little headway. But four strokes was my limit. I was annoyed with myself, for I knew we had some water sequences to film later on, and disliked feeling so afraid.

That afternoon I asked Armand to watch me. I turned over on my back and floated.

"That's fine," he said. "Now propel yourself along like this." And he showed me an easy overarm stroke.

I did as he said—and suddenly I was swimming!

At the first stroke my fear went. It was forgotten in the delightful sensation of being able to move through clear water, of being buoyed up by it.

"Oh, splendid, darling!"

Armand was beaming with pleasure. He knew what the effort had cost me.

"Now try to swim like that to me."

He swam in a little way and I went up to him—on my back, admittedly, but swimming all the same. And that is how I swim to this day. If I turn over on to my stomach all sense of balance deserts me, and down I go.

That night I found three coconuts on my bed.

"Are these a reward for my swimming efforts?" I asked Armand.

"Those coconuts nearly cost a good cameraman," he replied.

Apparently Des Bartlett had climbed one of the highest palm trees on the island to pick them for me, as he knew I loved them. A frond gave way, and he fell from the top of the tree on to the back of his neck. Miraculously, he escaped with a few bad bruises.

Next morning we were out on the beach filming. My job was to scare away seagulls from newly hatched turtles —a job of which I thoroughly approved, for I knew the torment turtles endure to ensure life and a measure of safety to the new generation—which they will never see.

Once a year the female turtles come to land and crawl painfully up the beach at sunset. Their flippers are not made for propulsion on land; they are so heavy with eggs that their tails drag behind them, cutting deep furrows in the sand. With heartbreaking effort they laboriously dig out a deep hole in the sand, lay a hundred or more eggs, cover them and scatter the sand so expertly that no trace is left of the hiding place.

Exhausted the females drag themselves to a fresh stretch of sand, where they disarrange the surface to deceive would-be egg-stealers. Then they make their way back to the sea. In due course the eggs are hatched out by the heat of the sun. The baby turtles dig their way out to the surface, and instinctively hurry towards the sea. But hundreds, in the first few minutes of their lives, in the hurrying race from nest to protecting ocean, are taken by seagulls.

I thought of the heroic performance of the mother turtle; I could not bear the thought of the seagulls killing the babies. The seagulls would not starve; food was plentiful on this coast.

While I kept the seagulls off the beach, Armand went out to the edge of the reef, equipped with goggles and breathing apparatus and his heavy lead belt slung round his waist to keep him below the surface. He was off to look for underwater locations.

I watched him submerge and then lost sight of him. Then I saw cutting through the water a sinister triangular fin.

I jumped up, my heart in my mouth.

Instantly, I flew down the beach on to the coral, screaming, "Armand! Armand! Quick! Shark! Shark!"

The water was so clear that I could see Armand swimming over the coral beds, weighed down by his lead belt.

To attract his attention, and also to frighten off the shark, which was now about a hundred feet from him, I splashed the water violently. At last he surfaced and heard my agitated shouts.

"Shark! Shark!" I yelled at the top of my voice, pointing towards it.

He saw it and began swimming towards me. I was in an agony of apprehension. Wading deeper into the shallows I splashed the water again, shouting with all my lung power, for I knew that sharks are afraid of noise.

I weighed up the chances. My swimming was rudimentary; if I plunged in, Armand would feel he had to rescue me, and that would delay him. The shark might get us both.

The fin was now less than fifty feet away from him. Then suddenly it seemed to spurt ahead.

In a flash I measured the distance between Armand and the shore. He had about twenty yards to go. In my desperation, I broke off a piece of coral and waited. Then I hurled it with all my strength.

It fell with a plop between Armand and the shark.

I saw the shroud-grey back and flat ugly head as Armand began to wade over the sand and coral. The shark veered away and gave him time to scramble up a little higher.

I was still shouting and splashing at the water's edge when Armand flopped down beside me, undid the lead belt and let it fall on to the sand.

The shark hesitated, not fifteen yards from the shore, then turned and cruised slowly off along the edge of the reefs.

"That was a near one," said Armand, cheerfully, as he freed himself of goggles and breathing mask. "Thanks very much. Let's hope we can get some pictures—too bad we had no underwater camera on this!"

Someone came up and said, "You might have been killed!"

"Don't you believe it," answered Armand, and added, turning to me: "We have charmed lives, haven't we, darling?"

I could only nod dumbly. I suppose we have. But danger on land is something I can deal with; the sea—although I can now swim—will always remain for me an alien element.

CHAPTER THIRTEEN

MY JUNGLE PETS

MY LOVE of animals dates back to a very early age; I cannot remember a time when I was without pets—birds, dogs, cats, or insects. I collected them as some children collect postage stamps, and I have continued to do so all through our travels in the jungles and deserts of the world.

I have previously touched on my early years in London, when my ambition was to set up a zoo of my own, with elephants and tigers and bears. This childish ambition never faded even when I was working as a fashion designer in New York; but it seemed wildly improbable that I should ever have a chance to realize it.

Then I met Armand Denis and a new life opened for me. Getting close to wild animals was the most exciting of the adventures that I was to share with him. In the space of a few weeks I found that my childhood dreams had become real.

I believe that some power binds all living creatures together and that, to some extent, all are conscious of it. Call it love, if you like; without love there can certainly be no understanding. But I think the power goes even beyond love; it works only through those who acknowledge and submit to it without question or conscious effort.

Only the odd person here and there gets close enough to wild animals to recognize that, like human beings, untamed animals possess distinct personalities—that one green snake differs from other green snakes as well as one leopard from other leopards.

I called him Monsieur Robert. Successor to the baby vervet who died during the filming of *King Solomon's Mines* at Murchison Falls, he was a bat-eared fox, almost half-grown, who had been given to me by a white hunter after our return to Nairobi.

I saw a small bundle of silver-flecked fur and thought what a handsome little creature he was, with his enormous dark ears which ran to a point. His pelt would hardly have covered the shoulders of a doll, for he was no larger than a biggish kitten. He had a delicate and sensitive face, lit with bright beady eyes, and slim, graceful forepaws. His bushy tail was tipped with white.

When I spoke to him he replied with a soft whinny.

Unable to resist him, I bent down to stroke him between the ears. Instantly he sank his teeth into my forefinger and drew blood.

The white hunter told me that these little foxes had more teeth than any other mammal of East Africa.

"So I see," I said, ruefully.

"Do you still want him?" he asked, staring at my bitten finger.

I nodded, and so Monsieur Robert became mine.

Our first introduction hardly promised enduring comradeship, but I thought he could be fitted into our gypsy household. I knew that these little bat-eared foxes were very wary and wild, but I knew of some that had been caught young enough and reared with a litter of puppies, and had been tamed.

Borrowing a pair of stout gauntlet gloves, I picked up the squirming little creature, determined to come to an understanding with him in spite of his sharp teeth.

Like all his kind he was nervous and watchful, and no wonder, for in his jungle home he was prey for the big cats. He and his ancestors may almost be said to have been born on the alert.

As he came to know me better, Monsieur Robert would

241

suffer me to pick him up, but I had to be cautious with him. I would slip my hand under his back legs and support his paws in front. I was thus able to stroke him so long as my hand was out of sight. Then he would close his eyes and relax; but let a finger flick into his vision and he would have his teeth into it like a flash.

There was, of course, nothing personal in it. He bit from an uncontrollable reflex action.

Yet he never seriously objected to a collar and leash, and he seemed to enjoy trotting beside me along the streets of Nairobi. When I lunched at the Lobster Pot, he would sit on my lap, patiently waiting for a saucer of milk with which he was always rewarded. People were charmed by him, but they invariably got bitten when they tried to stroke him before I had a chance to warn them. They often mistook him for a cat or a special breed of dog.

One day while out walking, with Monsieur Robert nestled on my arm, I met Mervyn Cowie, Director of the National Parks in Kenya.

"What a dear little fox!" he exclaimed. "Wow!"

He quickly withdrew his bitten hand and tried again —with the same result. Altogether, Monsieur Robert nailed the preserver of wild animal life five times until Cowie called it a day.

"I'm sorry that he should be so naughty," I said.

Cowie smiled ruefully.

"Perhaps he doesn't know who I am," he said.

While we were staying in a friend's cottage, Monsieur Robert dug a hole under the bathtub and made a nest for himself, for he loved comfort. Everything he could lay his paws on was dragged into the nest—Armand's sweaters, woollen socks, newspapers, ends of film, and even one of my cherished sable-hair paint brushes. He had the nerve to scuttle into our bedroom one morning and try to drag a blanket off the bed, but in the midst of the tug-of-war Shabani came in with morning tea. A saucerful of it made Monsieur Robert forget his urge to steal blankets.

He loved tea as much as any English spinster and would sit up and beg for it. When he retired to his nest under the bathtub and refused to come out for a walk, I would put a saucer of sweetened milky tea down by the bath and wait. Soon I would see his little pointed face peeping out, and then he would approach it cautiously, walking round and round. Then he would settle down and, with warning growls, start to lap. While lapping milk he would be so absorbed as to allow me to slip the leash on him and walk him off.

He was good company and I missed him greatly when I had to go into hospital with amoebic dysentery. During my absence he had to be boarded out with three other of my pets. When I returned home he had become so wild that nobody could touch him.

Armand persuaded me that Monsieur Robert was too big to travel with, anyway, and although I felt that, given time, I could have got him back into the old routine again, we left him with our friend Bobby Cade, who promised to send him to one of the modern zoos where animals are provided with paddocks and big runs.

It was inadvisable to free him, because after so long a period in captivity he might not have been able to fend for himself. In any case, he would most likely have been regarded as an interloper by other animals, and killed.

Monsieur Robert was a rare little character. Even though he was prone to bite the hand that tried to caress him, he was intelligent and responsive to kindness.

Another of my pets was Monsieur Camille, a chameleon.

Africans believe that this sub-order of lizards is poisonous, and I feared at first that we should lose our boys on his account. Whenever I went out, with Monsieur

Camille half-raised on my hand like a figure in bronze, they would let out terrified howls and sprint madly away. Then from a safe distance they would stare in amazement as I walked round with the chameleon, and failed to drop dead. To them it was magic that I remained unhurt. Shabani and Mucharia later grew to tolerate his presence, but nothing could persuade them to touch him.

Social note in the local newspaper: "Seen at the Lobster Pot—Mrs. Armand Denis in a dark red velvet suit and wearing a chameleon on her lapel."

Monsieur Camille used to curl up in my handbag, which was made of sisal, whenever he wanted to sleep. He was taken out every day to feed himself on flies— his favourite dish—and usually he stayed on the same twig, occasionally shooting out his tongue at a fly with unerring and deadly aim, until we took him in again.

He was wonderful to look at when he did the chameleon camouflage act. It was fascinating to watch him switch from pattern to pattern. His skin varied from deep black to a bold yellow motif and to a greenish-blue symmetrical cross-hatching. He would swivel one eye to me as if to see if I was duly observing his chromatic performance, but the other eye would continue to roam the landscape in search of flies. When he was angry his throat distended until it was a bright red sac with yellow spots —almost like a strawberry.

Inevitably, the day came when he vanished. Perhaps he felt there was no romance in his life and that somewhere a girl chameleon waited to be courted.

Although Monsieur Camille was a decorative and tractable pet, he was not as lively as a warm-blooded creature. The boys, I suspect, were glad to see the last of him. They were much friendlier to Monsieur Tikki, a small mongoose which was sent to us from Mombasa.

We had asked an Indian there to find a mongoose for us and arranged for him to be kept by some friends in

Nairobi if he arrived while we were on safari. One day our friends had a phone call from the railway station.

"There's a live rat here and it's addressed to the Denises," said a disgusted Indian voice.

It was our mongoose. Our friends collected him and sent him over to us.

Monsieur Tikki at once made himself at home. The boys loved him and gave him so many titbits that soon he had rolls of fat on the back of his neck, like an aged gourmand. The fireplace fascinated him; he would creep into it whenever he could, whether there was a fire burning or not. We would find him curled up asleep among the hot embers and, consequently, he lost most of his fur and good looks.

He had a mind of his own and his habits could not be changed. For instance, he decided to sleep with Monsieur Emile, the bush baby, who really preferred being left alone, but was unable to defend his privacy. Every morning we found them cuddled up together with the bush baby's chin resting on Monsieur Tikki's head.

Like all mongooses, once he had chosen a place for his convenience, he always went back to it. Instead of using the garden, he selected a vacant site in a bookcase and we couldn't break him of the habit. We would put a newspaper down for him, for it was awkward when we had visitors, especially as Shabani always announced in a loud stage whisper to me, "Mongoosi has gone W.C. in bookcase, Memsahib."

Monsieur Tikki died of a seizure while in the garden, brought on probably by overfeeding: a sad end for a lively little creature.

Monsieur Emile, our bush baby, was given to us while we were staying on the coast, at Malindi, about thirty miles from Mombasa.

The bush baby, or galago, is an East African lemur. This one had fur very like that of a chinchilla and a long white tail which he rolled up into a tight curl. When I took him out on a lead, he would bounce up and down, running and springing, his tail uncurling and flowing out behind him. He had extremely delicate ears which reacted to sound by folding and unfolding.

Although lemurs are creatures of the night, Monsieur Emile was at his liveliest during the day time, which was most unusual. So was his wonderfully sweet disposition. For bush babies, in spite of their round-eyed look of innocence, are generally of uncertain temper, and a bite from one of them is never a half-hearted affair.

Drink has been the downfall of many a bush baby. I don't know how, or in what circumstances, it was discovered that they are natural tipplers; but for a long time now they have been trapped by alcohol.

A cupful of drink, placed at the foot of a tree, or in the branches, never fails to lure the guzzling bush baby. As soon as he has finished the potion, he will shin up the tree without a care in the world. Soon the alcohol begins to work. Feeling exhilarated, he indulges in ambitious gambolling, but seldom manages it without missing his hold and tumbling down into the nets of his captors.

This is the only reliable way of catching bush babies, for they are as lively as gibbons. They vanish out of sight and reach so quickly that the observer is lucky if he can catch a glimpse of the huge luminous eyes in the tiny pointed faces.

But I had one baby that couldn't be seduced by fire-water. That was Tshui, the African leopard, who gave me the title of this book.

When he was small and in need of affection I nursed him on my knees by the hour. Armand often asked me what I would do with him when he grew up and wanted to sit on me, but the choice really lay with Tshui himself.

At first he was so small that I could nurse the whole of him in my lap. When he was half-grown he still came up to me to be cuddled; even then he was big enough to smother me, so that only my legs could be seen.

When he grew larger there was no camp chair strong enough to bear our combined weight, and I had to nurse my affectionate pet sitting on the ground. He was always my favourite among the larger animals.

His beauty was breathtaking. For an African leopard he had an extraordinarily handsome coat, clear yellow and black. His eyes were a greenish-amber.

Leopards vary greatly in colour; some are yellow, others tawny; and they are invisible when lying in the amber-tinted grass of the plains. Quite frequently they are confused with cheetahs; but having kept both animals at the same time, I soon learnt to distinguish between them on safari. The cheetah has black lines running on each side of its face from eyes to mouth; its legs are slimmer, its coat of a different texture. The leopard's fur is silky, but the cheetah's coat is harsh as a doormat and decorated with much smaller spots.

Tshui accompanied us everywhere. He travelled in the small truck which had been across Africa with us. The portable cage with fresh straw was an ideal travelling home for him. At stops during our journeys, I would loop a rope to his collar and tie him on a long leash to a tree. A cheetah would have entangled himself in the leash, but Tshui was far too smart for that.

When we left him he would either sit in the shade of the tree, his wonderful eyes alive with interest in his new surroundings, or climb up the tree and stretch his full length along a thick branch.

I find it impossible to describe the loveliness of his climb; he seemed to pour himself up the tree trunk, a stream of bone, muscle and fur, and then suddenly become still as evening waters in a black and gold sunset.

When I knew that there was no likelihood of visitors or strangers coming into the camp, I allowed him to roam freely. I became so accustomed to taking him about with me that when Armand and I went to see how the building of our Kenya house was progressing, he would bound on ahead of us up the wide central staircase like a huge dog. Often he would launch himself into mid-air with one of his liquid leaps and land in an upstairs room by way of the connecting arch.

Once, when the house was nearly completed, the plumber arrived to discuss the size of pipes we wanted. Armand and I had decided to have a bigger size than those in general use, and the matter was soon settled. The plumber was half-way down the stairs when I remembered that Tshui was unleashed.

I ran to the top of the stairs and called down to him.

"Be careful of the leopard in the garden!"

The man looked at me as if I was crazy. First, one-inch pipes—who ever heard of such things?—and now a leopard in the garden! He went on stolidly unable to appreciate the joke! I ran down the stairs after him.

"Be careful of the leopard!" I repeated. "He's near the guest house, probably in one of the trees."

That shook him, and he waited for me. We walked into the garden together.

"Stay here," I said.

I went on ahead. A few yards farther on I crouched down and Tshui landed on my shoulders from the tree in which he had been lying. I was used to this little game of his and braced myself to take his weight. The game was not without danger, for if I lost my balance, his claws would dig into me like those of a domestic cat that tries to hold on.

Tshui, of course, didn't know how vulnerable was human flesh; he just treated me as if I were another leopard with a strong protective coat. As I crouched lower he rolled off my back on to the ground and then put his head in my lap to utter his usual growl of welcome. He couldn't talk a lot but what he said was clear enough and full of intense feeling.

I couldn't see the plumber, but I knew that the scene must have taken his breath away. However, he was not

248

without courage. He walked towards Tshui and me.

The leopard turned like a flash and sprang, shoulder height, at the poor fellow, with every claw unfurled. Two thoughts raced through my mind: had the jungle call at last caught up with my pet, or could it be that his instinct to kill was aroused because he felt I needed protection?

The plumber stood white-faced. Tshui's claws had torn his raincoat into tatters. I spoke softly and took the leopard by the collar and tail, and pulled him off, squatting down to tickle him by the ears. He yawned, his savage mood vanished, and he began to purr sleepily and contentedly.

I fastened him up and took the shaken plumber indoors for a drink. I apologized and offered to replace his ruined raincoat. He refused, politely enough, saying that the coat was an old one, anyway, but he left hurriedly.

Although I knew that Tshui loved me, I never took liberties with him. At feeding time I was especially careful. When he ate he didn't want to know me; if I went near him he would neither release the meat he was eating nor raise his head; his broad nose would wrinkle wickedly and his lips curl up, exposing long shining teeth. His growl seemed to come up from the very depths of his being, full of menace and forgotten friendship.

During the filming of *Below the Sahara* we were presented with a couple of cheetahs. I was delighted, for after having reared Tshui to friendship I wanted to try my hand at making a pet of one of these attractive animals.

I pointed out to Armand how beautiful they were and how friendly they seemed. He smiled sceptically and said he had kept cheetahs before and found them as stupid as sheep and obstinate as mules. However, I was not to be deterred.

I sought the advice of Raymond Hook, who probably

knew more about cheetahs than any man in Africa. He had lived many years in Kenya, a few miles outside Nanyuki, where he interested himself in improving the strains of goats, sheep and cattle. He bred the strangest animal I ever saw—a cross between a zebra and a horse, but larger than either, with black stripes on its chestnut coat.

Hook trained cheetahs for the Indian maharajahs and at one time trained cheetahs for K. C. Gandar Dower, who wanted to race them in England against greyhounds. The cheetah's speed has been clocked in Britain at over sixty-two miles an hour; there could be no race against the far slower greyhounds. If in the mood, the cheetah would overtake the greyhounds, which had been given a head start of many yards, and contemptuously leap over them, passing them in one bound; but he was equally apt to sit down in the middle of the track and let the electric hare go hang.

The cheetah is altogether an odd animal. Although it belongs to the cat family, it differs from other felines in many ways. For instance, it cannot retract its claws; and it is not nocturnal like the other cats. It becomes quite tame and responds to training much more quickly than either a lion or a leopard, though it is less intelligent and reacts only to deeply inculcated orders.

Our cheetahs purred loudly with pleasure whenever they were stroked, but their eyes remained quite expressionless. How unlike Tshui who appeared to smile when I caressed him and who would rub his head against my legs in gratitude.

No cheetah I ever owned would make such a spontaneous gesture of affection. Muni and Luni, my two favourite males, were brothers. They were greatly attached to one another and would lick each other unceasingly. They licked me also, but I always felt it was because I happened to be handy. Raymond Hook had never been deceived by them. He was right when he said that the only thing a cheetah is interested in are things appertaining to cheetahs.

I watched Hook's training technique closely. First the animal had to be taught its name. He used what he called an educating spoon, actually a home-made wooden spoon with a handle about a yard long, big enough to hold a chunk of meat. The cheetah was repeatedly called by his name as the trainer moved slowly away from him. The animal would follow and take the meat; then the routine would be repeated. After a few days the cheetahs associated their names with food and came at once when called.

A similar technique was used to train them to race. The cheetahs were boxed and carted by ox-wagon to the training ground. There a man on horseback gave them the scent of a large piece of meat which he dragged behind him on a long rope. When the rider was far enough ahead, the trap doors were opened and the cheetahs shot out at an incredible speed.

They caught up with the bait in a flash. Then came the job of getting them back into their boxes. It took three of us to corner one of them; each of us held a frame covered with wire mesh, and while the animal was eating we formed a triangular cage round him, and one of us would hold out the wooden spoon with another piece of meat. As the animal moved towards it, the cage moved too—until the travelling box was reached. According to Hook's theory, the cheetah would then jump into it without further trouble.

He was usually right in his judgments; but the day came when one of our cheetahs, an independent female answering to the name of Helen, upset his calculations.

Helen was being photographed by Tom Stobart as she raced after the bait. She caught it—and then the trouble started. The boys approached her with the screens. She stopped licking the meat, looked at them, gathered herself up and shot away with a great bound.

Tom came up with an enquiring look on his face. Hook pushed his battered old hat to the back of his head and said in an outraged voice: "But cheetahs just don't do that!"

Armand and I trained Muni and Luni to race. I have never seen any creature run a faster hundred yards. And the beauty of their running has to be seen to be believed.

Of the two, Luni was the more docile. Muni had a bad reputation for biting, but he never tried to bite me. When I took them out on long leads they would walk along as sedately as trained collies—until they saw anything move in the grass. Then they would plunge forward in different directions, while I stuck my heels in the ground trying to hold them and keep the leads from tangling.

I dared not let them both free, for I would never have seen them again; but because of their affection for each other, it was perfectly safe to release one, knowing that he would never wander far from his companion.

Sometimes they were tractable enough to allow a friend's dog to come along with us, but they were apt to turn suddenly and floor the dog with slapping paws and send him off howling.

In the end I had to admit that Armand was right. Cheetahs are not to be kept as pets; they are too cold and impersonal to inspire and return affection. One can never be quite certain what they will do at any given moment, and this makes them difficult to work with.

I remember a film scene that still makes me smile. We did a shot of our five cheetahs together, leashed. They looked docile and beautiful and the commentator was inspired to explain blandly:

"Soon they were tamed and became as gentle as great cats."

No sooner had the shot been taken than the formidable Helen—who was certainly the most quarrelsome cheetah

I have known—turned on her neighbour with a snarl and began a savage brawl, in which all five joined.

I have no idea what touched off the quarrel, but they were all highly-strung and they lashed themselves into such a fury that they bit and clawed at anything in range. Their leashes became entangled, and it was pure luck that in dragging the infuriated animals apart nobody was seriously hurt.

Bad as it was, this experience did not finish me with cheetahs. The last straw came when Tom Stobart and I played nursemaids to Luni and Muni on a visit to the Wanderobo tribe, close relations of the Masai.

A mechanic had built a special body for our largest truck. It looked like a caravan and was almost sound-proof. It had windows which, we imagined, could be opened, and a hatch in the ceiling designed to allow a photographer to get his head and shoulders out to take pictures while we were on the move.

The cheetahs had to be transported in this truck. Cheetahs are jittery travellers, so Tom and I volunteered to stay with them. We sat on rolls of bedding with backs to the door. Soon we were travelling over a boulder-strewn road, the truck bouncing like a rubber ball. The cheetahs were badly shaken up. In addition, soon the inside of the truck became as hot as an oven. The animals reacted to this, fore and aft, rolled helplessly on the generously soiled floor, and then tried to settle in our laps.

We couldn't get the window open, nor the hatch. Surely, I thought, this is a foretaste of hell. Tom looked green; I wondered how I looked. He was hammering away at the partition behind the driver. We must have travelled at least fifteen miles before Armand and the driver guessed that something was wrong.

The truck stopped and somebody opened the door. Tom and I fell out, gasping for air. We looked as if we had been dragged through a sewer. After that, all four of us crowded into the driver's cabin for the rest of the journey.

I had always wanted to be surrounded by my pets, even when on the move, but I soon realized that this was impossible. Apart from our Bassenji dogs—the barkless dogs of the Congo—there were not many we could take with us; so Armand and I tried to come to terms on the problem.

What sort of animal was portable, able to pass from country to country without quarantine difficulties, and not large or fierce enough to cause a panic if it escaped?

The answer seemed to be Priscilla.

She was a beautiful green snake of the constrictor type from the Central Highlands of New Guinea. I managed to tame her and often carried her around in my arms; but she could not be trusted much with anyone else.

While taming a snake I hold the head and tail to prevent it slipping through my fingers, and I have found this the best way to handle all snakes. I carry snakes in a bag, and this is the way Priscilla travelled. The bag is secured by a draw-string while we are on the march. I always tried to keep her as cool as possible and keep her supplied with plenty of water.

When we left the Central Highlands and journeyed back towards civilized Papua, Armand began to express doubts about Priscilla's suitability as a hotel guest. She had grown to five feet—big enough to upset some people if she ever did get away in any of the Burn-Philps hotels.

I defended her character warmly and reminded Armand that it was his idea that she would be an ideal travelling pet. Hadn't he given her to me? It was no use. Armand shook his head and told me firmly that Priscilla could go no further with us. It was a harsh decision and for a while I could not find it in my heart to accept it. So I kept Priscilla hidden beneath the undies in my suitcase for some days. But deceiving Armand made me unhappy and I realized I could never keep up this sort of double life. Reluctantly, therefore, I had to leave her behind with one of the *tul-tuls*—a headman whose little daughter I had nursed through an illness—and I warned him that Priscilla was not to be eaten under pain of the most awful curses I knew.

CHAPTER FOURTEEN

THE ROUGH AND THE SMOOTH

WHEN I was small, I was always fascinated by the horizon. What lay beyond? But it takes money to see what lies beyond the horizon.

The Spaniards have a proverb: " 'Take what you want,' said God, 'and pay for it'." I took travel—and paid for it. I worked as a fashion designer and saved. When I had enough money I used it to travel—first of all, to explore the United States. Later, I went farther afield, and found myself up in the Andes, tracking down Indian artifacts and ornaments, ceramics and textiles. I did a good deal of sketching and painting on these trips, hoping to incorporate the intricate patterns I came across into my fashion designing.

On these journeys I grew impervious to discomfort. I found that I preferred to sleep on the ground, with or without a mosquito net. It refreshed me, this close contact with the earth, giving me a feeling of strength and of being at one with the universe. To-day, after living so much out of doors and sleeping rough, I suffer from insomnia when Armand and I return to civilization. The sky seems roofed off. I am insulated from the earth, trapped within walls. Many times I have rolled off my hotel bed, taking all the clothes with me, to settle comfortably on the hard floor. What a scramble next morning to get back in again before the maid brought us our tea!

One of the journeys I made before my marriage was to a tiny village called Santo Domingo in Ecuador. Travelling by truck from Quito, nine thousand feet

Left: Aborigine woman and her handiwork. This bag, boomerangs and spear - throwers (woomera) were all we ever saw the Aborigines make. Note the characteristic position of the foot

Right: Wallaby corroboree (Australian Aborigine)

Central Australian Aborigine man. Anthropologists regard the Australian Aborigines as the most primitive people left on earth

above sea-level, I dropped down from the wind-swept heights of the Andes to a land of soft grass.

Down farther still the vegetation became lush and tropical. Santo Domingo lay in the midst of forest, a cluster of huts, including three hotels, one of which was proudly called the Waldorf-Astoria. In spite of its name, however, it had no sanitation.

I chose the Waldorf-Astoria because it was near the bank. The bank had the only toilet in the village, and it could be used during banking hours. The meals were simple, with one single staple dish for breakfast, lunch or dinner—a piece of goat's meat with a fried egg on top. I might have got used to it if I hadn't looked into the kitchen which opened off the verandah with no dividing door. There on the ground lay my next day's meals—a slaughtered goat with its yellow entrails lying in a puddle of blood. A small child was running through the mess, with flies rising from her feet.

After that I ate the rice I had brought with me from Quito, with fruit—papaya, bananas or an occasional orange.

The upstairs rooms were small stalls of unpainted wood. I shared mine with three spiders, one of which had legs spectacularly striped in yellow and blue. The bed had no mattress, sheets or blankets, but luckily I had brought a blanket with me. The hard bed suited me all right and I slept well. There were no visible washing facilities, so I asked my landlady—a huge uncorseted woman with beautiful liquid black eyes—where I could wash. She took me to the flat-topped roof and pointed to a jug half-full of cold water and an enamel bowl on a small table. These amenities were, of course, in full view of the street.

Soon an audience collected to watch me at my ablutions, whistling and waving to their friends to join them. I brushed my teeth, washed my feet, face and neck and left it at that. The expectant intakes of breath on

the part of some of the men as I undid a button or two decided me. The crowd gathered every morning to see me clean my teeth and wash. They may have thought that a woman crazy enough to travel alone in their country might well some day take a bath in public.

While I was in Santo Domingo, I decided to visit the Colorado Indians and do some paintings of them; so, hiring a man and a horse, and loading up with supplies, I set out. Armand had arrived in the same district, with three assistants, to film the Indians, so we journeyed off together.

I am not too happy on horseback. Of all the animals I know, the horse alone gives me an acute feeling of inferiority. I think the animal senses my indifference to horsemanship and resents it. For about the only thing that can be said about my riding is that I manage to stay on.

The mare I rode on this trip was a nursing mother and, of course, had her foal with her. Three or four times an hour the foal would put its little head under the mother's belly and take a long drink. Our speed was regulated by the young one's insatiable appetite and temperament. When it galloped, we galloped, when it dawdled we did the same.

A few miles out of Santo Domingo we passed into thick forest where the trees met overhead. Tracks were few and far between. We rode on in perpetual twilight and a hot-house temperature. I had never before seen such beautiful flowers and foliage as in this forest of the Amazon. Huge green oval-shaped leaves, with patterns etched on them in light yellow or cyclamen, spread under the trees. There were tendrils which hung down, heavy with large red buds; orchids glinted in the bright moss.

My sightseeing had to be done with caution, for my mare had discovered another trick to add to my discomfiture. The branches came down so low that if I failed to

keep a firm hand on the reins, she passed beneath them and dislodged me. I outwitted her by lying full length on her back. Once the foal ran off the track and plunged into the jungle. The mare dashed after it. Branches snapped across my face and tore my hands and arms as I tried to control her. She stopped at last and we both stood still in the green silence that might have been at the bottom of the sea. The foal came up and took another drink.

Behind me, far in the impenetrable green, I could hear a voice crying, "Señorita, señorita! Not that way! Come back!"

But how? All around us was undergrowth dense as a green fog. The branches through which I had ploughed had snapped back and left no indication of the way we had come. I heard my guide's voice again, muffled by the vegetation. I shouted back but my voice seemed to beat against the walls of my green prison and be absorbed. I knew that I would never find my way out. My only hope was the horse's instinct coming to our rescue, perhaps she would find her way back to the other horses. She looked dejected. I patted her and said, "Get us out of here."

Pricking her ears, the mare started forward, made a weaving movement, first to the left, then to the right, followed by the wayward foal. For some minutes we picked our way through low-hanging branches; then I heard a sharp whinny on my left. We were back on the track again.

My guide scolded me. He looked shaken and kept on grumbling, though he need not have feared that I should stray off the track again. Soon we came across the first of the Colorados. They do not live in villages; each family has a hut of bamboo thatch and wood. Colorado society is patriarchal.

They are a strikingly handsome, light-skinned people. The men are generally tall with broad shoulders and narrow hips, but the most striking thing about them is the bright vermilion paint which covers them. At first glance the men's hair looks like a cap; it is painted bright red with the achioto colouring and cropped in the pudding-basin style. Around their waists they wear a piece of white, navy and red cloth, and both men and women decorate themselves with silver or tin bracelets. The women have long black hair parted in the centre and hanging down on either side of their faces past their waists.

They get their name from their love of the colour red. *Colorado* is Spanish for the light vermilion red. They paint their faces this colour and add stripes of navy blue in a regular pattern.

I called on the local witch doctor in his hut. My interpreter told me that he and all his family were suffering from a mysterious disease. When I talked with the witch doctor he coughed convulsively and a peculiar whooping sound came from his throat. I recognized the symptom. He had whooping cough.

The Colorado Indians are not addicted to strong drink like those I had seen around Quito. Their married couples drink on alternate Sundays. Both go out together, but only one gets drunk. When it is the wife's turn, she gives her hat to her husband who wears it on top of his own; on his day to get drunk, it is she who wears both hats. The trilby hats which both men and women wear are far too precious to be lost in a drunken spree.

Every morning I bathed with the Colorado Indian women and admired their Gauguin-like beauty of colour and form, their long hanging hair and striped faces. They splashed about in the crystal clear water and we somehow managed to exchange gossip, although I knew only one or two words of their language. While Armand and his men filmed, I made sketches of the Indians or watched the women weaving the striped material they wore. The thread they used interested me; it looked like some sort of vegetable fibre, though I thought it might have been wool.

One day I was examining a tree at the edge of a clearing and noticed that it had spiky seed pods. One of the young Indians broke off a spray and opened up a seed pod for me to examine. Inside were small seeds from which a vermilion juice oozed out—this was the source of their dyes and paints. I tried the colour on my lips and found it had a pleasant taste.

The young Indian watched me with interest. When I pointed to the navy stripes on his face, he showed me a round fruit, slightly larger than an orange. One of the women nearby cut the fruit in half and took out large whitish seeds which she heated in a pot on the fire. Gradually the seeds turned to an indigo colour.

I was soon able to test the lasting properties of this blue dye, when the Colorados offered to initiate Armand and me into their tribe. We agreed and were both painted with red achioto. Armand's hair was plastered with it and his face and mine were duly painted in stripes. We dined together in an hotel in Quito a week later striped like zebras. The indigo stripes were almost indelible.

To my horror, when we started on our journey back to Quito, I found the horses covered with blood. My guide assured me that there was nothing to worry about. Vampire bats had attacked them during the night. He himself had been attacked, he told me, when one of his feet lay outside the mosquito net as he was sleeping. He awoke with the pleasurable sensation of floating. When he opened his eyes he saw a tiger vampire bat greedily sucking the blood from his big toe.

On our return, Armand and I were astonished to learn that there was a theatre in Santo Domingo, housed in a barn-like wooden building. It had the oddly incongruous air of a schoolhouse. This impression was strengthened by the sight of a striking looking woman with long black hair curling down past her shoulders, ringing a big metal handbell, intoning like a school mistress, "The show is about to start! Hurry along, hurry along!"

We paid our pesetas and groped our way inside. Presently our eyes became accustomed to the dim light and we were able to see the faces of the audience. The place was half-full of the handsome but highly diversified people who live in scattered communities in this part of Ecuador; dark, aquiline features of Spaniards, flat-boned Negro faces, and the almond-shaped eyes of Ecuadorian Indians. They looked for all the world like a crowd of extras on a Hollywood set.

We sat on hard wooden benches arranged in rows. A tattered curtain was drawn across the far end of the room. I got into conversation with my neighbour, an impressive looking negress. Her three children, restless under the long wait, fell over my feet from time to time. She apologized for them, and I brought out one of my few Spanish phrases—*ne nada*—it doesn't matter. She beamed and broke into torrents of Spanish. I complimented her on her beautiful children, pointing to each in turn and exclaiming with much feeling and gesture, *"Bonita! bonita!"*

Armand grew impatient with the delay. He added his shouts to those of the audience, which had greatly grown since our arrival. The place was now packed to the last sweating inch and there was an uproar of shouting and stamping feet. After more than an hour's wait, the handbell outside stopped ringing. By now almost the entire population of Santo Domingo, except the bedridden and the drunk, had been rounded up by the inexorable female barker. She entered the hut, placed the bell on a side table and pulled from beneath it a coil of rope. An assistant came forward with a lantern. Together they tried to throw the rope, now attached to the lantern, over one of the crossbeams that supported the roof. After many ineffectual throws, my neighbour's husband, a colossal negro, elbowed his way forward, seized the rope and, with a casual, expert flick, sent it over the beam. He sat down again by his wife to loud applause, grinning broadly.

Once the lantern was in position, the audience hushed. From behind the curtains came a tall man who might have been either Ecuadorian or Chinese. Dressed in a gaudy mandarin coat, he acknowledged with a bow the terrific applause that greeted him.

Armand whispered to me that he was a magician and the only turn of the evening; in fact, he was the show. The curtains parted slowly with squeaks and groans. Once more the magician was revealed, this time flanked on one side by a table piled with paraphernalia. On the other side of him stood a small boy of about eleven years old. With a flourish the magician went into his routine.

He took yards and yards of coloured paper from the boy's nose, mouth and ears, and made eggs disappear up his sleeve. The audience were delighted, for these were simple people and a show of this kind was a rare treat. During the second half of the performance the magician announced with great solemnity that he would hypnotize his young assistant. He made passes in front of the boy's face with his hands. Soon the lad's eyes took on a glassy, staring look. He became rigid. The magician drew up two wooden boxes and placed them a little distance from each other. The boy was laid, stiff as a ramrod, across them. Tremendous applause. He then set the boy on his feet again. More stamping and clapping.

Delighted with his success, the magician now began to put various questions to his rigid assistant. The boy replied in a mechanical voice. Neither Armand nor I could understand this part of the performance, but it evoked a great deal of laughter from the audience. It all looked most convincing.

From where we were sitting, we saw the boy lightly relax his left hand and feel furtively in his pocket. In a flash he popped a sweet into his mouth and then was as still as before. I doubt whether anyone else in that spellbound audience spotted this, although from now on the boy's answers sounded definitely muffled. Then, to prove that his assistant really was hypnotized, the magician gave him a smart tap on the back. The sweet bounced out of the boy's mouth and rolled on the floor at his feet. The audience rocked with laughter, but the magician, who had not noticed, went on with his act as seriously as before.

The boy entered into the spirit of the fun. He started to grin at the audience. Fond of children like all South Americans, they did not dream of giving him away.

The show ended after the hypnotist had made a few passes before the boy's eyes to "wake him up." Then they both took their bows. Down went the naughty boy on his hands and knees to retrieve the sweet. He popped it into his mouth to a general shout of delight.

It was a hot night when we at last emerged, but the air seemed cool after the throbbing heat of the theatre. I was tired after the long ride of the morning and the ordeal of waiting for the performance. The hotel, however, was near at hand. I said good night to Armand and made my way up the wooden stairs with the aid of a flashlight.

In my room I lighted the half candle. One of the three spiders I had seen on the wall that morning had moved closer to my bed. It was the one with the blue and yellow striped legs. As there were no curtains, I closed the shutters and crawled thankfully on to the bare wooden boards of my bed, pulling the blanket over myself, tired and happy after the long day.

I fell asleep. Almost at once, it seemed, I was awakened by a tremendous hammering noise. Glancing at my watch I saw that it was nearly four o'clock. I listened in a half-dazed state, until I gradually worked out what the noise could be. It sounded like bare knuckles pounding on the wooden door of a room not far away from mine.

These rooms were eight in a line, facing on to a narrow corridor open to the street on one side. From below came shouts. Had a revolution broken out? Suddenly there was a pause, then more rapping—much nearer this time.

A man's voice yelled: "Señor Fernandez! Señor Fernandez!"

A terrible oath split the air from a disturbed sleeper. Undeterred, the intruder went on to the next door and began to hammer. Again, enraged denials came in a profane stream. Someone threw something with a loud clatter down the narrow passage. By now I was waiting for knocking on my own door.

Who was Fernandez? Why was he so urgently sought at this hour in the chilly dawn?

I was obviously the only woman in this row of rooms. Wouldn't it shock the nocturnal searcher if I called out in my unmistakably feminine voice? Peruvians and Ecuadorians were always amazed to see a woman travelling unescorted in their countries. Their own women lived extremely secluded lives.

Suddenly the hammering fell on my door. I kept silent. This provoked a hoarse, frustrated shout from the intruder, which echoed through the hotel. Then my shutters were burst open and a lantern was stuck through. I mouthed my prepared words voicelessly, and the light fell away, as if its holder was scared. My shutters were banged to and away went the voice down the corridor, bellowing astonishment.

Señor Fernandez was finally located in the last room of all. A clatter of boots down wooden stairs, a revving up of a motor in the street, shouts, grunts, backfiring. At last a truck drove away into the lifting night.

In the morning I asked the landlady what it was all about. She replied off-handedly that Señor Fernandez was a truck driver. His mate had come to call him. She shrugged. It was merely a case of over-sleeping!

Since those early days of solitary travel, I have visited a great many other places, and had even odder and more unexpected experiences. Luckily Armand and I share this love of adventure, this sloughing off of civilized values, and it is always with a sense of release that we leave the big cities and return once more to our roving life. With us we take along one or two picked companions, and the animals that form part of our family.

What kind of people, then, make the ideal expedition personnel? Amateurs, or those who wish to learn the business quickly, can hardly hope to make the grade. The requirements involve professional experience extending over a number of years. Any expedition is a costly business. The responsibilities which must be assumed for each member are great—fares, insurance, and countless additional expenses besides the salary. The leader of the expedition—whatever its purpose may be —must be certain that his investment in each member of the party is a reasonably sound one. A poor cameraman, for instance, can cause the loss of thousands of pounds, for his work cannot be properly assessed on the spot. We, for instance, don't see our film until we arrive back in London or New York.

To be a member of a photographic or film unit, a cameraman must not only be good at his chosen job, but must possess other qualifications as well. Consider Tom Stobart, who once worked with us. He has a Cambridge degree in zoology and is also a specialist in marine biology. Before he joined us he had been on three expeditions and won warm recommendations. After leaving us he filmed the triumphant Everest expedition. Desmond Bartlett, Armand's Australian assistant, had worked as a cameraman and as a technician with the Australian Information Service for years before he came to us. He is highly intelligent and well fitted for responsibility and command. Trained from youth by his father, a keen naturalist, Des Bartlett knows as much about birds as any professional ornithologist.

Apart from these qualifications, both Tom and Des had one other important asset: they were bachelors.

Preferably, expedition members should be single. Married men are never completely happy when they are separated from their wives and children. They worry when letters fail to reach them, their wives worry, then they worry because their wives worry, and this has an unsettling effect on them and soon on everybody.

One must be fairly stoical where pain is concerned. Cuts and bruises are common and must be considered as part of the day's work. Pain can be endured in silence up to a point, but if one becomes irritable it is better to be human and admit you are suffering. Again—up to a point—illness must be smiled away. A sick person on an expedition is an added burden to the others, since every member of the party has a full-time job on his hands. If possible, complete harmony must be aimed at—which means that mutual tolerance is essential.

Another essential: the ability to amuse oneself. This is so important that I cannot stress it enough. Once boredom sets in, petty quarrels can disrupt the entire working group. I remember an occasion when an argument over a glass of malted milk caused a heated outburst between two men, and the fussier of the two was forever after called "aunty" by everyone!

Armand always seemed indifferent to such matters. He has the ideal temperament for work in wild places and I have rarely seen him ruffled. As the work of an expedition such as ours consists of furious bursts of energy alternating with long waits—ten per cent action to ninety per cent waiting about (like detective work)— it is essential to be able to occupy yourself, and essential to be patient.

Armand and I have waited for months in a place for the right conditions in which to do our work; we have been caught by rains and bogged down for weeks. All the books we brought with us had been read—often several times. There is no radio, for only essential equipment can be carried. You are therefore driven back on your own interests.

A knowledge of the natural sciences—geology, botany, zoology—is invaluable if boredom is to be kept at bay.

During long waiting periods, I occupy myself by my writing and by observing animals. Whole days have passed watching ants and birds and taming my animals. I have been entranced watching the countless dramas of wild life and entering into them through my eyes and imagination.

What other virtues must an aspiring expedition member possess? He must be able to dispense with his daily bath or at least to achieve a bath in a cupful of boiled water, in a muddy waterhole or a river brimming with crocodiles. In a dry area you may go four or five days without washing. I carry with me a bottle of soda water to clean my teeth, as I dislike it as a drink, and it is less of a temptation to drink it when water supplies are low. I try always to look well groomed, as my morale is wonderfully uplifted by a little lipstick, neat hair, and a clean shirt. I remember once bathing—if one can call it that—on the edge of a waterhole which was three-quarters mud. I sat on the edge, dipping an enamel bowl in the warm, soupy liquid where, not long before, we had struggled to bring ashore sixty-eight crocodiles. The temperature was over 110. The men were not far away. If I heard anyone approaching, I yelled at the top of my voice. If I kept too near the water's edge a crocodile might get me. But these things one soon learns to take all in the day's work.

Washing in rivers can be dangerous. Bilharzia abounds. This is a tiny germ that attacks the liver and then invades the bloodstream. It can be absorbed through the skin and any cut or abrasion. So—in Africa particularly—washing water, as well as drinking water, must be boiled. Canvas safari baths stand about six inches from the ground, stretched on a wooden frame. We usually hollow out the earth beneath the canvas to make it steadier. Washing basins also are made of canvas, stretched on wooden stands. Laundry problems can be complicated. In Africa, however, native boys are part of the safari personnel. We carry heavy irons which open up to hold glowing charcoal embers. Nylon is a godsend, as it needs no ironing at all.

A safari, by the way, is not necessarily an expedition. Safari is Swahili for "journey." An expedition takes months; anything from six to sixteen, so the wise traveller takes everything likely to be needed, from evening clothes to toothpaste. What one has not taken one has to do without.

What about food? In New York or London I am a good housekeeper and like clean food, but out on safari I have eaten—and liked—pancakes crawling with flies. I don't recommend this diet for dainty palates or weak stomachs, but in some of the wild areas of the world you have to eat that way or starve.

If you go on safari you will probably hire a safari organizer or white hunter. He will shoot game for food for your native boys as well as for you; but you take many provisions with you, besides. Eggs dipped in isinglass and carefully packed. A certain amount of tinned food; tea, sugar, coffee, milk, and crates of vegetables. Armand and I take our favourite drinks—the makings of sweet Martinis; two bottles each last us a month.

Clothes are an important item. For safari I pack khaki clothes and quantities of nylon; I have to be glamorous at a moment's notice. A district commissioner or governor may invite us to dinner as we come into his territory—it is a godsend, thanks to nylon, to be able to wash a dress myself and have it dry within half an hour.

On my first expedition I wore G.I. pants which fitted well, when I had taken them in a little at the waist. In Nairobi I have a Goanese tailor who copies these pants for me. They have no pleats on the tummy, which is an important consideration when one is photographed. They can be washed regularly, and beaten on stones, which is the native way of washing, without going threadbare; notwithstanding this rather rough treatment, they last quite a while.

This costume of mine has caused some speculation among Africans in remote places. They have often mistaken my sex, calling me "Bwana" (Master) instead of "Memsahib" (Mrs.), in Swahili.

Shoes are important. For the rough and hilly country in New Guinea, where it was nearly always raining, I wore ordinary spiked golf shoes. In South America I had a wonderful pair with composition soles, which lasted for several expeditions. At last, however, the cotton thread rotted in the tropical climate, and they came apart.

A foot safari is tough on shoes. I buy all mine from a famous London firm; for jungle walking I usually wear sneakers, which most travellers condemn, but they suit me. The old settlers look at them and shake their heads.

"Those shoes are no good," they say, "you'll have fungus—you'll be pierced by a thorn—a snake will get you."

But it's sneakers for me—they are soft and pliable and give me the feeling of walking on bare feet. In this way I manage to keep up with the natives, matching my steps to theirs. I love walking with them, for when the rest of the party is left behind, they will imitate the mannerisms of some of the members, and they can be very funny. Now that I understand Swahili I can appreciate what wonderful mimics they are, and how excellent is their sense of humour.

For bush country I wear stout English walking shoes of the non-slip variety. My baggage includes glamour shoes, which are worn occasionally. Feet are precious and must be pampered. Once a year I go to my favourite shop in Bond Street and buy both walking and visiting shoes.

Coloured clothes are useless if you want to observe wild animals: they spot any primary colour at once.

I advise people who are going on a serious safari to buy their clothes locally. Nairobi is the best place to equip for an East African expedition, and to get sensible equipment. In contrast, I have seen the most incredible clothes on people just arrived in Nairobi. Beanies and shorts, and hibiscus flowered shirts! These are neither becoming nor suitable; they are the badges of the tourist.

Jeans are no good because of their colour. One thing a woman in the tropics must not forget; one does not wear safari clothes in any town, however small, through which one may pass. The people living there would take a very poor view of it and regard a woman who lounges in slacks as socially unacceptable.

I don't bother about hats. Once I arrived back in New York and had an appointment the same evening. A hat was indicated. What could I do? I rummaged through my luggage and fished out one of the Jivaro hats that had been given to us by the head hunters in Peru: a wonderfully gaudy thing built of the wings of macaws and the bills of toucans. I wore it and everybody thought it was the latest creation from Paris.

Before each expedition, medical check-ups are necessary. Blood counts, blood pressure, heart, lungs, teeth, injections. You have to be in tip-top condition. But we never take a doctor with us; tropical medicine is now so

271

advanced that we feel confident with our regular doses of paludrine, an anti-malaria preparation. Apart from Armand's tick typhus in East Africa, and my scurvy in Australia—with an uncomfortable few months of amoebic dysentery thrown in—we have been lucky.

In Africa you must look out for chiggers. These are tiny insects which burrow round the toenails and lay their eggs in the flesh. A white blister appears; if you look closely you will see a black head inside. It is quite a painful business to dig the whole egg-sac out. But that is the only way to prevent a severe toe infection. If chiggers are allowed to hatch, infection sets in and you are in danger of losing your toes.

Jewellery is another of my personal problems. I have never been able to make up my mind about it. Formerly I took it everywhere with me to wear when we reached a city. I had necklaces, rings, watches, pendants, earrings —a whole treasure chest kept in a biscuit tin.

Armand would often say: "Why, in heaven's name, don't you sell all this stuff?" But I couldn't bear the idea. My Russian grandmother left me some beautiful pieces which I simply couldn't part with. I should, of course, have insured my jewellery, but really I couldn't afford it, and I knew that Armand wouldn't approve.

Then the problem was suddenly solved for me—for ever. This happened at the time when our house was being built at Langata, about eleven miles from Nairobi. We had been down to South Africa to photograph sea-lions, and on our return picked up the biscuit tin (containing my treasures) from Mr. Hassan, our hotel keeper in Nairobi, who had kept it in his safe for me. The same day, Armand, Tom Stobart and I drove out to Langata, to see how our house was getting on.

I carried the biscuit tin while we walked round the building. It was so exciting to see it rising from the ground, realizing our dreams and plans. The house was designed by ourselves in the old Portuguese colonial style, and built of pink-tinged stone quarried on the land we had bought and so often camped on. I was enchanted with the progress of the work. The last details were being carried out.

Kikuyu workmen and Sikh carpenters were squatting on their haunches, hammering away. I was so interested watching them that I casually put the heavy biscuit tin down in our dressing-room.

We returned to Nairobi shortly afterwards and as the car pulled up outside the hotel I suddenly cried:

"Armand! The box. I've left my box."

"I'll drive you back straight away," said Tom Stobart.

"Nonsense!" broke in Armand. "Let's have dinner. We can go back first thing in the morning."

I feebly agreed.

Tom was at the house about nine-thirty the next morning. The phone bell rang in our hotel room.

"That you, Michaela? There's no box here. What was in it?"

"Thousands of pounds worth of jewellery, that's all," I said. Then I hung up.

Tom at once reported the loss to the police, but it was too late. The jewels had disappeared.

The loss that grieved me most was the first present I had from Armand—a silver necklace, earrings and a bracelet from Peru. It had a *motif* of filigree circles with a little llama—the national emblem of Peru—inside. There was also a strangely shaped gold pin which I had myself excavated in Bolivia. Another lovely piece was a two-thousand-year-old bird, a present from Germans who had lived with the Jivaro Indians for eight years and whom we had met in the jungle—Nazis in hiding, I strongly suspected.

The C.I.D. did their best. They were energetic, especially a nice woman inspector whom I now count among my friends. But the box was not found. The C.I.D. suspected that the jewellery had been smuggled out of the country within twenty-four hours. I was shocked when I saw the police list of people in Nairobi suspected of receiving stolen goods; it covered eleven double-sided pages in the record book!

In despair I decided to consult a Mganga (a witch doctor). I should, of course, have done this at once, but I knew that the police authorities frowned upon white people enlisting the help of the native witch doctors. However, I knew that the Mganga seldom fail to find a thief and make him return the stolen goods, and I wanted my jewellery. I can't explain their powers; they may have an occult basis, or they may come from deep psychological knowledge.

My two African boys drove with me to a small village some miles away and asked for the Mganga. This Mganga was a woman. She sat meditating under a tall acacia tree. She was a beautiful woman, with a finely chiselled face and almond eyes. We shook hands solemnly. Although I prefer to see Africans in their native costumes, this woman looked stately in a white European dress, edged with maroon, and with a white cloth thrown toga-fashion over one shoulder.

She signalled me to wait and went to her hut. She came back with an assistant, a younger woman, carrying a strange object, like a bow wrapped in serval cat skin. We all got into the car and drove to our house. When the African and Indian workmen saw the Mganga they ceased work and looked frightened.

I took her to my dressing-room.

"This is where you put the box," she declared, laying her hands on the exact spot where I had indeed left it.

She now unwrapped the bow-like object. Spreading its hide cover on the floor, she drew a circle (round the place where the box had stood) with yellow powder shaken from a gourd. Then she took another gourd and shook it as we shake dice; some beads and beans spun on to the hide and she began to chant.

I squatted beside her, watching. Soon heads appeared at the windows and stared into the room. She pointed at the beads and one of the boys translated for me.

"This is a Hindi," she intoned. "There are five Hindi here." (Hindi is the Swahili word for Indian.) "There are five Hindi working here and one of them has taken the box. He is the tallest Hindi and he is the one who gives orders."

Armand, who had joined us, confirmed that there were indeed five Indians and that the foreman was the tallest of them. We called him in. While he was being sent for the Mganga took the bow, which had a gourd in the middle and a string across it, and struck the string with a long knitting needle. It gave out a weird but melodious sound. As the string vibrated, she put one end of the knitting needle on it and held the other end to her ear.

"He is the thief," she exclaimed.

The tall Indian entered the room, pale but dignified. The Mganga looked at him without interest and without any embarrassment.

"He is the thief," she repeated.

The Indian said no words of denial. He merely stood, as if transfixed, very pale.

"I want you to curse the man who has stolen, unless he returns the jewels within three days," I said.

This was in the approved African tradition. I thought if the Indian believed in such things he might return my jewellery. If by any chance he was not guilty, no harm would be done. The Mganga took my hand, palm upwards, in hers. She spat into it and shook some yellow powder into the hollow of my hand. She took the Indian's hand and put it on mine. I felt my strength drained from all parts of my body into my wrist. I could not snatch away my hand—it was as though the Indian and I were invisibly joined. The Mganga waited, and then she tapped me lightly on my shoulder. I broke the grasp, feeling emptied.

The Indian got up dazedly. He returned to his work, the Mganga swept up the beans and beads into the gourd, and wrapped up the strange bow-shaped instrument in the serval cat skin.

I returned to the house the next day; the Africans and Indians watched me surreptitiously, and I saw the accused Indian walking directly in front of me as I walked out of the house. His face paled as he saw me.

The second day I thought he looked drawn and exhausted. On the third day my jewellery had not been returned to me. When I drove over to the house I found the boys silent and frightened. The Indian headman had had a bad fall—from the top of the house to the ground —and had been carried home with a broken leg. The Kikuyus were whispering and I caught the word "Mganga".

Pity for the injured Indian swept over me. I had a vision of his family and their wails of anguish when he was taken home. Confusedly I felt responsible for his injury. My jewellery, I decided, was not worth a man's life and the sorrow of his family.

The next day I went to the Mganga. She knew at once why I had come to see her, but she waited for me to speak. I gave her a present and, with the help of an interpreter, told her that I wanted to lift the curse. She looked at me with narrowed eyes, and shrugged her shoulders.

"Then I must go with you to the house of the Hindi," she said.

We found the house crowded with friends and relations. As we entered they drew away. The Indian's wife pleaded with me, first in Gujrati and then in English, to lift the spell from her husband. He lay staring at us with dilated eyes, his leg in splints.

"I know my husband has done wrong," said his wife, and she started to weep.

I tried to make her understand that everything would

be all right and motioned the Mganga forward. She put the powder in my hand, spat into it, and directed me to clasp the Indian's hand. Then a gourd of water was brought and the powder was ceremoniously washed off.

The Indian thanked me with his eyes; his wife bowed to me and left the room. She returned with incense which she laid at my feet. She offered me a chupatty; I took it as a mark of good will. As I reached the door to leave, the Indian called me back.

"I cannot tell you where the jewels have gone, Memsahib—they would kill me."

He lay back, sorrowful and exhausted. I guessed "they" must mean the fences—the dealers in stolen property.

I knew that I had lost my jewellery for ever. But I had been shown that, in the scheme of human things, my cherished jewels were not very important after all.

I told Armand all that had happened, and asked him if I had done right in lifting the curse. He said he thought I had, and he looked unwontedly serious as he said it.

There's a moral, of course. A woman on safari had best leave her jewellery at home.

CHAPTER FIFTEEN

COURAGE IS LIFE

WHEN THIS book goes to press we leave again on our travels. Our aim, once more, will be to return with living records of peoples still beyond the frontiers of what we are pleased to call civilization, and of the wild creatures which inhabit the jungles and grasslands, the mountains and seas of this inexhaustible world of ours.

To this aim Armand and I seem to have dedicated our lives. Under the pressures of modern civilization the world has shrunk like that fatal piece of wild ass's skin until we are left with only fragments of the primordial past, in which ancient peoples and wild animals are still engaged in the naked struggle for survival. We have approached them with love and they have accepted us. What measure of success we have achieved has been due to a wholehearted devotion to our work. We have lived outside the routines of civilization and sought, in adventures in wild places, the self-fulfilment without which life is meaningless.

Years have come and gone and left us concentrated on our task. We have forgotten what holidays are like. Our work has occupied us for sixteen hours a day or more for months on end, without any form of conventional relaxation. Any success that has come to us is the result of a mode of life which has demanded all our powers of endurance and our powers of love for the peoples and animals that are our subjects.

But for me success is not a personal achievement; it is a triumph of the things for which we stand and which, I hope, we faithfully represent.

278

We set out from the first to make a break with the old approach of the white man to the wild and its inhabitants. It was strange, we thought, that people who loved domesticated animals should regard those of the jungle as enemies. We were convinced that if we approached them with love and without fear, we could learn to understand their true natures and thus—in however small a measure—win their confidence.

I think our work proves that we were right.

Our films, I am sure, are informed by the spirit that inspired us when we first set out on our adventures. They do not depict the brutalities of frightened men or hunters driven by blood lust. We were told that the public wanted cruel sensationalism, but we pursued our own course because we loved our subjects and did not desire the sort of fame that comes from a morbid exploitation of their agonies.

Our aim was, above all, to enable city people who saw our films to share in the feelings that inspired us, as they followed us into strange worlds made beautiful by the untainted air, the good earth, the majestic prospects of mountain and plain, the mysterious magic of the jungle, and the miracle of life as it is expressed in free peoples and untamed animals.

We worked for the first years together in the production of feature films. Hundreds of thousands of people saw them and participated in what I think can be justly called the moral side of our work. Eventually we came to England, on a routine trip, for the promotion of our film *Below the Sahara*. Then a new phase was opened up to us. We were asked to do a television show.

Over-night we became the familiar friends of the great British television public. Their response confirmed what I had known since I was a child in London, that the British people are passionate lovers of animals.

Occasionally a critic would comment on the entertainment value of our television shows, but for us that was only half the story. We believed we could entertain without resorting to the cheap tricks which have for so long disfigured the face of Africa, New Guinea and other lands as areas where danger and death lurks in every shadow.

Nature can be cruel, but Nature can also be kind and beneficent. We wished to give adventure, yes, but also the beauty of the world and of life—the lioness's tenderness for her cubs, the elephant's for her calves. Literature and the visual arts had hitherto been mainly concerned with the more savage aspects of wild life. We had learned something of the deeper nature of animals and found there emotions that bind them to all living things, including mankind.

Quite apart from what we tried to do for animals by showing their real characters, we hoped to reveal some larger aspects of primitive life from which people can renew their faith by dwelling on the essential goodness of things. We live at a time full of peril and fear which can give rise to hatred and suspicion of life itself, and which can be destructive of faith.

How sad it is to have nothing to believe in; how sad to drift into the evil courses which follow lack of faith. If our travels have taught me anything it is that the worst dangers come not from simple people and wild animals but from surrender to danger, from despair, and from forgetting that there can be no failure if faith in life is unshaken.

I have often thought how much easier life would be if one decided that there is only one person to please and that is oneself. To be the person one wants to be—that is the important thing. Never mind about "what others think of me". The acid test should be: what do I think of myself.

Be the person you yourself want to be; rise above the world's jealousy and ridicule. If you are sincere and feel

you are doing the right thing, you will find satisfaction
and happiness in work; you will be happy yourself and
give happiness to others. There is no job in life, I have
found, too humble to make a full life for those who find
supreme satisfaction in serving others.

To some has fallen the task of moulding many lives,
to others of moulding only the lives of a few; but the
important thing is to strive to do your best; that is the
highest offering one can make to life, and it is never
rejected, though full acceptance may be delayed. That
is the testing-time of the spirit.

At this point I remember Pat Putnam, an extraordinary
character, who had gone to the Congo on a Harvard
expedition and thrown up the chance of a brilliant
scientific career in order to live among the pygmy people
and devote himself to their welfare. He intended to write
a book about them but became so absorbed in his day-
to-day work that he never got down to it.

When we met him in a Congo forest he had lived with
the pygmies for twenty years and made himself a home
there. Five huge trees had been cleared to make a site
for his house by the river. Its enormous thatched roof
sloped up steeply from the mud and wattle walls which
were distempered a pinkish orange.

Putnam's first wife, who was interested in "natural
architecture", had designed and built the house. It fitted
into its surroundings perfectly. No jarring European
note destroyed the illusion of a native dwelling. The fire
was laid in the centre of the brick floor, and the smoke
filtered through the thatch.

Pat spoke French and Lingala as well as the pygmy
language. He lived on the same food as the little people
and was almost as skilful a hunter as they were; but he
had paid a heavy physical price for his devotion to their
interests. I was struck by his pallor and weakness; he
was so weak, indeed, that he had to be carried everywhere
by tipoye. I can see him now, with his dark hair and beard

and his sunken cheeks. He died a few months after we left.

Through Pat Putnam we were able to get into close contact with the pygmies and, at the risk of digressing, I would like to recount an adventure that befell us in their company. But first let me describe them. The men are about the size of an average eight-year-old European child, the women somewhat smaller. They attach themselves to various African tribes—in fact, any tribe they happen to come across—and speak the language of their hosts as well as their own.

They are great hunters. The pygmy antelope is their favourite game, but they occasionally kill elephants by means of poisoned arrows. In return for bananas and corn, they supply the tribe to whom they are attached with meat.

Normal size Africans do not regard the pygmies as "people"; the little people, on their part, do not resent being thought of as different from other Africans—they seem to accept it as part of the settled order of Nature. Our boys, Mucharia and Shabani, were completely mystified by them and uncertain as to whether they were real men and women.

Pygmies are rather lighter in colour than the ordinary Africans—a yellowish-brown shade. Their most characteristic feature is a short and broad nose. Their voices have a sing-song quality which runs the gamut of about five notes. Musical in a primitive way, their five-man orchestras are made up of pipes which produce only one note each.

They do not paint themselves. Their dress consists of a piece of bark drawn between the legs and tied round the waist. It is made by stripping bark from a tree and pounding it on a log with a piece of wood until it becomes thin enough to be used as cloth, which it resembles. Sometimes the garment is stained with a vegetable dye.

Armand and I visited the pygmies at one of their little camps. Their dwellings are beehive-shaped huts made of leaves and vines, and very comfortable they look.

Our attention was drawn to a very old pygmy woman. About the size of a six-year-old European child, she was incredibly wrinkled and the whole of her upper lip perforated with holes. When she saw Armand, she crowed with glee, and reminded him, through our interpreter, that when he had last been in the forest he had promised to procure some honey for her.

She knew of a tree, she said, where there was a beehive, so we asked her to lead us to it. Pygmies often raid the hives for honey, which they consider a great delicacy.

Soon the whole village was mustered for the honey expedition. All the little men and women accompanied us along the narrow forest track which was flanked by immensely tall trees. After we had gone some distance, the old woman stopped by one of the forest giants, and pointed upwards. It seemed impossible that any human being could climb such a tree, let alone a tiny pygmy.

But the little men were undaunted. One of them took a vine which he made into a loop and passed it round the tree at the height of about twelve feet. He left just enough slack in the loop for a pygmy to sit in. Then, with truly amazing agility, he pulled himself up by the looped vine, pushing with his feet. Up he went, with no branches to help him, to a height of perhaps forty or fifty feet. I watched fascinated as he reached the first fork in the tree and began to fumble in a satchel he carried slung across his shoulders.

From the satchel he took something bound up in a leaf. It was a smoking ember of wood. He thrust the ember into the beehive and at once began to fan his face vigorously with his hand. I soon saw why. Out poured the bees from the hive and swarmed round him; his fanning hand beat them off.

Down below we were also active. Cameras had been

set up to record the scene and were now being operated. When the hive was empty, the little man up in the tree started to rifle it. Soon he was throwing down the honey, wax and all, to those on the ground. They were wild with excitement.

I noticed one tiny woman who was so emotionally overcome that she kept clutching at her breast, unconsciously squeezing it so hard that her finger-marks showed in the flesh.

Chunks of honeycomb fell among a sea of clutching hands, to be grabbed and swallowed with indescribable speed. My eyes fell on our little old woman and I wondered if she was getting her fair share; but she was so agile that she appeared to be getting more than anyone else. It was wonderful to watch her antics.

All through the scene the pygmies kept up a continual shout of excitement, and we soon found ourselves yelling with them—but for a different reason. The bees, infuriated by the raid on their hive, were attacking us. They found their way into our shirts and up our slacks; they swarmed into our ears and up our noses; they made mass assaults on our heads. We were stung mercilessly but could do nothing about it.

The scene was so interesting that we simply had to go on filming. As for the pygmies, they must have been stung much worse than ourselves, but they took no notice. I marvelled at their indifference to pain as I watched them stuffing lumps of honeycomb, black with bees, into their mouths. I shuddered to think what was happening inside their stomachs. Our little old woman now sat all by herself, like an ancient mongoose, fanning herself with a large forest leaf in one hand, while she thrust honey into her mouth with the other. I have never seen such a rapturous look on the face of any human being.

I look back on the beautiful places I have known in remote Africa, in the hidden areas of New Guinea, in the waste lands of Australia and the forests of South Africa.

All their varied beauties make a unity that is the world.

Part of the world, too, are the great cities in the civilized centres and the homes of their peoples. The same spirit is at work there, although one cannot always apprehend it, since it is less tangible than a tree on a lonely height, a bird on the wing, or the skyline of a mountain range. But it is there—the same animation, the same purpose which guides everything.

It is in the great cities, however, that I feel the people—all of us—struggle under a sense of being cheated. The hard-won thing we call civilization—where has it led us? To fear of annihilation by the hydrogen bomb. The lucky ones, who live in forests, who have no access to news of any kind—these people live at peace, untroubled by the events which cloud our horizon with evil spectres.

Soon I shall be back in my beloved Africa and I shall carry with me the wish that even in the strange environment which civilized people have created for themselves, they should have the same security, the same sense of permanence, as those primitive folk among whom I shall live.

Is this possible? I believe it is. People everywhere are eager for it. The course of history has been changed before by the desire of the people. It may happen that way again. By will and work terror can be cast out of our hearts.

Above all, let us get back to admiring what is demonstrably good, after we have proved that it has changed our values for the better. We can then enthrone it above the cheap deceptions which have betrayed us for so long.

Material things can never be an end in themselves, though they need not be spurned. The great need is to keep them in their place and to follow the impulses that lead away from violence and self-glorification. This is the way of love.

I often think how much the world might benefit if the statesmen would leave their dusty conference rooms—those dens of frustration and despair—and hold their meetings in some of the places I know. Under tall silver trees, by the banks of a great river, or in the gentle undulations of grassland—there the world's statesmen might be blessed and moved to confer blessings on the whole of mankind.

Mind, without guns. That would be essential. If they walked fearlessly into the jungle of international politics, as Armand and I have entered African forests, they would not think of killing one another; but they would unite to face, with courage and understanding, any menace that might lie before them and their peoples. Without guns, they would not go hunting; a higher purpose would emerge from their adventure.

Man is not the be-all and end-all of existence. Life itself is the ultimate. In trying to make man into a god, we are in danger of destroying him.

In the relatively short time that man has been on earth, can we truly say that he has added to the beauty of the world? Has he created anything as beautiful as the texture, the shape, the functions of a tree or an animal or a bird?

Up to now the historical course of man has been one of mastery over weaker things, of destruction of all that stood in the way of mastery—and often of violence for the sake of violence.

It may well be that the world is moving into another phase—a more humane phase—in which violence will be replaced by understanding and the mania for mastery will pass. Even in our own brief time something of the sort has happened and is still happening in Africa. Truly civilized opinion has now made it impossible for those possessed by greed and blood-lust to give unrestricted play to their evil will as they did less than a century ago, when animals were slaughtered senselessly and primitive forests were the scenes of human hunts.

With love and understanding it is possible to meet simple people and wild animals on terms of peace, provided one respects their natures and the circumstances which have shaped them. But if one approaches them with the desire to kill or dominate them, then there is almost bound to be trouble and bloodshed.

The full meaning of tolerance can hardly be grasped unless one has been thrown into circumstances that normally do not arise in the great civilized centres, where the sanctions of law too often take the place of understanding and sympathy between man and man.

I have slept with a snake without knowing it, and no harm came to me; but if I had been conscious of its presence, and shown resentment and fear, there might have been a very different story to tell. If I had known that the snake was in my bed, I hope I should have had enough sense to tolerate its presence, knowing that intolerance might well have led to disaster.

I think there is an important lesson to be drawn from this experience—a lesson particularly applicable to mankind at the present time.

The historical course could be changed to one of preservation and protection. By wisdom and control a new historical period could be ushered in—one from which the ancient evils would be banished. Then and only then shall we arrive at real sanity and achieve real peace of mind.

I know by the thousands of letters we have received that I am not alone in my hopes of a new world. Millions share them and the number is swelled daily. This is, I think, an assurance that the hopes will be realized, even if it takes a generation or more to do it.

Go back into history and mark its horrors; then think of how human beings, just like ourselves, conquered them and opened up new eras.

There are, however, backward as well as forward movements in the march of history. The consequences of a backward movement now can hardly be contemplated. My own belief is that the tide is turning. Here and there, but more especially in the will and hopes of the great mass of mankind, one can discern the ripples that mark the beginning of the forward flow.

Meanwhile, we have the good earth and the miraculous beauty of all created things. These demand respect for life; they draw forth love and tenderness from all normal men and women. From them comes understanding and courage, and a philosophy that brings calmness and strength. It has been my happy lot in the short span of my lifetime to have learned such a philosophy. It has sustained me in some of the darkest places of the earth. Through it I have survived and been enabled to add my contribution to what I hope is the sum of human good.

I return to Africa in an undimmed spirit of adventure at the heart of which, I repeat, lies self-fulfilment, yet with the sense of going back to a secure home where I am one with Nature and all living things. Life can offer nothing richer than this; all that we mean by worldly wealth is poor in comparison.

Yet there are dangers everywhere—dangers to be met and overcome before peace is established in the heart.

If I were asked to express my philosophy in a few words, I should say: Courage is life. Fear, and be slain.